PENGUIN BOOKS

INDIAN COUNTRY

Peter Matthiessen was born in New York City in 1927 and had already begun his writing career by the time he graduated from Yale University in 1950. The following year, he was a founder of *The Paris Review*. Besides *At Play in the Fields of the Lord*, which was nominated for the National Book Award, he has published five other novels, including *Killing Mister Watson*. Mr. Matthiessen's unique career as a naturalist and explorer has resulted in numerous and widely acclaimed books of nonfiction, among them *The Tree Where Man Was Born* (with Eliot Porter), which was nominated for the National Book Award, and *The Snow Leopard*, which won it. His other works of nonfiction include *The Cloud Forest* and *Under the Mountain Wall* (which together received an Award of Merit from the National Institute of Arts and Letters), *The Wind Birds*, *Blue Meridian*, *Sand Rivers*, *Men's Lives*, and *African Silences*. He edited George Catlin's *North American Indians* for the Penguin Nature Library.

INDIAN COUNTRY

PETER MATTHIESSEN

PENGUIN BOOKS

PENGUIN BOOKS
Published by the Penguin Group
Viking Penguin, a division of Penguin Books USA Inc.,
375 Hudson Street, New York, New York 10014, U.S.A.
Penguin Books Ltd, 27 Wrights Lane,
London W8 5TZ, England
Penguin Books Australia Ltd, Ringwood,
Victoria, Australia
Penguin Books Canada Ltd, 10 Alcorn Avenue, Suite 300,
Toronto, Ontario, Canada M4V 3B2
Penguin Books (N.Z.) Ltd, 182–190 Wairau Road,
Auckland 10, New Zealand

Penguin Books Ltd, Registered Offices:
Harmondsworth, Middlesex, England

First published in the United States of America by
The Viking Press 1984
Published in Penguin Books 1992

1 3 5 7 9 10 8 6 4 2

Portions of this book appeared originally in slightly different form, in *Audubon; Geo;* "Tropic
Magic," Sunday Supplement, *Miami Herald; The Nation; The New York Review of Books;
The New York Times; Newsweek, Parabola; Rocky Mountain* magazine; and *The Washington
Post.*

Grateful acknowledgment is made to Professor Simon J. Ortiz for permission to reprint a
selection from "Fight Back: For the Sake of the People, for the Sake of the Land," by Simon J.
Ortiz, INAD-UNM, 1980.

THE LIBRARY OF CONGRESS HAS CATALOGUED THE HARDCOVER AS FOLLOWS:
Matthiessen, Peter.
Indian country.
Includes index.
1. Indians of North America — Religion and mythology.
2. Indians of North America — Land tenure.   3. Human ecology —
North America.   I. Title.
E98R3M33   1984
304.2'08997073   83–47996
ISBN 0-670-39787-3 (hc.)
ISBN 0 14 01.3023 3 (pbk.)

Printed in the United States of America
Set in Garamond
Designed by Mary A. Wirth
Map by David Lindroth

To Craig Carpenter, my teacher and guide on my first
journeys into Indian Country, whose fierce encouragement of the last traditionals among his people is one
good reason why they still exist.

ACKNOWLEDGMENTS

In general, those who helped most with this book are the Indian people who appear in the following pages, and I thank them all for their patience, their teachings, and their hospitality; I also wish to thank Mad Bear Anderson and Dan Budnik. Tim Coulter and others at the Indian Law Resource Center in Washington, D.C., reviewed many of these chapters, and made a number of valuable comments and corrections. They are not responsible for any errors that may remain. Warm thanks are due to Lucas Matthiessen, who provided important assistance with the editing, and to Maria Matthiessen, whose generous forbearance permitted my long disappearances in Indian Country.

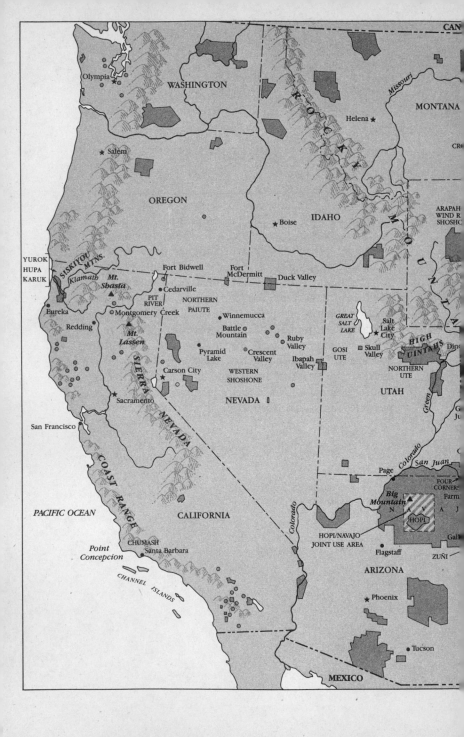

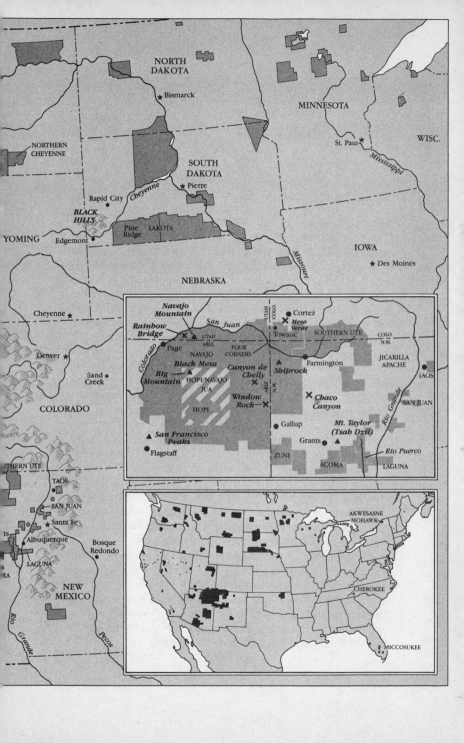

How can you buy or sell the sky—the warmth of the land? The idea is strange to us. We do not own the freshness of the air or the sparkle of the water. How can you buy them from us? . . . We know that the white man does not understand our way. One portion of the land is the same to him as the next, for he is a stranger who comes in the night and takes from the land whatever he needs. The earth is not his brother but his enemy, and when he has conquered it, he moves on. He leaves his fathers' graves, and his children's birthright is forgotten. . . .

There is no quiet place in the white man's cities. No place to hear the leaves of spring or the rustle of insect's wings. But perhaps because I am a savage and do not understand, the clatter only seems to insult the ears. And what is there to life if a man cannot hear the lovely cry of a whippoorwill or the arguments of the frogs around a pond at night? The Indian prefers the soft sound of the wind darting over the face of the pond, and the smell of the wind itself cleansed by a midday rain, or scented with a piñon pine. The air is precious to the red man. For all things share the same breath—the beasts, the trees, the man. The white man does not seem to notice the air he breathes. Like a man dying for many days, he is numb to the stench. . . .

When the last red man has vanished from the earth, and the memory is only the shadow of a cloud moving across the prairie, these shores and forests will still hold the spirits of my people, for they love this earth as the newborn loves its mother's heartbeat. . . . One thing we know—our God is the same. This earth is precious to Him. Even the white man cannot be exempt from the common destiny.

—Sealth, a Duwamish chief, 1865

FOREWORD

The desperate struggles of the Indian people for survival in this century are too widespread and various to be treated in a single volume; those dealt with here may be taken as representative of many others in "the New Indian Wars" which, it is hoped, will eventually attract the attention they deserve. A number of battles, past and present, have been well described elsewhere—for example, the fishing-rights fights of the Puyallup-Nisqually and other tribes in the Pacific Northwest, the Great Lakes, and elsewhere; the eastern land claims of the Passamaquoddy, Penobscot, Oneida, and many others; the bitter violence among political factions in the Lakota nation; the water-rights litigation of the Crow, Papago, Pyramid Lake Paiute, and nearly fifty other Indian groups, from southern California and Arizona to the northern Great Plains; the fights against destruction and pollution of earth, air, and water by numerous Indian communities in the United States and Canada; the continuing persecution and repression of many indigenous peoples in Central and South America. Basic source material (to which Rex Weyler's *Blood of the Land* [1982] and Alvin M. Josephy's *Now That the Buffalo's Gone* [1983] should now be added) is listed in *In the Spirit of Crazy Horse* (1983), which provides background for many of the topics and events referred to but not explored in the present book.

Some of these chapters, in different form, appeared in *Audubon, Geo, The New York Review of Books, The Nation, Parabola, Rocky Mountain*, and the Sunday magazines of *The New York Times, The Washington Post*, and the Miami *Herald*, in an attempt to draw wider attention to transgressions on Indian land and life all over the country. Although history is drawn upon for background and perspective, *Indian Country* is essentially a journal of travels and encounters with Indian people over the past decade. My hope is that these Indian voices, eloquent and bitter, humorous and sad, will provide what history and statistics cannot, a sense of that profound "life way" which could illuminate our own dispirited consumer culture. Hear these voices, listen carefully: the Indian spirit is the very breath of the Americas.

CONTENTS

· 1 ·

NATIVE EARTH

Christopher Columbus, going ashore in the Antilles, was struck by the profound well-being of the island Arawak. ("There is not in the world a better nation. They love their neighbors as themselves, and their discourse is ever sweet and gentle.") It has been suggested that he named them Indios not because he imagined them to be inhabitants of India (which in the fifteenth century was still called Hindustan) but because he recognized that the friendly, generous Taino people lived in blessed harmony with their surroundings—*una gente in Dios,* a people in God. Within a decade of Columbus's arrival, these people had been slaughtered and enslaved throughout the Caribbean region, and are now extinct.

Columbus's admiration of the native peoples was shared by many Europeans, before and after, from the eleventh-century Vikings who attacked the Skraelings (the Inuit) in Labrador to the Dutch, English, French, and Spanish colonists farther south, but the fate of the Indios was always the same. Despite the great kindness and assistance they received from the Algonkin-speaking peoples, from Plymouth to Manhattan to Jamestown, despite the abundance of the land and waters that the native peoples were so glad to share, the Europeans were appalled by the might of nature in a huge land without the mark of man, and with the departure of their ships, they felt homeless, cast away. They had not been prepared for the fierce extremes of climate, and they were dismayed by the huge dark wall of virgin forest, the huge silence; hiding unknown dangers from their view, it was perceived as oppressive and dangerous, even malevolent. As William Bradford wrote from the Plymouth Colony, "What could they see but a hideous and desolate wilderness, full of wild beasts and wild men? And what multitudes there might be of them, they knew not."

Yet Bradford recognized the "wild men" as a "special instrument sent of God for their good beyond their expectation," and also, no doubt, the expectation of those three seamen of Drake's expedition who, left behind in Mexico in 1568, made their way unharmed all the way across the continent to Cape Breton Island, where they found passage home. The Indians strove to live honorably and responsibly as well as generously, and perhaps it was the very goodness of a "heathen" people, so civilized in all meaningful ways, that was so disturbing to religious men who had to wrestle with the bestiality in their own natures. Since they intended to usurp the Indians' country, it must have soothed the Puritanical conscience to dismiss these open-hearted folk as "wolves endewed with men's braines" (Roger Williams)—or "hounds of hell," in Cotton Mather's term—to be cleared from God's path as speedily as possible. Thus Captain John Mason, who led the villainous attack on a sleeping Pequot village in 1634, exulted in "burning them up in the fire of His wrath, and dunging the ground with their flesh. It was the Lord's doings, and marvelous in our eyes!"

The Indians soon realized that their hospitality had been repaid in greed and treachery, and those Algonkins of Virginia, described in 1584 (by a Captain Barlow) as "most gentle, loving, faithful, void of all guile and treason, and such as live after the manner of the Golden Age," were the same people who destroyed the Roanoke Colony a few years later. The Spanish, too, lost friendship after friendship, from the Florida Apalachee to the Pawnee on the Great Plains to the Yuma who eventually closed down their overland trail from Mexico to California; even the French, who entertained romantic visions of the noble savage (reflected in the work of the painter Rousseau and the romancier Chateaubriand) and managed their affairs more skillfully, encouraging the Indian nations to war upon one another, were much weakened in the Mississippi Valley by conflict with the powerful Natchez, an event that led inevitably to the relinquishment of the Louisiana Territory and the opening of the American West. And the "Americans" would inherit much of this animosity, in addition to what they invited on their own; an Indian people described by Coronado's chronicler (in 1541) as "gentle . . . not cruel, faithful in friendship," became the fierce Apache bands that resisted the whites so bitterly in the Southwest.

Having roused the hostility of the Indians, the Europeans had good reason to fear these "demons of the forest," who could have easily hurled them back into the sea. To exterminate Indians by whatever means—and plague and alcohol served as well as war and slavery—would not only assuage this dread but facilitate seizure of their territories. Lord Jeffrey Amherst, in the French and Indian War, offered the Indians pox-infected blankets (most of Canada's Indians would die of smallpox in 1780) and Benjamin Franklin praised the efficacy of rum in the systematic extirpation of "these savages" as their usefulness as allies came to an end. Because the white men were outnumbered, they were forced until the nineteenth century to deal with the Indians as sovereign nations, but increasingly, as the whites achieved dominion (and the red men were lumped with other mammals in the New World natural histories), it was perceived that "savages" had no claim to lands that were going to waste as wilderness, as hunting grounds. Few bothered to notice that most of the tribes were agriculturists, not hunter—gatherers, with a strong sense of home country, and that their right to stand upon this land, to be a part of it, was ancient and inalienable; instead, the Indians' own sense of land and life was used against them. As they said themselves, the People belonged to the Mother Earth, not the reverse, they *were* the earth, so how could they own this earth as property, how could they own the deer or air or water? "[This] way of life . . . views land as the most vital part of man's existence. . . . It supports them, tells them where they live, and defines for them *how* they live. . . . It provides a center of the universe for the group that lives on it. As such, the people who hold land in this way always have a home to go to. Their identity is secure. They live with it and do not abstract themselves from it."* It was only because the white men would not understand this that the Indian nations had to define in formal treaties what was essentially a country of the mind.

· · ·

The first treaty signed by the United States, in 1778, determined the boundaries of the Lenape or Delaware Nation, which would all but vanish within thirty years; those Algonkin nations of New England and the Atlantic states which had not already been obliterated were soon to follow. Even the powerful Cherokee and Creek, the "Civilized Nations" that had welcomed the English in the Southeast, even the Oneida and Seneca of the Six Nations "Iroquois" Confederacy so feared and courted by George Washington, had been driven west or penned on reservations, together with the Shawnee, Winnebago, Potawatomi, and many other peoples from the regions south of the Great Lakes, in a great disruption and displacement that caused wars among the Indians all the

*Vine DeLoria, Jr., *We Talk, You Listen* (New York, 1970).

way west to the Great Plains. The Indian Territory that had earlier described all that great land beyond the Appalachian frontier, and later broad regions west of the Mississippi, was ever more isolated, narrow, and remote, until finally all those stolen and lost lands were lands of myth, without boundaries and without horizons. "Indian country" no longer meant much to the white man, although as meaningful and still immediate to the Indian as his own heart.

As late as the early nineteenth century, Lewis and Clark, encountering Indians of many nations who were still unfamiliar with white men, were sheltered and aided all the way to the Pacific. Yet President Jefferson, who sent them west, had long since referred (in the Declaration of Independence) to the "merciless Indian Savages," and a century later, there was still talk of exterminating the first Americans. The historian Francis Parkman described these formerly admired people as "man, wolf, and devil, all in one" (he wrote of the "homicidal fury" of the Iroquois, whose Six Nations parliamentary system, so admired by Benjamin Franklin and the Founding Fathers, was incorporated in his country's constitution); Mark Twain dismissed the "Goshoots" (the Gosi Utes) of western Utah with disgust, and the naturalist Witmer Stone, in 1902, observed in passing that the Arctic fox was "the equal if not the superior" of the Eskimo "at least in matters of forethought, cleverness, and morality." In the late nineteenth century, the slogan of the Savage Arms Company, printed above a likeness of Sitting Bull, was "Savage Rifles make bad Indians good." (A century later, in 1982, Americans were offered a jolly board game called "Custer's Revenge," in which victory was achieved when a naked white man caught and "ravished" an Indian woman; in 1983, a group of Indians who were refused service at a country-and-western nightclub in Albuquerque reported a sign that read "No Indians Allowed.") After four hundred years, the defeated and defenseless "people in God" had been dehumanized, and the national shame of it erodes our spirit to the present day.

Seemingly, the fear and guilt that drove us to make enemies of the red man were reflected in frontier attitudes toward that "hideous and desolate wilderness" of the Pilgrims. Daniel Boone, breaking the so-called Wilderness Trail across the Cumberland Gap into Kentucky, referred to "the horror" of this wilderness, which was everywhere met with a frenzy of land-clearing far beyond any practical need. In the nineteenth century, among intellectuals, an identity of "God" with "Nature" was perceived, but the idea made small impression on the frontier. To judge from the ruthless treatment of "the wild men" and the wasteful and destructive exploitation of the continent, the view of primordial nature as a wilderness to be tamed and dominated has persisted in North America to the present day.

The American Indian, of course, had no such concept: the only wild place was the realm of spirits and of talking animals entered by shamans, who sought power at the ancient source of the old ways. The wilderness was merely uninhabited, a place "where we do not live," a farther part of home; it was "only unknown when one's communion with it had not yet been revealed." The Indians' lack of interest in modifying nature, their ability to live happily at one with it, seemed to the beleaguered colonists the most outlandish thing about them. In 1796, an Indian told the governor of Pennsylvania, "We love quiet. . . . When the winds are rustled by the wind, we fear not." For after all, the wind is the voice of the Creator. Asked what it said, an old shaman of the Netsilik Inuit replied that the message was always the same: Have no fear of the Universe.* As far north as Baffin Island, where the summer tundra and the winter pack ice provide so bountifully for the Inuit; as far south as the cold, hard plain of Tierra del Fuego, where the few trees are twisted and flattened by the ceaseless winds, where landmarks were commemorated by the white men with such names as "Famine Mountain" and "Desolation Cove," the indigenous peoples understood the rightness of nature, in which nothing is out of place. One astonished missionary heard an Ona, gazing out across the "uttermost part of the earth," murmur rapturously, *"Yak haruin"*—"my country!" (When forced to move, the Ona could not tolerate the relocation from their native earth and died off within weeks; like most Indian peoples of the Argentine, they are now extinct.) The northern spruce muskeg of James Bay, described by whites in recent years as "barren, uninhabited, fit only for flooding," is known to the Cree as Kistikani, the Garden. In the huge dripping evergreens of the Pacific Northwest, washed by sea fogs, wind, and cold, remorseless rain, a

---

*Cited by Peter Nabokov in *America as Holy Land* (a work in progress). See also Joseph Epes Brown, *The Spiritual Legacy of the American Indian* (New York, 1982), another recent work in related subject matter.

Duwamish chief said, "Every part of this earth is sacred to my people. Every shining pine needle, every sandy shore, every mist in the dark woods, every clearing and humming insect is holy in the memory and experience of my people."

. . .

An Indian friend in California once told me how much she hated the phrase "wild Indian" in the books of American history that she was given to read in school: "We were never 'wild,' " she said. "We were just natural." Traditional people, still in harmony with the world around them, do not isolate themselves from other living things, nor consider one creature superior to another. This was also true of Europeans, before the discoveries of science made them observers, manipulators of the natural world, instead of un-selfconscious participants. By seeking to dominate it, the white men set themselves in opposition to a vital, healing force of which they were a part and thereby mislaid a whole dimension of existence.

> One thing we know which the white man may one day discover. Our God is the same God. You may think now that you own Him as you wish to own our land. But you cannot. He is the body of man. And His compassion is equal for the red man and the white. This earth is precious to Him. And to harm the earth is to heap contempt on its creator. The whites too shall pass—perhaps sooner than other tribes. Continue to contaminate your bed, and you will one night suffocate in your own waste. When the buffalo are all slaughtered, the wild horses all tamed, the secret corners of the forest heavy with the scent of many men, and the view of the ripe hills blotted by talking wires, where is the thicket? Gone. Where is the eagle? Gone. And what is it to say good-by to the swift and the hunt, the end of living and the beginning of survival?

In such utterances as these and many, many others, there is a clarity and a quiet beauty that is stunning. We can no longer pretend—as we did for so long—that Indians are a primitive people: no, they are a traditional people, that is, a "first" or "original" people, a primal people, the inheritors of a profound and exquisite wisdom distilled by long ages on this earth. The Indian concept of earth and spirit has been patronizingly dismissed as simple-hearted "naturalism" or "animism," when in fact it derives from a holistic vision known to all mystics and great teachers of the most venerated religions of the world.

This universal and profound intuitive knowledge may have come to North America with the first peoples to arrive from Asia, although Indians say it was the other way around, that the assumption of white historians that a nomadic people made a one-way journey across the Bering Strait from Asia and down into America, and never attempted to travel the other way, makes little sense. Today most Indians believe that they originated on this continent: at the very least, there was travel in both directions. (In recent years, this theory has been given support by a young anthropologist who, on the basis of stone tools and skull measurements as well as pictographs and cave drawings, goes so far as to suggest that the Cro-Magnon—the first truly modern men—who came out of nowhere to displace the Neanderthals in Eurasia perhaps 40,000 years ago were a pre-Indian people from North America.*) According to the Hopi, runners were sent west across the Bering Strait as messengers and couriers, and information was exchanged between North America and Eurasia in very early times, long before European history had begun.

The Old Way—what the Lakota call *wouncage*, "our way of doing"—is very consistent throughout the Indian nations, despite the great variety of cultures. The Indian cannot love the Creator and desecrate the earth, for Indian existence is not separable from Indian religion, which is not separable from the natural world. It is not a matter of "worshiping nature," as anthropologists suggest: to worship nature, one must stand apart from it and call it "nature" or "the human habitat" or "the environment." For the Indian, there is no separation. Man is an aspect of nature, and nature itself is a manifestation of primordial religion. Even the word "religion" makes an unnecessary separation, and there is no word for it in the Indian tongues. Nature is the "Great Mysterious," the "religion before religion," the profound intuitive apprehension of the true nature of existence attained by sages of all epochs, everywhere on earth: the whole universe is sacred, man is the whole universe,

*Jeffrey Goodman, *American Genesis* (New York, 1981).

and the religious ceremony is life itself, the miraculous common acts of every day. Respect for nature is reverence for the Creator, and it is also self-respecting, since man and nature, though not the same thing, are not different. (Thus, a leader of the Coyote Clan, the Thunder Clan, may be referred to as the Thunder, or the Coyote; the kachina dancer does not represent the deity or spirit, he *becomes* that spirit.) Plants and animals that must be used are thanked with ceremony, and rocks are not moved carelessly from their own places. Every morning, prayers are offered to the sun, earth, and the powers of the four directions, the water that brings life, and the Creator; this earth teaches us, takes care of us, and nothing is wasted, even the common clay. "When we make pottery, we are very careful, and do not waste anything, because we know where it comes from." And this love of earth, this respectful awareness of the world around, of its warnings and its affirmations, brings a joyous humility, a *simplicity* that spares the Indian the great restlessness and loneliness that the alienated white men have brought down upon themselves.

"There was no such thing as emptiness in the world," a Lakota says. "Even in the sky there were no vacant places. Everywhere there was life, visible and invisible, and every object gave us a great interest to life. Even without human companionship one was never alone. The world teemed with life and wisdom, there was no solitude for the Lakota."*

The Indian people had no "horror of the wilderness," and they did not disrespect the deer killed or the plant harvested, the graves of the Old Ones, the land and life that also belong to future generations. ("Think not forever of yourselves, o chiefs, nor of your own generation," said Deganawidah, who led in the formation of the Six Nations Confederacy. "Think of the continuing generations of our families, think of grandchildren and of those yet unborn, whose faces are coming from beneath the ground.")

Consider this Paiute song, as rendered by the Acoma poet, Simon Ortiz. Ortiz is talking about a sacred spring:

Something from there, from down in there, is talking to you.
You could hear it if you listen.
Listen!

*Luther Standing Bear, *Land of the Spotted Eagle* (Lincoln: Univ. of Nebraska Press, 1978).

You can hear it.
The stones in the earth rattling together,
The stones down there moving around each other.
When we pray, when we sing,
When we talk with the stones rattling in the ground,
And the stones moving in the ground,
That's the place Indians talk about. . . .

Oh, we stay there for some days.
You can hear it talking from far.
From far away inside, they're moving, from far away.
Come to us, coming to us pretty soon.
Getting closer, getting close, the power is getting close
And the ground is hot and shaking.
Something is doing that,
And the people know that.
They have to keep talking, praying.

That's the Indian way.
Singing,
That's the Indian way!
And pretty soon it's there.
You know it's all around, it's right there.
And the people are right there. . . .

The people talking, telling the power to come to them
And pretty soon, it will come, it will come,
The moving power of the voice,
The moving power of the earth,
The moving power of the people.
That's the place Indian People talk about.

·   ·   ·

Mitakuye iyasin!, the Lakota says: All my relations! meaning all one's relations with everything on earth. Indian healing ceremonies are based on the idea of restoring those relations, including the balance of body and spirit—they are not different—that are out of harmony with the world around. In the Western world today, few understand natural matters that are taken for granted by traditional peoples, and few among the Indians themselves know how to listen to the earth; for most present-day

Indians (the traditional people say) the world is a dead thing. Like the white man, they have no home. All this was foretold by Sweet Medicine, the great Cheyenne prophet, who tried to warn his people: "They will keep pushing forward, going all the time. They will tear up the earth, and at last you will do it with them. When you do, you will become crazy, and forget all that I am teaching you."

> The white man does not understand the Indian for the reason that he does not understand America. He is too far removed from its formative processes. The roots of the tree of his life have not yet grasped the rock and soil. The white man is still troubled with primitive fears; he still has in his consciousness the perils of this frontier continent, some of its fastnesses not yet having yielded to his questing footsteps and inquiring eyes. He shudders still with the memory of the loss of his forefathers upon its scorching deserts and forbidding mountaintops. The man from Europe is still a foreigner and an alien. And he still hates the man who questioned his path across the continent.
>
> But in the Indian the spirit of the land is still vested; it will be until other men are able to divine and meet its rhythm. Men must be born and reborn to belong. Their bodies must be formed of the dust of their forefathers' bones.*

Most Indian nations have—or used to have—similar attitudes toward earth. Yet to this day, we dismiss those attitudes as something archaic, picturesque, to be pushed aside by that lunatic insistence on "progress," on "growth," on gross national product, that is destroying the land and air and water, the wild animals and plants, the countryside, small towns and small business and small farmers, not to speak of quality and craftsmanship, birdsong, silence, night, and the very soul of man.

At the end of an old John Wayne movie called *Hondo*, the Apaches are defeated and the actor says, "It's the end of a way of life—a good way. NOW GET THOSE WAGONS MOVING!" Those wagons of Progress are still moving, riding roughshod over what is left of the beautiful American Canaan. Not only have we failed to learn from the Indian's "good way of life," we are still in the process of destroying it through acculturation, relocation, the

*Ibid.

recurrent termination legislation, the theft and pollution of earth and air and water, and the disreputable leasing policies and land-claim settlements that dispossess the Indian people from their sacred earth.

Elders and spiritual leaders in many places in the United States and Canada say that traditional religion, while no longer forbidden, is frowned upon and interfered with by many if not most of the bureaucrats in the government agencies (who are often of missionary background) and that disruption of sacred places—mountains, valleys, isolated rocks and springs, and even burial grounds—is not the exception but the rule, even where there is nothing extra to be gained by the alliance of industry, federal agencies, and acculturated Indians that dominates the economy of most reservations. More often than not, the transgression of sacred ground is also an environmental transgression, which Indians—who do not share our view of the environment as something apart from ourselves—perceive as the same thing: one cannot love the Creator and desecrate Creation.

Traditional peoples the world over have much to teach a spiritually crippled race which, as Lame Deer said, sees "only with one eye." This half-blindness has been the curse of Europeans as long as the Indians have known us, but we have not always been accursed; at one time, we, too, were at one with the *mysterium tremendum*. And we must feel awe again if we are to return to a harmonious existence with our own habitat, and survive; we must consider this life-essence that is all about us, manifesting in each moment—the music of the stars, the color of the wind, the dead stillness between tides at dead of night, the birds, trees, sea pearls and manure, the moment-by-moment miracle of our existence.

"All is God," D. H. Lawrence said, describing the religion of the Taos Pueblo. "The whole life-effort of man is to get his life into direct contact with the elemental life of the cosmos." It isn't enough to admire Indian teachings; we *need* them. We belong to this earth, it does not belong to us; it cares for us, and we must care for it. If our time on earth is to endure, we must love the earth in the strong, unsentimental way of traditional peoples, not seeking to exploit but to live in balance with the natural world. When modern man has regained his reverence for land and life, then the lost Paradise, the Golden Age in the race memories of all peoples will come again, and all men will be *"in Dios,"* people of God.

· 2 ·

THE LONG RIVER

One morning in early March, I walked south from the slash pine strands of the old Loop Road into the scrub cypress and wet prairie that extends southward into the sawgrass of Lostman's Slough. There was no sign of man, no smoke, no intrusive note of inorganic color, and every mile or so I stopped to absorb such emptiness, listening, sniffing the coarse marsh air, turning beneath the sky in a slow circle, aware of the skeleton of ancient limestones through the pale marl under my feet. The sun that rose over the Everglades brought a hard sparkle to small isolated hammocks of saw palmetto and groundsel bush, wax myrtle and poisonwood, like dark islets in the yellow sea of grass. Bluebirds and spring warblers were already arriving in the piney woods and hardwood hammocks back there on the Loop Road, but the birds out here on the sawgrass prairie were hardy winter species—a bittern, kingfishers, a red-shouldered hawk, swallows and meadowlarks, a shrike, and always the slow egrets and ibis, in silhouette on the shining eastern skies. The spring song of the meadowlark was the voice of this first warm day after a norther that had caused the aestivating tree snails to fall from their wood niches in the hammocks.

In the winter grass the spring flowers were still solitary, scattered—marsh pink and small blue-eyed iris, redroot and tickseed aster, a bluebell known as bay lobelia—and from a small pool on the south side of a willow copse rose the odd white blossom of the aquatic arrowhead. I stooped to look at it, extending my hand at the same time to pick up the bronze shell of an apple snail, and at that moment another odd white flower opened, just the length of my forearm away. There was no hiss, nor even the soft whipping of a scaly tail on the grass tussock, only the two white petals of the shiny mouth.

Slowly I straightened, aware of a surrounding silence; feeling a need to get my bearings, I gazed about me. To the west was the low gray forest of small cypress; to the south and east, in the broad sawgrass slough known as Shark River, was the archipelago of hardwood hammocks that had sheltered the last Indians in the south Everglades. This prairie extended south to the old Calusa Indian mounds on Lostman's River, which like the Shark, flowed out eventually among the mangroves of the Ten Thousand Islands, on the Gulf of Mexico. Perhaps four miles away, off to the north, was the Loop Road and the relict shacks of Pinecrest, which had been condemned in the creation of the Big Cypress National Preserve in 1974. When I first came here in the mid-sixties, the Loop Road was already decaying after years of sun and weeds and water, releasing white fossil seashells from its marl; it was summer then, and fish were swimming across the broken pavement to the swamps on either side.

Because of the hard cold of recent days, I had not expected to see snakes, and in fact, this one that had climbed out onto a tussock to get warm was still so torpid that it did not move away, merely opened its white mouth without hissing when I hunkered down again to have a better look at it. In memory of boyhood days when my brother and I collected copperheads, I considered catching it, but there was no stick handy, and no purpose. I left the cold snake warming where it lay and headed north again, moving now with more attention and respect. For all of man's intrusions, this vast cypress and sawgrass marsh between Lake Okeechobee and Cape Sable has retained at least a whisper of its former wildness; a few cougar, bear, and crocodile survive here, and multitudes of alligator, and this cotton-mouth moccasin that I had not seen until it warned me was only one of the four species of poisonous snakes found in the region.

The people who know this country best are Indians, many of them full bloods who speak their own language: not many such people are left in North America. Their culture has survived because of an ability and will to endure and fight and hide in an inhospitable and trackless reach of swamp and marsh where heat and humidity, deer flies and mosquitoes, and the tall, razor-edged sedge called sawgrass all became their formidable allies; it persists because of an unrelenting mistrust of the white man. In terms of men as well as money, the United States fought the longest and most costly of its Indian Wars before abandoning its efforts to clear the last Indian out of Florida, and for a century thereafter, the Everglades and the Big Cypress hid from the world the scattered fires of these people. Even when it was safe to reappear, the Indians preferred their isolation. But in recent years, they have been driven out into the open, not by soldiers but by bureaucrats and politicians; the white man had simply usurped the land that was theirs by right and by prior occupation. Never defeated but no longer acknowledged, they found themselves homeless in their own country.*

In the eighteenth and early nineteenth centuries, as pressures from European colonists increased, various bands of southeastern Indians of the great Creek Confederacy drifted or fled southward into the peninsula left empty by the aboriginal tribes; the fierce Calusa, who killed Ponce de Leon in 1521, had been all but destroyed by diseases of the Spanish. The first newcomers were small bands of fierce Hitchiti-speaking hunters, the traditional enemies of the agricultural Creeks who appeared later. One Hitchiti band settled for a time near present-day Tallahassee, at a lake called Miccosukee, or "Mikasuki." Eventually this name became attached to those Indians who spoke Hitchiti, a dialect unintelligible to the Muskogee-speaking Creeks that has now vanished everywhere except south Florida. Few people, in fact, have ever heard of the Miccosukee Indians, who are generally included among the "Seminole"—from *siminoli*, a Muskogee word variously translated by white ethnologists as "wild" or "outcast," "undomesticated," and by the Muskogee clans themselves as "people of the distant fires."

The Spanish who laid claim to Florida for nearly three hundred years, over the protests of both France and England, recognized the Miccosukee by that name at least as early as the Treaty of Walnut Hills of 1793, but to the new American colonists of Georgia and Carolina, the Miccosukee and Florida Creeks were all unruly "Seminoles" who had not only been friendly to the British during the Revolutionary War (when Britain had dominion over Florida) but had given sanctuary to the numerous runaway slaves. These blacks—mostly warlike Ashanti, not long out of Africa, whom the Indians valued as allies against the whites—had been permitted to establish their own villages, and to a large degree had adopted the agricultural Muskogee culture. After 1808, when the Atlantic slave trade was prohibited, expeditions into Spanish territory (now virtually devoid of Spaniards) were sent south to

---

*Excellent bibliographies relating to the Florida Indian peoples may be found in W. C. Sturtevant, *The Mikasuki Seminole: Medical Beliefs and Practices* (Yale University, 1955), and in J. O. Buswell III, "Florida Seminole Religious Ritual: Resistance and Change" (unpublished doctoral dissertation, St. Louis University, 1972; available from University Microfilms, Ann Arbor, Michigan). See also I. M. Peithmann, *The Unconquered Seminole Indians* (St. Petersburg, Fla.: Great Outdoors Publishing Co., 1957), and Virginia B. Peters, *The Florida Wars* (Hamden, Conn.: Archon Books, 1979) for general historical background.

retrieve these slaves and capture any other individuals who might be sold off as their descendants; the negligible interbreeding between Indians and blacks was exaggerated from the start to justify seizing Indians as slaves. In 1811, the beleaguered Seminole were approached by the great Shawnee leader, Tecumseh, who wished them to join in a great Indian confederation against further encroachment by the Americans; like the Cherokee, the Seminole failed to respond. Within two years, the white men's raids had the support of four hundred Tennessee cavalry under Colonel Douglas Clinch, whose orders to "chastise the Indians, plunder and burn their homes and property, and drive in their cattle" are a fair indication of the ruthless attitudes on the new frontier.

The Creeks of Georgia and Alabama had been fatally defeated by Andrew Jackson and the Cherokees in the Creek War of 1813–1814; with most of their lands turned over to the American settlers, many Creeks were now reduced to serving Jackson's Florida forays as soldiers and scouts. (In fact, it is estimated that over half of Jackson's force were Creeks led by a half-breed known as McIntosh, who was later executed by his people for surrendering Creek lands to the whites in violation of the tribal law.) In the course of what came to be called the First Seminole War of 1817–1818, General Jackson's forces were attacked by Miccosukee warriors as they forded the lake for which the band was named. In 1819, the absentee Spanish sold the peninsula to the United States for five million dollars, but those clauses in the Treaty of Cession by which the Spanish guaranteed Indian rights were ignored by Jackson, who was appointed governor of Florida in 1821. The new governor made few distinctions in his broad dislike of Indians; he was already obsessed by the idea of "removing" the remnant southeastern Indians from the path of the clamoring settlers by banishing them across the Mississippi. But before Jackson could put this plan into effect, which he did speedily upon his accession to the Presidency, the United States had recognized that the Seminoles were a separate nation from the Creeks, and therefore had a valid claim on their own land.

According to the Treaty of Moultrie Creek, in 1823, all of Florida except one tract in the north-central part of the peninsula was acquired from certain chiefs who thought it best to accommodate the white men. Eneah Emathla, chief of a Miccosukee town, had protested to the Indian commissioners that they must not send his people to a southern country that lacked hickory nuts, acorns, and persimmons; when he realized that no mercy would be granted, he spoke as follows to William Duval, who had replaced Jackson as governor of Florida:

> Do you think . . . I am like a bat, that hangs by its claws in a dark cave, and that I can see nothing of what is going on around me? Ever since I was a small boy I have seen the white people steadily encroaching upon the Indians, and driving them from their homes and hunting grounds. When I was a boy, the Indians still roamed undisputed over the country lying between the Tennessee River and the great sea [Gulf of Mexico] of the south, and now, where there is nothing left them but the hunting grounds in Florida, the white men covet that. I will tell you plainly, if I had the power, I would tonight cut the throat of every white man in Florida.

The tract awarded to the Indians, by the admission of the fair-minded Duval, was "by far the poorest and most miserable region I ever beheld"; nevertheless, harassment of the Indians by slavers, settlers, and adventurers continued. By the terms of the Removal Act signed by President Jackson in 1830, all Indians remaining in the Southeast, including the President's allies, the Cherokee and Creek, were to be transported to the Arkansas Territory, and in 1832, the U.S. commissioners cajoled and threatened certain Seminole chiefs into agreeing to take their people west. However, these chiefs were repudiated by others who declared that the first group had no such authority and who balked at a clause tacked on to the so-called "Treaty of Payne's Landing" that bound them to deliver the "Seminole Negroes" into slavery. In this period, the Indians' black allies were led by a fierce old "Maroon"* called Abraham, who also acted as a war chief and as an interpreter in dealings with the whites.

In 1835, in an epochal opinion by Chief Justice John Marshall, the U.S. Supreme Court confirmed the validity of all treaties made between the Indians and Spanish, including the Treaty of Walnut Hills, and held that the United States was obliged to observe those clauses in the Treaty of Cession protecting the rights and sovereignty of the Indian nations, which were as binding as

*From *cimarrón,* a Spanish word for "renegade" or "wild."

the "supreme law of the land . . . inviolable by the power of Congress. . . . It would be an unwarranted construction of these treaties, laws, ordinances, and municipal regulations, were we to decide that the Indians were not to be maintained in the enjoyment of all the rights which they could have enjoyed under either, had the provinces remained under the dominion of Spain." Ignoring the Court, the government proceeded to carry out the three-year ultimatum imposed upon the Indians at Payne's Landing: as the angry President remarked, "The Chief Justice has made his law; now let him enforce it."

Violent resistance to emigration was led by a young Creek who seems to have fled south after the Creek Wars and who was raised among the Miccosukee. Called Asi-Yaholo ("Black Drink Crier") or "Osceola," and known to the whites as "Billy Powell," this young war leader executed a chief who had agreed to emigrate, and allegedly threw into the bushes the gold that this man had accepted for his cattle. The Indian agent at Fort King, General Wiley Thompson, in a letter to the Secretary of War, had already identified Osceola as "a bold and dashing young chief . . . vehemently opposed to removal"; he suspected that the volatile Osceola was influencing the Muskogee leader, Micanopy, to hold firm. On December 28, 1835, Osceola led fifty Miccosukee in an attack on Fort King and succeeded in killing Thompson, who had made the mistake of jailing him for his hostile attitude a few months earlier. That same day, all but three of a detachment of one hundred and ten men under Major Francis Dade that had been proceeding to Fort King were destroyed by a band of Indians and blacks led by Micanopy and his subchiefs, notably a war chief named Halpatter, or "Alligator." Three days later, U.S. troops were attacked on the Withlacoochee River by the combined forces of Osceola and Alligator, and the Second Seminole War was under way.

In February 1836, Osceola dictated a letter to General Douglas Clinch, whose men had been attacked on the Withlacoochee: "You have guns—so have we. You have powder and lead and so have we. Your men will fight, so will ours, till the last drop of Seminole blood has moistened the dust of his hunting ground."

General Thomas Jesup, who took over the command in Florida at the end of 1836, shortly received a very similar communication from Apayaka, or "Sam Jones," the old chief of the Miccosukee Seminole: although much less numerous than the

Muskogee, with whom they had been forced to make common cause, the Miccosukee were leading the resistance, and Apayaka later assisted Osceola in the abduction of Micanopy and other weary Muskogee chiefs who had agreed to lead their people west. Because of the fierce Miccosukee, resistance to emigration was soon so intense that even to listen to discussion of it was said to be punishable by death. "The country can be rid of them," General Jesup concluded, "only by exterminating them," and to this end, he tried foul means as well as fair.

In 1837, Osceola and his chiefs, presenting themselves in good faith for peace talks, were taken prisoner by the frustrated Jesup, who subsequently deceived a well-intentioned Cherokee delegation into serving as decoys to those chiefs remaining in the swamps; the Cherokee persuaded Micanopy, Cloud, and thirty others to come in for peace talks, only to see them arrested and held hostage at St. Augustine for the surrender of their followers and families. Demanding an interview with the captives, the Cherokee cleared themselves of any part in the betrayal, and later a Cherokee chief would testify that at this meeting, a Colonel Sherburne, representing General Jesup, had asked Osceola and the other chiefs if the Indians would accept a territory that included all of Florida south of a line drawn from Tampa Bay to the east coast; if so, would they come to Washington to ratify such a treaty? All immediately agreed to do so except old Chief Philip, grandson of a Spanish duke, who insisted on evidence that this time the Americans meant to keep their word. As he suspected, they did not; the chiefs were sent to Arkansas instead of Washington—all but Philip, who did not survive the journey, and Osceola, who died a few months later of white men's diseases at Fort Moultrie, South Carolina. (Before burial, the great war hero of the Miccosukee and Muskogee was beheaded by his physician, whose wife was the bereaved sister of Wiley Thompson. "Dr. Weedon was an unusual man," his great-granddaughter would admit many years later. "He used to hang the head of Osceola on the bedstead where his three little boys slept, and leave it there all night as a punishment for misbehavior.")

George Catlin, who completed Osceola's portrait just five days before his death, wrote of him as follows:

> I am fully convinced from all that I have seen, and learned from the lips of Osceola, and from the chiefs who are around

him, that he is a most extraordinary man, and one entitled to a better fate.

In stature he is about mediocrity with an elastic and graceful movement; in his face he is good looking, with rather an effeminate smile; but of so peculiar a character, that the world may be ransacked over without finding another just like it.

After the death of Osceola, the leadership of Seminole resistance had passed to Philip's son, the ferocious Coacoochee, known as "Wild Cat," who had also been betrayed into captivity but later made a remarkable escape that the Indians attributed to his shamanistic powers. On Christmas Day, 1837, Wild Cat rallied the wavering Seminoles for a great battle near Lake Okeechobee. Victory that day was credited to Colonel Zachary Taylor, "Old Rough and Ready," who, like "Old Hickory" before him, would be assisted to the Presidency by his exploits as an Indian-fighter. But in fact Taylor's force of more than 1,000 men was outfought and defeated by several hundred Indians under Wild Cat, Alligator, Apayaka, and Holata Micco, called "Billy Bowlegs," who harassed the soldiers from the cover of the forested terrain.

Many Americans, already annoyed that an expensive war against the Indians was being fought for the benefit of rich slave-owners and land speculators on the southern frontier, had protested the betrayal and death of Osceola, and Taylor's replacement, General Alexander Macomb, had orders to end the disgraceful and humiliating Florida campaign as soon as possible. Macomb's negotiations with the Indians, commencing in 1839, led eventually to a grant of five million acres in the wet, barren, and uninhabited southern peninsula, but because of a great uproar from the settlers, who wanted all Indians out of Florida, dead or alive, Congress would not ratify the treaty, the terms of which had been meticulously honored by the Seminole. To pacify local criticism of the Macomb Agreement, the Secretary of War announced that it had, in fact, been a device to pacify the Indians, the better to expedite their removal to the west. Shortly thereafter, the truce was broken when warriors led by a giant Indian named Chekika wiped out half a detachment of soldiers under Colonel William Harney, in a night attack on the Caloosahatchee River; Harney escaped into the bushes in his drawers. The following year this same band

attacked the settlement in the upper Keys known as Matanzas,*
killing seven whites, including the great botanist Henry Perrine,
after which Chekika returned to his hammock camp deep in the
Glades. (Indians say that Chekika had gone there to kill a buc-
caneer who had offered to kill Indians for the U.S. government
at two hundred dollars a head.) Colonel Harney, who had been
criticized for negligence on the Caloosahatchee, and who swore
he would have the scalp of "that piratical savage," took ninety men
and attacked Chekika's hammock, killing the huge Indian and
hanging his men. This punitive expedition continued westward,
emerging finally at what is now called Harney River; they were
the first white men ever to cross the sea of grass.

In addition to Jackson, Winfield Scott, Zachary Taylor, and
William Harney, the soldiers who engaged in the Seminole Wars
included Lieutenant William Tecumseh Sherman, later the head
of the U.S. Army. But perhaps the most distinguished service to
his country was offered by Ethan Allan Hitchcock, a young lieutenant whose first duty in Florida was to see the burial of Major
Dade and all his men (the officers went into one trench, the enlisted men into another). Despite this ordeal, some two months
after "the Dade Massacre," Hitchcock would write as follows in
his diary: "The Treaty of Payne's Landing in 1832 by which it was
attempted to remove the Indians was a fraud upon them and they
have in fact never agreed to emigrate. I say therefore that the
Indians are in the right to defend themselves in the country to
the best of their ability."

By 1840, he had not changed his poor opinion of his nation's
conduct, an opinion now shared by an increasing number of
thoughtful citizens. In a letter to his brother, Hitchcock declared:

In 1836—I thought when I heard of the massacre of Major
Dade and his command—that the Indians had made a treaty
to emigrate in good faith and had violated their engagements,
signalizing their violation of faith with the most wholesale
and barbarous murders. In that opinion, as you know, I entered Florida as a volunteer, being on furlough at the time.

*Matanzas, or "Killing Ground," was so named by the Spanish because four
hundred Frenchmen had apparently been killed there by the fierce Caloosas in
the early eighteenth century; it was later Dade Key, after Major Dade, and later
still "Indian Key," today a small island not far off the shore of Lower Matecumbe.

I no sooner reached Fort King and had access to officers who had been witnesses of the proceedings of the government than I entirely changed my mind. . . .

The Indians have always held one language in regard to their understanding of the treaty. They have from first to last uniformly declared that the deputation to examine the new country had no power to confirm the treaty, but were to return and report the result of their observations when they, the tribe, were to assent or dissent.

The deputation, however, was induced while at Fort Gibson (as I've heard, even under threats that they would not otherwise return to their friends) to sign a paper signifying that they were satisfied with the country designated for them in the treaty. This paper was regarded by President Jackson as completing the treaty and the Senate ignorantly ratifying it, it became, to appearance, the law of the land in '33 I believe. Two or three years were lost, however, before any decided step was taken by the government to enforce the treaty. . . . The war was then fairly entered upon and we are no nearer its termination than when we commenced; while Florida, from its present condition, opens a field of runaway Negroes and desperate white men, the Indians are growing stronger every day, and there is reasonable ground to doubt whether fewer than 20,000 men could quiet the country short of five years to come, and it might require ten years.

I give you this little sketch in order that you may estimate the feelings with which I now enter this country. Five years ago I became a volunteer, willing to make every effort in my power to be of service in "punishing," as I thought, the Indians. I now come with the persuasion that the Indians have been wronged and I enter upon one of the most hopeless tasks that was ever given a man to perform.

The skirmishing continued until 1842, by which time most of the Muskogee chiefs had been seized, tricked, bribed, and threatened into departing for that part of the Arkansas Territory that was later known as Oklahoma. Even Wild Cat and Alligator eventually resigned themselves to going west. Lieutenant W. T. Sherman saw to the arrest of Wild Cat, who spoke to Colonel William Worth as follows:

When I was a boy, I saw the white man afar off, and was told that he was my enemy. I could not shoot him as I would a wolf

or bear, yet he came upon me. My horses and fields he took from me.
He said he was my friend. He gave me his hand in friendship; I
took it, he had a snake in the other; his tongue was forked; he
lied and stung me. I asked for but a small piece of land, enough
to plant and live on far to the south—a spot where I could
place the ashes of my kindred—a place where my wife and child
could live. This was not granted me. I am about to leave Florida
forever and have done nothing to disgrace it. It was my home;
I have thrown away my rifle and have taken the hand of
the white man, and now I say take care of me!

The people had songs for the Removal, as they did for all events
in life:

> We are going with Washington.
> Which boat do we get in?
>
> They are taking us beyond the Calusa River.
> They are taking us to the end of our tribe.
> They are taking us to an old town in the west.

The few hundred Indians now remaining were scattered on remote
hammocks in the Big Cypress Swamp and Ten Thousand Islands.
There they were ordered to remain after August 11, 1842, when
"peace" was declared by Colonel Worth; Worth's name is attached
to what is now called the Macomb–Worth Agreement of 1842,
according to which the Florida Indians were given all of the southern peninsula south of Pease Creek (now Peace River) and west
of Lake Okeechobee. President John Tyler approved and ratified
the Agreement, and his successor, James Polk, in 1845, signed an
Executive Order directing that an additional "strip of the public
lands, twenty miles in width, around the District set apart for the
use and occupancy of the Seminoles of Florida, should be reserved
from survey and sale."

In 1843, Colonel Worth, estimating that the remaining "Seminoles, Mickasukis, Creeks, and Tallahassees" numbered about
three hundred, recorded his respect for the Indian warriors and
also his willingness to betray them.

> As yet, few have manifested a disposition to emigrate; and
> the time has not arrived to effect their removal by coercive

measures, as they are somewhat shy and distrustful of the whites. . . . These apprehensions, under the policy pursued, will soon wear away; when, if considered desirable, advantage may be taken of a favorable occasion to send off the whole. . . . When done, it must be thoroughly and effectually done; for if *ten* of these warriors remained, maddened to a spirit of hostility, they would suffice to break up and scatter the entire line of new settlements, although ten-fold their numbers. . . .

Since the pacification, August 14th, 1842, these people have observed perfect good faith, and strictly fulfilled their engagements; not an instance of rudeness towards the whites has yet occurred; they plant and hunt diligently; take their skins and game to the trading establishment at Tampa, procure the necessaries they desire, and return quietly to their grounds.

By 1845, the year that Florida became a state, most of the remnant Indian population was living dutifully on Macomb–Worth Agreement territory in the Big Cypress and the Everglades, a land that they assumed would be theirs forever. But even this poor land was wanted by the whites, and in 1850, Holata Micco—Billy Bowlegs—who had fought at the battle of Okeechobee and also in Chekika's raid on the Caloosahatchee, and who was probably the last chief recognized as such by both the Muskogee and the Miccosukee, was offered a bribe to take his people west. When he refused this, he was persuaded to make a visit to Washington, D.C., where he was registered in the hotel as "Mr. William B. Legs"; in Washington, said the Army captain charged with the duty of removing him by hook or crook from Florida, he was bound to be impressed by "the annuities and presents distributed periodically to [the] bands in Arkansas" and also by "the number and power of the white men." But unlike so many chiefs of so many tribes, before and after, who were taken off to Washington to be corrupted, Mr. Legs did not permit his enjoyment of the visit (nor his audience with Great White Father Millard Fillmore) to weaken his intention to remain in Florida. Later that year, the western Seminole had word from Billy Bowlegs that the Indians in Florida "would shoot any person who attempted to visit them for the purpose of influencing them to move west." In response, the General Assembly of Florida on January 12, 1853, declared it unlawful for any Indian "to remain within the limits of the State . . . and any Indians that may remain, or may be found within the limits of this State, shall be captured and sent west of the Mississippi."

In 1855, a U.S. Army scouting expedition in the Big Cypress, apparently sent to spy out the Indian villages, discovered and destroyed Billy Bowlegs's settlement and gardens, an act which brought Indian forbearance to an end: next morning, the party was attacked, with two men killed. After three years of raids and skirmishes that became known as the Third Seminole War, the United States realized that it had been foiled again, this time by a few small bands of Indians so adept at guerrilla warfare that in the words of Robert McClelland, the Secretary of the Interior Department (which had taken over administration of the Indians from the War Department six years before), they "had baffled the energetic efforts of our army to effect their subjugation and removal." Even the cynical use of other tribes—Creek, Shawnee, Choctaw, Delaware, and Sauk and Fox had all been sent in against their brothers at one time or another—had failed to defeat "this cunning race of Indians . . . so cruel, distrustful and superstitious." (The author of these disillusioned words, Captain J. T. Sprague, was none other than he who had befriended Billy Bowlegs with the intention of having him traduced in Washington.)

Eventually the weary Holata Micco was persuaded to accept a larger bribe, and late in 1858 his band of Muskogee, together with forty-odd captive Indians, was sent to Arkansas; the next year, he returned as an agent of the white man to persuade a last part of his people to go west.

The Miccosukee led by "Sam Jones," or Apayaka, now over one hundred years old, were the last undefeated band of Indians left in Florida. A few remnant Muskogee-speakers later turned up north of Lake Okeechobee, while the Miccosukee hid in the Big Cypress and Everglades in the far south. So few of these "southern Indians" had been captured and sent west that no Hitchiti-speaking band was ever established in the Seminole nation (established officially at Wewoka, Oklahoma, in 1868). Those left in Florida, after so many years of exploitation and betrayal, had learned to despise as well as fear these "Americans" who did not know how to keep their word. They also mistrusted the Muskogee Seminole, who had been enemies before they had been allies, who had always given in more easily to the whites, and whose leaders—even the great war chief, Alligator, even Billy Bowlegs—had come back regularly from Oklahoma as agents for the white men, trying to cajole them into going west.

As late as 1879, the office of Indian Affairs sent R. H. Pratt (founder of the Carlisle Indian School) to sound out the Florida Indians on the subject of removal; it was Pratt's report that finally discouraged further efforts. "Except by some unworthy trick, they could not be procured to go there. . . . To reach them in their present divided state and exercise any authority as agent would be extremely difficult even should the Indians be willing to accept such authority." At a meeting organized at Fort Myers in July of 1879 with the help of Captain F. A. Hendry, one of the few whites trusted by the Indians, Pratt's offer of federal assistance and schooling was coldly refused. The Indians wanted no white man's education, no help, and no money; they only wanted to be left alone, and they punished any Indian who disagreed. According to the first ethnological report, written five years later, "the birth day of a white half-breed would be followed by the death of the Indian mother at the hands of her own people."*

The ethnological report of 1884 made no distinction between the two separate groups of Indians, but the Indians themselves had no such problem. The Muskogee Seminole, joining gradually into a single band of agricultural inclination, would become known as the "Cow Creeks" or "Creeks" (after Cow Creek, north of Okeechobee), while the Hitchiti-speaking Miccosukee returned to a life based on fishing and hunting, in a remote region of the Big Cypress near Sam Jones Old Town, and also in the Shark River–Ten Thousand Islands mangrove region in the far southwestern reaches of the Everglades.

Once again the long seasons of both tribes revolved around the Green Corn Dance, when the power of the medicine bundle that carried the spiritual well-being of the people was renewed. The Green Corn Dance fulfilled every wish and need for tribal government, but the settlers could not let well enough alone. In 1891, an Indian Agency was set up at Immokalee, and numerous sincere attempts were made by the uneasy white people to set

---

*Clay MacCauley, "Seminole Indians of Florida" (Washington, D.C.: Bureau of American Ethnology, 1887).

aside land, preach against the whiskey that other white people were providing, and otherwise extend the hand of friendship to these exceptionally unfriendly Indians. But for many years no two white groups could agree on which piece of land was poor enough to give them, and anyway, the Indians wanted no boundaried tract, knowing as they did that the earth was like the air, and could not be owned. Even as late as 1920, the Miccosukee refused to gather on the "Seminole" reservation that was finally established in the Big Cypress. Apart from being a scraggy land as ill-suited for hunting as it was for gardens, the reservation had to be shared with the Cow Creeks, and anyway, it was much too close to the ever-increasing activities of the white man, who might decide at any time to round up the redskins, as they were popularly known, and pack them off to Oklahoma. The Miccosukee remained hidden in another waste reserved for them in 1917, consisting of sloughs and brackish marshes in the remote southwest reaches of Shark River.

The isolation and intransigence of this people would spare them the stunning poverty and spiritual degradation that had eroded the spirit and the pride of defeated Indians all across the country. This isolation was enforced by their own strict laws; an Indian named Billie Conapatchie nearly lost his life for associating with the family of the aforementioned Captain Hendry in the 1890's. At outlying trading posts such as Chokoloksee Island, alligator hides and egret plumes and furs were exchanged for rifles, liquor, pots, and cloth; otherwise, the Indians rarely ventured from the inhospitable and roadless reaches of Atsi-na-hufa (the Big Cypress) and Pa-hay-okee (the Everglades), which held out almost no attraction for the white man. Also, they steadfastly refused all money or any other aid from the U.S. government, made available to them in one form or another after 1879; excepting liquor and ammunition, there was little that they needed that they could not make for themselves.

In some unknown year toward the century's end, the last wolf was exterminated in Florida. A few years later, the trade in egret plumes was banned, and eventually the trade in alligator hides, as well; restrictions on hunting and trapping increased as the wild creatures declined, and meanwhile the Indians were forced to compete with the better traps and better guns and mechanized equipment of the white men, who were pushing into the Everglades in increasing numbers, and were not averse to taking shots at Indians who got in their way. The last great stands of bald cypress and pine were disappearing, and so were the white-tailed deer, which had been exterminated all over south Florida in a mistaken effort to control tick fever in cattle. With the deer all but gone, the cougar also vanished, and big game hunters were replaced by collectors of the beautiful tree snails and rare orchids, together with oil prospectors, poachers, smugglers, and fugitives of every description.

In Pa-hay-okee—"the Grassy River"—the water no longer flowed as it had before. A canal between the east coast ridge and high land near Cape Sable had been proposed by the ill-fated Dr. Perrine in the 1830's, and as early as 1848, Generals Jesup and Harney, among others, recommended the drainage of the Everglades for agriculture. The first meddling with this unique ecosystem commenced after the Civil War, with the dredging and deepening of the Caloosahatchee to drain off the rich mucklands around Okeechobee; in 1906, and again in 1913, canals were dug to drain the eastern Glades. The Great War slowed down the destruction, but by 1920 there were more canals, and the real estate boom on the east coast had begun. In the country around Okeechobee, the sawgrass river gave way rapidly to cattle pasture and citrus and sugar cane plantations. The Army Corps of Engineers, ignoring the natural overflow channels of this vast, shallow lake, erected misplaced dikes and built up floodwaters that, in 1928, in a great hurricane, caused heavy loss of life and property; in a pattern of "progress" that became typical, the disaster served as an excuse for the construction of additional, much larger levees all around Okeechobee's southern shore. Since Okeechobee (and the Kissimmee River which flows into it from the north) are its main headwaters, the entire Everglades and its human and animal inhabitants have been subjected ever since to alternating cycles of flood and drought that have less to do with rainfall and the seasons than with gross folly and mismanagement.

Between 1926 and 1928, with the construction across south Florida of the Tampa–Miami Road, or "Tamiami Trail," the Indians' old way of life came to an end. The Trail laid wide this glittering and fragile wilderness to the destruction approaching from both coasts. With water levels increasingly unstable due to the drainage activities farther north, the old canoe routes that had once led from one coast to the other fell into weed-choked disuse; unnatural floods submerged the hammock gardens, unnatural fires caused by man-made drought destroyed the hardwoods and burned the peaty soil down to the limestone. A number of those Indians drawn in curiosity to the disturbance were hired as laborers in Trail construction, being adapted to the mosquitoes and the heat, and some of the families which camped along the roadbed remained there after the construction crews had gone; the day of the "Trail Indians" had begun.

In 1934, through the Indian Reorganization Act, the U.S. government extended a whole program of benefits, including education, to Indian tribes willing to submit to western-style incorporation under federally directed "tribal councils." The following year, on the hundredth anniversary of the Second Seminole War, Secretary of the Interior Harold Ickes and Indian Commissioner John Collier met in West Palm Beach with a number of Seminole, mostly Cow Creek, to whom they explained the economic advantages of registering as an incorporated tribe under the auspices of the IRA. They also spoke about the proposed national park, which was to absorb a large tract in the Shark River region, set aside by the state as a hunting ground for the "southern Indians" some years before. In the Secretary's opinion, the Seminole should retain the right to hunt and fish within the park, and should always have preference in any jobs that might be created. Meanwhile, they were encouraged to petition for a permanent reservation or homeland, north of the new park, which Ickes said might come to as much as 200,000 acres.

Though the Cow Creek from north of Okeechobee were scarcely affected by the new park, they promptly petitioned for all lands presently occupied or used but not owned by the Indians, including the Big Cypress Swamp inhabited by the Miccosukee; they also requested a monthly allowance of fifteen dollars per person, in return for which they would "swear allegiance to the United States of America." Since the Interior Department was anxious to lay all Indian land claims to rest, the petition would doubtless have been granted, had it not been for its prompt repudiation by a group of Miccosukee, or "true Seminole," led by Cory Osceola and including Josie Billie (a controversial medicine man, son of the aforementioned Billie Conapatchie, who was later the source of virtually all anthropological information on this close-mouthed people).

> We, the Chiefs, Leaders, Medicine Men, being the duly constituted authority to speak for and on behalf of the true Seminole Indians who live in the Big Cypress country . . . desire to call attention . . . to the fact that the Seminoles are not at peace and have never signed any Peace Treaty with the Government of the United States of America. . . . We do hereby protest against the aforesaid Legislation, desiring to live as our fathers lived, giving our lives to that end in honoring their memory and courage, never surrendering the heritage they gave us; always defending our rights and continuing our peaceful pursuits free from the ever-changing and hindering policies of the white man.

Because the "true Seminole" had had the assistance of a lawyer in composing their statement, it was suggested by the Bureau of Indian Affairs that they were simply a few malcontents, manipulated by troublemaking whites, and that they did not represent the Seminole people; everywhere in Indian country, this charge is used as an excuse to ignore those "traditional" Indians who resist the acculturating policies of the BIA. Negotiations between state and federal governments proceeded without the consent of the region's only inhabitants, and the hunting grounds north of Shark River were duly included in the new park; the Indians were recompensed by a tract of similar size adjoining the Seminole reservation at Big Cypress—mostly useless land, long since shot out by the hunters, which could be taken away from the Indians at any time. In 1936, when the governor of Florida paid a visit to the Trail Indians, it was Cory Osceola who was their spokesman; he said to the governor, "*Pohaan chekish* [Leave us alone]." The following year, over the protests of Cory Osceola, Josie Billie, and many others (including the new Seminole Agency superintendent, who declared in a letter to John Collier that despite claims to the contrary by park promoters, the loss of their good hunting ground would bring severe hardship to the Indians), the eviction of the Everglades people was begun, and in the next decade, the last Indians were forced out of Pa-hay-okee. Even so, some Miccosukee turned up at the town of Everglades in December 1947, when the new park was dedicated by President Truman.

The silent, stone-faced Indians stared with dislike and disapproval at the colorfully dressed "Cow Creek" Seminole, brought into Miccosukee territory for the occasion; in the course of the festivities, very suddenly, these Miccosukee disappeared.

Since the Miccosukee, or "true Seminole," were still unrecognized as a separate tribe, and since they refused to join in any dealings with the state or federal government made by the Cow Creek (who were much influenced by the Creek-led Muskogee Seminole of Oklahoma), they still had no land they could claim in their own name. Evicted from their hunting grounds in the south Everglades, they set up camps along the Tamiami Trail, where a few made a living as hunting guides. Some gigged frogs for the Miami restaurants, others eked out a marginal existence in craft shops and "Indian villages" and ragtag zoos where they placed themselves on exhibit among the monkeys and the alligators; the entirely inauthentic stunt of "alligator wrestling" for the edification of the tourists was added later to the small list of attractions. Yet it was these Trail Indians, exposed in the most ignominious way to the loud voices and rude stares of the whites, who most fiercely maintained their isolation. Even with customers, they remained cold-faced and remote; their children, kept away from the white man's schools, were forbidden to write, read, or speak English. On the other hand, those Miccosukee who moved onto the Big Cypress Seminole reservation, an inhospitable scrubland remote from the roads, seemed to give up the fierce spirit of independence that had sustained this band for over one hundred years. Some found jobs as ranch hands or harvest workers, or in the howling sawmills that were devouring the last giant trees in the Big Cypress; others dejectedly succumbed to alcohol and also to Christianity, brought not by white ministers, who were still mistrusted, but by Seminole preachers out of Oklahoma.

With the creation of the Indian Claims Commission (1946), designed to eliminate Indian land claims by means of monetary settlement, the BIA persuaded twelve Cow Creek to sue the federal government on behalf of the whole tribe for compensation for the treaty land taken away. Immediately, the "true Seminole," or Miccosukee, disassociated themselves from the Muskogee claim, which was initiated in 1950, and once again, they found themselves ignored. Unsophisticated, proud, and idealistic, the Trail people persisted in a course that was to ensure their displacement from their land. Formal letters were sent to the ICC, the Commissioner of Indian Affairs, and the Attorney General stating yet again that "it is not their desire or intention, now or in the future, to accept any money from the United States government"; a sworn statement in opposition to the Muskogee claim was signed by Ingraham Billie, Head Medicine Man (Josie's brother), and Buffalo Tiger, Official Interpreter. The following year, still unrecognized by the ICC, the traditionals presented a formal petition to President Eisenhower. Called the Buckskin Declaration, it made a statement of the traditionals' identity, together with tribal feelings about land and life. Dealing firmly and eloquently with neglected treaty obligations, it pointed out "the deliberate confusion of our Mikasuki Tribe of Seminole Indians . . . with the Muskogee Tribe of Seminole Indians in order to avoid recognition of our tribal government, independence, rights, and customs"; it expressed resentment of abuses and interference from government agents and officials, and asked that a special representative be sent so that a better understanding might be reached on all these matters.

President Eisenhower delegated the U.S. Indian Commissioner, Glenn Emmons, to investigate this old-fashioned situation. Emmons, echoed by the new Florida Indian Commissioner, Max Denton, concluded that the Indian right to live and hunt in a traditional way in the Everglades region should have been preserved at the time that their former hunting territory in the Shark River region had been ceded to the federal government by the state of Florida, as had been promised by Interior Secretary Ickes as well as by the National Park Service and the state. Following a meeting with "the Everglades Miccosukee General Council," held on the Trail in December 1954, the U.S. government acknowledged for the first time the separate identity of the Miccosukee Seminole and recognized that these people were not merely "squatters along the Trail" (as the BIA reports repeatedly suggested) but were on the contrary convinced of their prior right to occupy south Florida, unbound by any land claim that the white people might make. In the words of medicine man Sam Jones, as interpreted by Buffalo Tiger, "The land I stand on is my body, and I want you to help me keep it." Nonetheless, the extensive report that issued from this meeting was ignored by the ICC, which persisted in its refusal to recognize the traditional Miccosukee as a separate group, or hear the petitions submitted by their attorney.

As for the promised right to hunt within the park, it was refused by the National Park Service Director, and his superiors failed to overrule him.

In 1957, a number of demoralized reservation Miccosukee signed up with the Muskogee in the incorporated "Seminole Tribe" in order to become eligible for federal benefits. Since the days of the last Seminole removal, the Hitchiti-speakers had outnumbered the Muskogee-speakers still in Florida by more than two to one, but increasingly, through intermarriage and the custom in both tribes that young men live with their wives' people, the designation "Muskogee" or "Miccosukee" had come to refer less to one's ancestry or language than to one's attitude toward Indian way and toward the white man. Whatever their language, those reservation Indians who had registered in "the Florida Seminole Tribe" in 1957 and were so recognized by the U.S. government, pursuant to the Indian Reorganization Act of 1934, immediately became eligible for federal benefits; they were soon far more prosperous than the traditionals along the Trail, who were beginning to separate into bitter factions. The negotiations of the "Everglades Miccosukee General Council" had never been joined by Cory Osceola and his people, who mistrusted the increasing involvement with U.S. government representatives. Nor did this group join the General Council in requesting the state of Florida to grant the Miccosukee a 143,500-acre tract just north of the Trail in the region of their camps around Forty-Mile Bend, where they might try to preserve their traditional way of life. When it wasn't a dry and grassy waste, most of this tract was underwater, but even so, the request was turned down by the state, which persisted in its refusal to recognize a legal distinction between Seminole and Miccosukee; any of the Trail people who wished to live on the Seminole reservations or come in and register for Seminole benefits were free to do so, while those Indians dissatisfied with what had been done on their behalf might care to move to another state. This suggestion immediately reawakened the old fears of betrayal and removal to Oklahoma, and meanwhile, the Miccosukee had been threatened by discussion in the U.S. Congress of the recurrent "termination" legislation, designed to end all federal responsibility and support for the Indian nations, making "Americans" out of the Indians while making their lands available to whites. Among those who testified against such legislation at congressional hearings was Buffalo Tiger, who took over as head of the General Council in 1957.

By now, the Miccosukee attorney had unearthed the old treaties with Britain and Spain that laid the foundation for the land claims later affirmed at Moultrie Creek in 1823 and in the Macomb–Worth Agreement of 1842. Encouraged by Wallace "Mad Bear" Anderson (the Tuscarora activist celebrated in Edmund Wilson's *Apologies to the Iroquois* and now a leader in the Indian Rebirth Movement that had started a few years earlier among the Hopi), the increasingly sophisticated Miccosukee declared themselves a sovereign nation, and in 1958, armed with their treaties, they threatened to bring suit against the United States at the International Court of Justice at The Hague. In 1959, Buffalo Tiger and Howard Osceola, together with other Miccosukee spokesmen, met with Mad Bear in Washington, and later that year they accompanied him to Cuba, where on behalf of the Miccosukee Nation they signed a treaty of friendship with Fidel Castro. In response to this disconcerting publicity, promoted by Mad Bear as a goad to "Washington," the state of Florida in 1960 decided to recognize the Miccosukee after all, and lease them that land in their own name that had been refused to them three years before. In the same period, the U.S. government intensified its efforts to bring these Indians under federal supervision, and before long, Buffalo Tiger had been persuaded that negotiation with the United States was the only real hope for obtaining land. But Ingraham Billie and his group, convinced that Tiger and attorney Morton Silver were compromising the people's independence, withdrew all support from the General Council, aligning themselves once again with Cory Osceola.

Then, in September 1960, hurricane Donna flooded the Everglades, causing enormous devastation in the Miccosukee camps and gardens, and driving all but a last few from the drowned hammocks into the already impoverished community on the Trail. This calamity overcame much of the resistance to Buffalo Tiger's negotiation with "Washington," and as a first step, the Bureau of Indian Affairs was invited by Tiger to establish a clinic and a school. Two years later, when "the Miccosukee Tribe of Indians of Florida" was formally incorporated, with Buffalo Tiger as its chairman, the enrolled members of the new tribe numbered less than three hundred out of an estimated two thousand Hitchiti-speakers; almost that many traditionals had refused to register, and most of the rest were reservation people, already signed up as Seminole with the Cow Creek. The Department of the Interior, through the Bureau of Indian Affairs, awarded the new tribe a narrow strip of "reservation," five miles long by five hundred feet deep, along the south side of the Trail at Forty-Mile Bend, not in perpetuity but on lease from the National Park; in the fall of that year, for the first time in the tribe's history, Miccosukee children were taught English in the growing complex of tribal administration offices, school, clinic, library, and other facilities with which "progressive" Indians all over the land had been rewarded.

With the imminent incorporation of the new tribe, in 1961, Buffalo Tiger had been repudiated by almost all the remaining members of what once had been the General Council, including his fellow spokesman, Howard Osceola, who was to denounce what he considered a betrayal in a public letter in December 1961, and again in 1976, when the Seminole Tribe was awarded a monetary settlement by the Indian Claims Commission. In the bitter view of the traditionals, a fatal compromise had now been made, and still the Miccosukee had no homeland; even the lease to the narrow strip might be terminated by the Park Service at the end of fifty years, should Buffalo Tiger's "new tribe" fail to behave itself. Avoiding the strip, the traditionals scattered west along the Trail; signs identify the small tourist attractions thay have managed to keep going in competition with the subsidized "culture center" of "the tribe" as "traditional Miccosukee" and "traditional Seminole," so anxious are they not to be confused with the incorporated Miccosukee.

The traditionals had not forgotten that until 1962 their people could fairly call themselves "the last unconquered Indian tribe"; even the Hopi, whose traditional leaders are regarded all over Indian America as the least corrupted and most true to Indian way, have lived for many years on a reservation. And in the same way that those Indians who hid out in the Glades mistrusted those who finally consented to emigrate from Florida, the traditionals now mistrusted those who had submitted themselves to the mercies of the Bureau of Indian Affairs. As the Hopi and Navajo, the Lakota and Paiute, and many other Indian peoples had discovered, the BIA was all too easily prevailed upon to set aside the best interests of the Indians whom it was chartered to protect wherever these got in the way of commercial enterprise, which in south Florida was sprawling out in all directions.

Florida's population growth had already become the highest in the nation, a proud boast that excited ambitious dreams among politicians, developers, and other promoters of unwise short-term progress. In 1947, the increasing demands of the big farmers and developers, together with timely hurricane floods, had encouraged the Army Corps of Engineers to centralize its "management" of water under the Central and South Florida Flood Control District—the FCD—which proceeded with the construction of an oppressive grid of levees, floodgates, and canals; this ambitious project broke the flow of the whole Everglades drainage, from the brooding riverain forest of the Kissimmee River south to Cape Sable and the mangrove estuaries of the Ten Thousand Islands.

In 1962 the Corps completed an immense levee along the Tamiami Trail, separating the FCD's water catchment areas from the National Park. Although a drought was already in progress, the four FCD floodgates were immediately closed, and they remained almost entirely closed until late 1965, by which time thousands of desperate small creatures had been killed by cars while crossing the highway to the water in the FCD "Conservation Areas" to the north. The alligators, collecting in the last pools, had decreased by half due to drought and poachers, the otter had all but disappeared, and the populations of great water birds were scattered and dying. Yet throughout this long period of drought and dangerous fires the FCD, in a peculiar euphoria of vainglory and incompetence, was diverting billions of gallons of precious fresh water every year into its system of East Coast canals, where it poured away into the Atlantic Ocean.

In the 1960's, no doubt inspired by the FCD example, the Dade County Port Authority came up with a plan to bury in cement some thirty-six square miles of the Big Cypress, in a "jetport complex" somewhat larger than the international airports of New York, Chicago, Los Angeles, and Washington combined. "We will do our best to meet . . . the responsibilities of all men," declared one visionary, "to exercise dominion over the land, sea, and air above us as the higher order of man intends."

By this time, dominion by this higher order of men had already polluted much of the land and sea of southern Florida, and not a small part of its air as well. To justify its colossal appropriations, the FCD required ever more tons of steel and concrete and gigantesque machines, including a fearsome thing known as the River-Eater, which actually straightened the soft bends of the Kissimmee and made it a hard-edged ditch fifty miles long. The cascades of fertilizer, pesticides, and sewage that came cascading down this tunnel soon saturated and poisoned Lake Okeechobee; the new Everglades Park had been gutted by drought and fire; and the great breeding grounds of fish and shrimp in the brackish estuaries—already much damaged by the Corps of Engineers' promiscuous issue of dredge-and-fill permits to prospering developers all around the southern coastline—had sadly deteriorated for want of fresh water, causing near-ruin of a fishery that had been famous ever since the time of the first explorers. In the underground aquifers, a disastrous intrusion of salt water had begun, due to the massive loss of the fresh water that the FCD had been set up to conserve.

It must have been in 1947—the year that the National Park was opened, the year that the great concrete follies of the FCD got underway—that I made my own first visit to the Everglades. I was still young then, vitally interested in birds and snakes, and like most visitors in that period when Indians all over the country were lying low, I was all but oblivious of the Miccosukee; except as a touch of local color, I scarcely remember their thatch-roofed *chekes*, or "chickees," scattered here and there along the Trail. What I do remember was my first sight of the superb swallow-tailed kite on the burning blue, hawking back and forth over the highway in the bright sun of early spring. In those days, there was still a little space between the cars that stream across Florida like ants over a melon, biting at the vulnerable places, and I can remember running back and forth across the Trail, waving binoculars and yipping with excitement. That day my imagination was imprinted by the light of those big skies, the blowing gray-gold flow of sawgrass in the glittering fresh *glaeds* that stretched away forever, north and south, to the mysterious, dark hammock isles on the horizon. In later years, I would return here many times, to write about the FCD's destruction of the Kissimmee River that hastened the destruction of Lake Okeechobee; to support the acquisition by the National Audubon Society of the last great stand of bald cypress in the Corkscrew Swamp; to write a report for the Secretary of the Interior on the threatened ruin of the Everglades

Park caused by the Park Service's weak response to FCD operations to the north; to investigate the threat to the Big Cypress posed by the grandiose Miami jetport. But even then, in the late 1960's, it had not occurred to me that these Trail Indians had as much right here as the wild creatures whose environment I was so anxious to defend, that they were inseparable from this soil and water, and that setting aside in perpetuity an Indian homeland that could not be obliterated by Florida's greedy, feverish, and awful growth was the best hope for this rare wilderness.

*   *   *

In November 1972, Chairman Buffalo Tiger, speaking on behalf of "dignified reservation Indians," had dutifully deplored the Indian protest march on Washington called The Trail of Broken Treaties, involving Indians of many factions from all over the country, including his old associate Mad Bear Anderson. Nevertheless, his new group of incorporated Indians still pursued the Miccosukee land claim, deploring the acquisitive attitude of the incorporated Seminole, who in 1964 had waived all further land claims in return for the promised Claims Commission payment. On April 27, 1976, the Indian Claims Commission announced a final award of sixteen million dollars to "the Seminole Indians." While the Seminole tribes of Florida and Oklahoma squabbled over the allocation of the settlement, the Miccosukee Seminole rejected it entirely, not because the payment was so small but on the principle that the earth was sacred and could not be sold. So did the "Everglades Miccosukee Executive Council," whose spokesman was Howard Osceola, and so did the "Traditional Seminole," whose current spokesman was Cory Osceola's son. "We asked Howard to rejoin us," Guy Osceola told me, "but I guess he was just too fed up to work with anybody."

In 1977, the Indian Law Resource Center in Washington, D.C., unearthed a map in the National Archives that confirmed President Polk's Executive Order creating the Seminole reservation; that order has never been altered, abrogated, or changed. According to the ILRC director, a young Potawatomi attorney named Tim Coulter, "The Traditional Seminole are among the only Indians I know who continue to operate in the real Indian way in regard to land. They don't want to *own* land; at the same time, they must have free access to it. They are interested in land rights, but not necessarily the *title* to the land, so important in the white man's legal system. In other words, they don't want a batch of land assigned to them any more than you would like a batch of air assigned to *you*; you would resent someone who presumed to parcel out air, but that doesn't mean you aren't entitled to it, that you don't need it to survive." Coulter, whose office also represents traditional groups in the Six Nations Confederacy, the Lakota, the Western Shoshone, and the Hopi, takes a dim view not only of incorporated BIA Indians but also of Indian activists who only demand equal rights and justice within the white man's economic system; in fact, most of his clients are tribes that will settle for nothing less than the sovereign status as separate nations recognized by the U.S. government as they were until 1871, when further treaty-making with these nations was forbidden. In Coulter's opinion, sovereign status is "the only real hope for the Indian." As he points out, the Macomb–Worth Agreement, ratified by President Tyler, was completed well before 1871 and the reservation has never been "disestablished"; therefore, those Indians who have never accepted compensation from the U.S. government are the rightful owners of all of southwest Florida.

Most of the so-called Traditional Seminole have moved away toward the west end of the Trail, near Big Cypress Bend. Although they still live on their land, they do not appear in any government record, welfare roll, or census, will accept no government aid, have no reservation, and refuse to name or list their people, who are estimated at about two hundred; one of their leaders, Bobby Clay, contested the compulsory education of his children in the Naples public schools. "Trouble is," Guy Osceola says, "most of our people don't speak English; I do most of the talking for them. And if the land is ever released back to us, we're going to need police protection along the borders just to keep out all those white hunters; there just aren't enough of us left to go around." The Traditional Seminole do not endorse Buffalo Tiger's land claim, which is burdened with too many concessions and restrictions. "We want to be free to hunt and fish as we always did, to live here without restrictions or red tape. We want no attachment to the federal government, and no help from it. That is our right. We don't 'want' land, not the way white people want it. We don't believe in ownership of a certain area, and we don't have a claim, but one of these days we may be forced to make one." Guy Osceola sighed. "Among Seminole people, the only group that means anything these days is the clan. These so-called Miccosukee can't tell you their Miccosukee lineage any more than we can; they were just named that by Buffalo Tiger, to distinguish his group from the rest. Well, we call ourselves the Traditional Seminole for the same reason. The name has changed, but we have always been here, we have never changed; it is those others who have gone away."

I first met Buffalo Tiger in December 1979 in his office in the tribal administration building, where he sits at a large desk in a large office in front of a copy of George Catlin's famous portrait of Osceola. A tall man with a stern, closed face, dressed formally in a string tie and colorful Seminole vest, Buffalo Tiger was very reserved at our first meeting, reminding me of the words of warning that in one form or another are found in almost all accounts of dealings with this people: "Whites are deeply distrusted and attempts to gain a knowledge of Mikasuki language and culture only serve to increase the hostility. . . ." Though he listened politely to my ideas for an article in support of the Miccosukee land claim, he stopped me at one point to inquire, in effect, What's in it for *you*? I told him that the Miccosukee claim interested me especially because I was also interested in the Everglades, and it seemed to me that the Everglades and its wildlife would be far better protected if Indians instead of ambitious bureaucrats had supervision of the water lands north of the Trail, which even on Park Service maps are described as "critical to Everglades National Park ecosystems." The Park Service is still evading the commitment made to the Indians in 1974, when the creation of the Big Cypress National Preserve absorbed still more of their ancestral lands; while acknowledging that the Indians have a right to fish and hunt and conduct ceremonies on this land (as was once promised them in regard to the National Park), the Park Service is challenging the provisions set out in Section 5 of PL 93-440, according to which the Miccosukee and the Seminole are entitled to continue "their usual and customary use and occupancy"; "customary occupancy" can only mean the right to occupy traditional chekes, camps, and gardens.

Similarly, the Miccosukee lease in the FCD's Conservation Area No. 3 had been called back for "renegotiation" by the state, apparently in response to that higher order of men who wish to develop three large "recreational facilities" in the area; after six years of negotiation, during which the Miccosukee made almost all of the concessions, the status of the land was still unresolved. The situation had been further complicated by the demands of the FCD that Indian rights be "subservient" to its own rights "to control water levels in the area described," presumably in the disastrous manner that has characterized Corps–FCD operations for fifty years.

Because any lease could later be revoked, or the land condemned for jetports or condominiums, the Indians could be displaced again, as they have been throughout their history with the white man; what they were seeking was assignment of the land in perpetual trust. For its part, the state was being careful "not to lose this opportunity to forever end the type of claims that Indians are making in other states"; it wanted assurance that whatever arrangement it made with the Miccosukee would quiet forever any claim that the Indians might make in the future.

As we talked, Buffalo Tiger's face seemed to relent a little. Perhaps, he said, it might be a good idea for me to listen to elders such as his brother Jimmie, who had a wide knowledge of Miccosukee tradition. Then, in a soft and thoughtful voice, he began to talk to me about the land. "We Indian people," he began slowly, "are not supposed to say, This land is mine. We only *use* it. It is the white man who buys land and puts a fence around it. Indians are not supposed to do that, because the land belongs to all Indians, it belongs to God, as you call it. The land is a part of our body, and we are a part of the land.

"So we don't want to say, This is Indian land. But we also know that if this land"—he pointed toward the north—"is not protected by making it a reservation for the Indian people, then the white man will use up all of it. Who is the white man to tell us where to live? He is not God. And the Miccosukee were never defeated; we never accepted defeat. Therefore our land should always be free land for us to live on, free of taxes, without white-man licenses to hunt our deer, without restrictions. And we will take good care of it; we want no concrete construction, we want it to be left just as it is. That is what the white people cannot understand: we do not want to 'improve' our land, we just wish to keep it as it is. It's hard for us to come to terms with the white man because our philosophy is so different. We think the land is there for everyone to use, the way our hand is there, a part of our own body."

Buffalo Tiger comes from a traditional family and was raised accordingly; the family name derives from *tigre,* as the early Spanish called the cougar. "We were not supposed to play with white children," he told me, "and we got whipped for using the white man's pencils, even to draw pictures!" In 1950, because of his traditional upbringing and the good English learned as a housepainter in Miami, he was asked to be a spokesman for his people by the medicine man Ingraham Billie. Buffalo Tiger does not regret his subsequent decision to lead his followers into dependence on the U.S. government—in effect, into a welfare state in which most jobs are offered by "the tribe"—but he speaks of a day when his people will be able to refuse government grants, as they did in 1879, and return once again to independence. (This is conceivable, of course; a few years ago, the Inuit of Umingmaktok, in the remote Northwest Territories, chose to return the welfare checks of the Canadian government when they saw how fast their loss of independence had eroded the traditional skills and spirit of the band.)

"White people think that Indians are unimportant; they have never learned how to make bullets or bombs. We are 'soft,' according to their way. Yet we survive, because we go with nature, we can bend, we are still attached to the earth. Now your way of life is no longer working, and so you are interested in our way. But if we tell you our way, then it will be polluted, we will have no medicine, and we will be destroyed as well as you."

Like many Indians all over North America, Buffalo Tiger believes that the end of this world is fast approaching, largely because of the "pollutions" of the white man, who has turned his back upon the earth. "When you see rain coming down like oil, as black as that, it means the world is nearing the end." He sighed. "We think the earth will always be here, but it will not. It has already been destroyed a few times; something happened to those earths before. But if only one person maintains the Old Way, and grows his crop with the proper ceremonies, man will survive; so it is not only for the red man that we must follow our way, but for the white man, too. Therefore, we are not too concerned about what the white man has done to us in the past; so long as Indian people can hold out another fifty or one hundred years, we will survive."

Buffalo Tiger has spent most of his life away from his own people, working in the Miami area where he still lives; he drives a gold Cadillac, and has had two marriages with white women who were the mothers of his five children, none of whom speak their ancestral tongue. "I am trying to balance between two worlds," he sighed, referring not to his own life but to his responsibilities to his people. "It is very difficult, and one must be very strong." Buffalo Tiger said this with no trace of complaint, and leaving his office, I had a confused feeling of respect and sadness. The chairman speaks of Indian way with eloquence, but what he is doing is another matter.

· · ·

Those Trail people who refuse to enroll themselves in the "Miccosukee Tribe of Indians of Florida" do not think it is possible to "balance between two worlds" without falling down between, and they scoff at the idea that the Miccosukee can ever achieve real independence within a competitive economy for which they have neither training nor inclination. Since the federal incorporation of the tribe, one Indian told me, the whole attitude of the people has been corrupted. "Money is all they care about over there," he says, and his feelings on this point are probably shared by the more far-sighted beneficiaries. A smart, tough, humorous young woman who is one of the most promising leaders at the center is also disturbed by the infections caused by money, though at first her worry was expressed in terms of the prosperous Muskogee Seminole, who are threatening to open up some local businesses to compete with the Miccosukee establishments along the Trail. "All them Seminoles think about is money, money, money!" she exclaimed one day in Sonnie Billie's restaurant. "They're really into money!" Asked if money could be a problem here as well, she gave me a brief hard look, then nodded. "It'll happen here, too." Frowning, she gazed out toward the highway, where the tourist cars went howling past in the bright sun; on the far side of the highway and canal, the shining grass and water of the land claimed by the Miccosukee stretched away into the north. "It's happening already," she murmured glumly, in a momentary loss of self-assurance.

Most of the enrolled Miccosukee have jobs within "the tribe," and in the tribal offices, one gets an impression of people sitting around in front of typewriters that are rarely used. Whether out of shyness or insecurity, or in the instinct that a display of aggressive "Indianness" in the form of arrogant hostility toward whites will somehow compensate for acceptance of white aid, BIA Indians all over the country seem a lot less sure of their own feelings than those who are managing on their own. A gentle Asian woman who worked at the Tribal Center for a number of years and is very well-liked by the Indians is occasionally upset by brusque, raw attitudes among people she regards as friends. "Why don't you quit, give an Indian your job," they used to say to her before she did so. I was present one day when she confused a boy's name with that of his brother, a natural mistake since she had laid eyes on neither of them in a year. This boy, one of her favorites, said to her coldly, "All Indians look alike, I guess. We're just savages anyway, right?" Rejecting the friendly greeting of a non-Indian, hurting her feelings, was his way of asserting an Indian identity in which, perhaps, he has lost confidence; it is not the way of traditional Indians, who are often very blunt but rarely rude.

White people who have lived for a long time on the Loop Road and knew many of the Indians before the advent of federal assistance tend to believe that government subsidies and make-work jobs have "prolonged the agony" of an assimilation into the white economy that has been inevitable for years; "they have just put off facing reality for another generation," one person told me. Nor has the new affluence made the Indians happy. "There used to be a lot more goings-on," another man said. "Like those big bathing parties in the canals; the Indians used to *laugh* much more! Now they're depressed. The only time they seem to laugh is when they drink." A number of suicides have occurred among the half-educated young Indians who found themselves wandering between two cultures, and one white employee of the tribe told me that the use of alcohol and drugs among young Indian children has risen drastically in the four years since my first visit here in 1979, and that the parents are too demoralized by drink and idleness to care.

Having been so recently exposed to a consumer economy,

Buffalo Tiger's people are still innocent about money, and take it for granted; if a new TV set doesn't work, it is as apt to be tossed into the canal as to be taken in to be repaired. A teacher who escorted some of the children to see the last stand of bald cypress forest at the Corkscrew Swamp said that the kids were bored to death. "All they wanted to do was get back to their junk-food lunches in the bus, and all they could talk about were the TV shows that they were missing, back in those new cinder-block houses on the Trail. It's very sad, but that's the way that things are going." And although this might be true of any child exposed to American education, and although, as she said, "You can't expect these people to turn back to *sofkee* [corn gruel] and mosquitoes," she could not entirely hide her disappointment.

Howard Osceola, the former spokesman for traditional Miccosukee who accompanied Buffalo Tiger to Washington and Cuba but refused to support him after he began the negotiations with the federal government that led to incorporation of the tribe, is a husky, white-haired man who works for the Park Service in general maintenance. He is also a guide along the nature trails, being acquainted with many if not most of the wild plants used in Indian medicine. Howard's father-in-law was the late Josie Billie, the controversial medicine man who was reputed to know the name and uses of some 250 species of plants. "We buried Josie last Thursday," Howard Osceola told me when we spoke one morning out on the Loop Road, and his shrug suggested that much of the Old Way had been buried with that old man.

Howard Osceola seems to say that his people are finished as an Indian tribe: even the land claim didn't mean much any more, although "thirty or forty years ago, that land would have been important to the tribe. In those days, the Indians wanted to be as far as possible from whites. That land we had down in Shark River, they gave us that because they thought it was a wasteland, but it was only a wasteland to the whites; the Indians knew how to use it, and they felt at home there." Now it was too late, he thought. The younger men in Buffalo's group did not even go frog-hunting any more, it was too much trouble; they just sat around waiting for the government handouts. He acknowledged the theoretical value of the land as a Miccosukee homeland that people could return to, a hunting ground and a place for traditional ceremonies such as the Green Corn Dance in the spring and the Hunting

Dance in autumn, a place where the people could retreat from the white man's noise and hurry and pollution: a homeland would hold the tribe together as nothing else could. "But they aren't going to give it to us anyway," he said, "so it doesn't matter." Howard Osceola sat back with his hands behind his head, trying to smile, but his eyes weren't smiling any more. "Maybe it's better if the old ways die out than to have them all mixed up, the way those people are teaching them up at that school. Those people are just pretending to be Indians." He was proud, he said, that he had not turned away from the real Indians. "At least I can sleep at night; at least I didn't sell out the Indian people for some chicken dinners. I'd rather just scrape along, the way I'm doing." He laughed in order to hide how bitterly he feels about what he sees as a typical "Washington" effort to divide his people into hostile factions: "The government just found out who liked money."

Howard admits that not many of his people share his feelings any more, and that some won't even talk to him: his sister Alice as well as his own children work for "the tribe." "Me and Mad Bear," he said with a sudden smile, cheered up again by the memory of his old friend. "Me and Mad Bear used to be the most hated Indians *around* here!"

According to Howard's nephew, Leroy Osceola, "Buffalo's bunch split away, moved east over there to Forty-Mile Bend, and those other people [Guy Osceola, Bobby Clay] moved west, over toward Naples, and started to call themselves 'traditional Seminoles,' to separate themselves from the Buffalo group, I guess. But there is no such thing as Seminole Indians: Seminole just means natural, wild in its own way, and no Indian who lives on a reservation can call himself '*siminoli*.'

"If only one traditional Miccosukee speaks for us in the correct way, that is enough to carry our tradition. We are still in the middle of our land, right where we always were, we haven't moved either east or west, and our people in the middle still have the buckskin. Buffalo's and Howard's mothers were sisters, and Buffalo's mother was very traditional; she would have hated what they have done over there with those cinder-block homes."

"Wild Bill" Osceola, who is Howard's brother, lives in a neat Indian camp not far west of the old jetport entrance at Fifty-Mile Bend; he is an expert silversmith and stone-carver who believes strongly in hard work. "A man doesn't work, he's not his own man no more; that's what's happening to them puppet Indians over there. A man gets in trouble and does things he regrets; he begins to steal." Saying this, his handsome, jolly face goes hard. He agrees that the Trail Indians, whatever they may call themselves, are all the same Miccosukee people, but with traditional insistence on each man's right to go his way, he had no use for my suggestion that his "traditional Miccosukee" group and the "traditional Seminole," who agree about almost everything, might be more effective if they worked together. Bill Osceola pointed his finger at his wife, his son, his daughter, who looked away quickly to avoid the gaze of a white stranger. "I'm not speaking for her, for him: I just speak for me. I live my way, and I'm going to die my way; if I got to starve to death, I'll starve my way, too." After a cold pause he said, "There are more real Indians than people think."

· · ·

Although Buffalo Tiger's family does not criticize the chairman, neither does it recognize him as tribal leader, for Indians are profoundly democratic. "He is not our leader, he is our mouthpiece with the whites," one of his brothers says, not meaning this in a derogatory way: in the old days this description would cover most of those Indians who were called "chiefs" by the whites, not because they had any real authority to speak for the tribe, far less sign treaties, but because they were the only ones able (or willing) to speak English, and could interpret the white man's ways for all the rest.

Three of Buffalo Tiger's brothers live at Forty-Mile Bend. The eldest, Jimmie (whose camp was used for the 1954 meeting at which the separate status of the Miccosukee Seminole was finally recognized by the U.S. government), now operates a fleet of airboats, taking tourists out to "camps" on nearby hammocks, where a few of his relatives, commuting from the Trail, sit around being Indians during the day. Bobby Tiger wrestles alligators behind his shop at the Miccosukee Culture Center, where a commercial Indian village has been set up. Tommie Tiger, a skilled carpenter, builds the thatched, airy, open-sided *chekes* not only for Indians but for local white people in the Miami area.

"The white man gives the Indian a little bit of candy, just a taste," Tommie Tiger told me, "and after that they try to lead the people around the way they want them." A fit, lean man in his mid-fifties who was fitting a new handle to his axe when I first met him, Tommie is the Tiger brother least comfortable with the new ways, spending more time out in the Glades than any of the others. "Jimmie likes to get away from this road," he says, as a way of expressing his own feelings. He is disturbed by the introduction of strange trees, which are pushing out the native plants across south Florida. "Indians never saw that tree," Tommie Tiger said, pointing at an Australian melaleuca. "Now it's everywhere along the Trail." He is outspoken about the damage done by white men to the natural balances of land and life in Pa-hay-okee; this year, for example, the FCD had flooded out the hammocks. "They are trying to play God," he said, "and it isn't working." Tommie Tiger feels that the manipulation of the natural flow of the Grassy River has harmed the wildlife a great deal more than hunting and trapping, though the present scarcity of buck deer on the hammocks was probably attributable to an over-population of white hunters.

A few days later, not fifty yards down the canal road from the place where Tommie Tiger was shaving cypress poles with his old-time two-handled plane, I watched an otter hump across from one canal bank to the other. Hearing of this, Tommie shrugged, commenting that both otter and deer have been declining, due to the many airboats that careened around the open, shallow waters; even the frogs were growing wary. "They scatter out into the sawgrass now when they hear those airboats coming," Tommie Tiger said, adding cryptically, "I guess *everything* learns its lesson, sooner or later."

On the afternoon of the day I encountered the cottonmouth moccasin, I went with Jimmie Tiger on a reconnaissance of the more isolated hammocks to the north, which were used by Indians long before the Everglades National Park or even the Tamiami Trail had been imagined. Though in his late sixties, Jimmie Tiger is strong and agile and still very active in his business. The first time I visited him, he was climbing around on top of an airboat that was perched on the back of his old pickup truck, spraying the engine and working parts with oil; the truck was parked in his family village on the south side of the Trail, where he lives with some of his twelve children in thatched dwellings fitted with electricity and with TV. For a long time he gave no sign that he had noticed my arrival, but when I failed to go away, he finally climbed down and led me into the cooking *cheke*, where we confronted each other across a rough wood table.

Jimmie Tiger is a big man whose gray hair stands up in a youthful sprout; he wears the old-fashioned neckerchief and bright patchwork Seminole shirt, and he knows a lot about Miccosukee traditions. As the chairman remarks rather often, "Jimmie could tell you about that." But like Tommie, he had to look me over a few times before he decided he could talk to me, far less take me out into the Glades. "I do not know if we will go out. I have to think about it," he had said at our first meeting. "Come and talk to me tomorrow and maybe I will tell you then." At the end of our second meeting, he agreed to spend an afternoon showing me food and medicine plants out in the hammocks; I should meet him here at a certain hour on the following day. When I did so, he appeared surprised to see me. "Oh, boy," he said, shaking his head. "I'm very busy," he said over his shoulder. "Maybe later."

Left standing at the edge of the canal, I wondered if these Trail people weren't simply too wary and suspicious to work with. Yet I knew that the superficial forms of what white people call good manners, including fulsome greetings and good-bys, are perceived by Indians as excessive, insincere, and that in some way I was being tested. In their tradition of hostility toward whites, in their lack of sophistication resulting from so many decades of isolation, in their limited understanding of the white man's language, the Trail people were not only shy and insecure but paranoid and unpredictable. A seemingly unfriendly attitude could be transformed quite suddenly into a friendly one; if I had patience, everything might fall into place.

Since the day was sunny, with a limpid breeze, it was fun to watch the scattered snail kites—I have seen as many as twelve of those uncommon birds at once, near Forty-Mile Bend—lifting and falling in the wind as they hawked across the shining grass and water. I kept an eye out for the swallow-tailed kite that I had seen here thirty years before, which would be arriving any day from South America. Two purple gallinules had joined the coots in the bullrush margins of the canal, a limpkin gave its strange wailing call, and every sector of the sky was crossed by tilting vultures, wind-blown crows, long strings of egrets, ibis, wood storks, a distant osprey, kingfishers, more crows, headed in the same direction as the first. Eventually Jimmie Tiger returned, saying "Oh, boy," when he saw I was still there. "Well, we can't go out all afternoon," he told me crossly. "Maybe an hour." And he pushed one of his smaller airboats off the bank, threw in some tools and a spare jerry can of gas, and climbed up onto the driver's seat in front of the motor.

The Glades airboat is a flat-bottomed skiff driven by an airplane motor with propeller, which is mounted high behind the boatman in a scaffolding built onto the boat's stern; this rig can all but fly on an inch of water, crossing patches of heavy sawgrass without difficulty, and would be an exhilarating way to travel were it not for its huge racketing noise, which eliminates all but shouted communication between travelers. Since it made no sense to try to talk, I sat back on a passenger bench to enjoy the ride. The water birds seem to have adapted to the noise, to judge from the calm demeanor of those we passed; even a snail kite perched with its prey on a dead snag did not shift its wings as the airboat came roaring past, less than a hundred yards away. "It's funny," Jimmie Tiger remarked later. "You go along out here and you never see those snails, but those birds see them."

Smallpox Tommie's, a hammock named for "my aunt's husband," lies well off to the north of Forty-Mile Bend. Smallpox Tommie lived here until about 1928, when a fire destroyed the hardwoods on this hammock; he moved to another hammock, then another, until finally all the changes that had come made life too difficult, and he moved down to the Trail. The camp lies hidden by a fringe of willows that surrounds the hammock, and a narrow walkway on small pilings, rotting now, leads through the willows to a small clearing on the highest point of ground, which this year is less than two feet above water level. Here a few decrepit *chekes* are still standing, and Jimmie showed me how the fire in the cooking *cheke* is maintained at the points of four big logs, representing the four directions, that are placed like spokes in "the circle of life," beginning with the log that is pointing east. A larger *cheke* sheltered the family platform, raised about three feet above the ground as a protection against rainwater and flood as well as snakes; here the people slept at night and worked during the day, when the bedding was stored on rafters under the eaves. On the platform sat the rusted skeleton of an old hand-cranked sewing machine, which had been used in other days by his Aunt Mary, and in the rafters lay some recent bedding belonging to his brother Tommie, who had used this camp since 1964. Tommie intended to rebuild these *chekes*, Jimmie said, "maybe next year."

Discussing the origin of *chekes*, Jimmie Tiger said that the Miccosukee people were originally "hatched" from the high banks of the Mississippi, and that the first man out of the earth spoke the word "Takoshi"; the word had no meaning, but as the first word, it had been adopted as the name of the clan to which his wife belonged. Moving southeastward, and coming eventually into Florida, the people had lived for a long time in the region of Tallahassee; the original Tallahassee or "Old Town," he said, had been a Miccosukee settlement. In those days, the people all lived in log cabins, like the Creek, but as they moved southward, building cypress dugouts to hunt and explore the water trails of the interior, they encountered strange open-sided huts used by an Old People who were here before. The Miccosukee had not mixed with these Old People; instead, they attacked one another, and after that the Miccosukee killed them on sight with blowguns and spear-throwers, since in those days they had no bows and arrows. The last band of these people was routed out of what is now known as Hawk Cypress, east of Immokalee, and after that they disappeared toward the south. "We always wondered where they went to," Jimmie said. According to his great-great-grandfather, who "taught him these things," a few might be left up there in the Big Cypress, although these people knew how to make themselves invisible. I asked if this was the Old People known as the Calusa— the Yaate Hampe, or Bad People, I said, as Jimmie nodded, giggling over my use of this term. "Bad mans! Of course they were not *all* bad. Some good, some bad, like Miccosukee. Maybe they called us Bad People, too!" He laughed again. "But the Calusa were very ugly people, very ugly, that is what my great-great-grandfather told me."

Because of the heat and also the scarcity of hardwood in the marshes, the Miccosukee soon adapted to the open-sided, thatched Calusa *chekes* of palm thatch and cypress poles, using smudge fires as a defense against mosquitoes. Jimmie thought that a few people had tried alligator oil, boiled down from the meat. "Smelled so strong, nobody come near you; you try to sleep with your wife, you got big trouble!" Jimmie said, and we burst out laughing.

I asked Jimmie the true meaning of the word "*siminoli*," which white ethnologists have translated as "outcast," "wild," or "undomesticated." He said, "*Siminoli*—that means wild, okay. To us it means *scared* wild, like a rabbit. In the wars, them Seminole run off like rabbits all the time—they was so scared, you know." He laughed to show me he was making a joke at the expense of the Muskogee, and his glee was infectious; we were beginning to enjoy ourselves.

The original hardwoods at Smallpox Tommie's had been replaced by a second growth of coco plum and pond apple, cabbage palm and gumbo limbo. Scattered among the small wild trees around the clearing were old sour orange, guava, and banana trees, and by the cook hut was a patch of domestic mint. There was also pond cypress, transplanted by Indians in order to grow poles for building *chekes*; according to Jimmie, this camp was very old, and a good deal of ancient pottery used to turn up here. But mainly the Indians had depended on the hammock trees and plants, one of the most valuable of which was the sabal, or cabbage palm, used not only for *cheke* thatching but for food: the "cabbage" root, about one foot underground, was very good to eat, and so was the "heart" or inner tip of the new growth. Also, he said—and he demonstrated—the frond served very well as a mat or plate for food, and the concave frond stem as a ladle or a spoon. Roots and tubers of common water plants such as bullrush and arrowroot were also good; the arrowroot was poisonous, but if it was peeled, sliced, and dried in the sun, then mortared in a pestle for three or four hours "until you don't hear that squishing sound no more, that gets the poison out; then you can spread it out again, dry it as flour."

Leading me around the clearing, Jimmie pointed out more of the common plants, together with their uses. "For white people," Jimmie Tiger said, "it may just be a lot of green out here, but I see a lot of food and a lot of medicine." This rubber tree (*Ficus*) provided medicine and string, its latex could be prepared as a kind of chewing gum, and its figs became ripe in July, as did the pond apples and coco plums and elderberries. The gumbo limbo was never to be used for firewood: "That smoke is very bad and burns your eyes." Spanish moss and the fiber of the saw palmetto had been used in other days for women's skirts. The moss was still used for scraping pots, and also as a preservative for storing deer's brains, used in tanning; deer's brains—or brains of any kind—were never eaten by the Indians, since they caused impotence. Jimmie Tiger expressed surprise at the white man's willingness to devour brains, not to mention snails and rabbits, frogs and rattlesnakes. A man could get cramps just from skinning one of these marsh rabbits; eating frog's legs would give you a weak frog's chest, perhaps TB, and snake meat brought on rashes and high fever. Returning to the airboat, he pointed out a place where the new marsh grass had been cropped by rabbit and deer; the rabbits had left their droppings everywhere on the old walkway, and the droppings lay among shells of apple snails discarded by the kites. Not far away, a string of snail eggs, like a cluster of small white grapes, was attached to an underwater stem of alligator flag.

Because I knew a little about plants and animals, it pleased Jimmie to show me something about Indian medicine. Out here in the Glades, away from the harassments of his business, he had cheered up a good deal, and he did not start home when we left Smallpox Tommie's but headed farther to the north and west, skimming swiftly across the grassy water to one of his old camps out on Big Hammock. On the high ground of this large island, perhaps five hundred yards back from the clearing, he had kept a garden of corn and pumpkins, beans and sugarcane, but now the high waters impounded by the floodgates had cut off the garden from the camp, and waterlogged it; no garden would be possible this spring. Instead of stabilizing the water level, Jimmie said, the white men were talking about bringing in more machines; they proposed to use drag lines to build up the level of the hammocks, as opposed to the much cheaper course of maintaining the water at its natural levels. But like most white-man solutions to red-man problems, this one had not come to very much. "Fifteen years ago, the government was telling us we could still live down there where they put the park—live in a natural way, I mean, no airboats, no guns, and no concrete, just making our camps like in the old days, fish and hunt frogs from canoes, kill a few deer with bows and arrows. Well, we're still waiting. There's plenty of Indians would go back into the Glades if they got the chance."

We bent to inspect the beautiful spiral skeleton of a snake. "Chicken hawk got'm," Jimmie said. Snakes were getting scarce out in the hammocks, he muttered without pleasure; man had overturned the seasons of almost all of the wild creatures. The coral snakes were very rare now, so were the big diamondbacks; even the moccasins and pygmy rattlers were much less common. The talk reminded me of the moccasin I had met that morning, and hearing about it, Jimmie gazed at me for the first time, as if considering the possibility of my human status. "Almost got you, huh?" He gave a small uneasy laugh, and we kept on going.

From Big Hammock, we continued west toward the edge of the Big Cypress, a low gray line as soft as mist; we passed a white man's hunting camp along the way. Like the Indian camps, this one was situated on the north end of its hammock; all these low teardrop islands formed by the southward flow of the Grassy River build up higher ground at the wide north end. But at this camp, the approaches through the sawgrass were broad and well-defined, as in a channel, whereas the approaches to the Indian camps seemed vague, as if people did not know the way, or wished to leave as little trace as possible. When I remarked on this, Jimmie Tiger nodded. "We leave ours hard to follow, very rough," Jimmie explained. "If we don't, those hunters come and scavenge *everything*." There was no pretty clearing at the hunters' camp, only a heavy plywood box set about by oil drums, wedged into the scrub on the hammock's edge. "Fifty or sixty of them white-man camps out here, and maybe more," Jimmie continued. "No place for the animals to rest." It was these hunters, expressing concern for the wild animals, who were leading the fight against the legal transfer of this uninhabited area to the Indians.

From his high perch, Jimmie guided the airboat through thick bronzy sedge that was well over my head; on the far side a great blue heron, windstream lifting its gray feathers, fixed us with its calm, fierce eye as we rushed past. Then we were sailing free again, over short gray-green wire grass and glittering water. Ahead, broad sun rays slanted down through distant rains, bringing a strange pinkish haze to the gray cypress. In this leafless time of the late winter, the nakedness of the pond cypress is made more stark by the spiky silhouettes of the bromeliads, which loom on the trees like strange parasitic growths. Off there not far behind the little trees lay the great "jetport" that, had it been completed, would have submerged the light and silence of Pa-hay-okee in a chaos of noise, fumes, and disruption, hastening the onset of that final day when rains would fall that were as "black as oil."

Where cypress knees began to nose out of the water, Jimmie

Tiger maneuvered his airboat with great skill into the abandoned camp called Jack Clay's Farm. Here he inspected the derelict fruit trees, guava, papaya, and key lime. "Coons get 'em all," he said, neither fed up nor approving. The old corn garden was overgrown by bracken, and for some reason, the high ground on this island was littered with the shells of small box turtles dismantled by raccoons. We inspected the shell of a large painted turtle, and a track and bubbles where an alligator made its home back in the slough, and a lovely, tall, pale willow bustic—what Jimmie called a "bow tree," since in the old days it was used to make bows and arrows.

Though the day was late, Jimmie Tiger made a final stop on the way home. Until lately this hammock had been used by the Miccosukee Tribe of Indians of Florida for "cultural outings" for its children, at which tribal elders attempted to transmit at least a hint of the old ways, but due to lack of interest on the part of the children—and also the elders' insistence upon payment—it was now to be returned to Jimmie's family. Like his brother Tommie (and like Howard Osceola), Jimmie was troubled by the growing ignorance of Indian way that was so evident in the young, the apathy and laziness, the dangerous gas-sniffing and the abuse of alcohol and drugs. In the days when the Tamiami Trail was built, the white contractors had welcomed Indian labor, not just because the Indians were tough and could handle the summer heat and the mosquitoes, but because they were excellent and dependable workers; in the drought fires of 1962, the Park Service had sought out Miccosukees, who were the best fire fighters they could find. Today, an Indian contractor who does much of the building around Forty-Mile Bend says that he hires whites whenever possible, because so few Indians can be depended on to show up for work.

"Today, nobody live right," Jimmie Tiger said. "And the young people don't listen anymore to their uncle and their grandfather. In the old days, the Indian man listened to the elders until he was forty years old, maybe fifty, and he stayed on the guide line that they gave him; when you strayed off, they tell you pretty quick, Hey, you go too far that way! And at the Green Corn Dance, now, you could get yourself a good scratching! You know about that? Oh, they scratched you *hard*!" He paused. "I'm *still* listening to my great-great-grandfather, you know," he said, after a moment, gazing at me to see if I had understood.

"Not so long ago, if an Indian here had any kind of an old car, he was doing pretty good; now these young people, they have to have new cars, they have to have *money*." Jimmie shook his head; although he is prosperous, one of the first and most successful businessmen along the Trail, he still prefers to live under a thatch roof, and he is content with his old pickup. "We don't need that new school over there; the Indian knows what God has told him, and that is enough."

At the edge of the clearing, a short-eared owl rose from a low bush and flopped away over the green wall of salt bush and wax myrtle. When I pointed at it, Jimmie acted vague; until now, his sharp eyes had missed nothing. Then I remembered his brother's intent listening, the previous evening, when a barred owl hooted out on the Loop Road. "Some of them are not owls," Tommie Tiger had said. "We know how to tell when it is Something Else. They give us signs." This respect for signs is nothing more than respect for the unseen in all of nature; among many Indians, as well as white people, such respect was dead.

Jimmie Tiger's camp has six *chekes* and a cornfield, and it pleased my companion that only last year a bear had come to feed upon the neglected guavas on this hammock. "Next year when you come back," he said, "you may find me living out here. I never got used to that highway over there—too damn much noise. Over here, it's always so quiet, you sleep as late as you want, talk to your family." He sighed. "Them old days were better days, you know: we only go to town maybe once a month. These days they always wanting to go, more and more and more." He stopped, shaking his head. "Oh, boy," he said. Bear or no bear, the abundance of those other days would not come back, and people who had grown accustomed to cars and airboats and electricity would not return to cypress dugouts and dark quiet evenings. But when I asked him if his people would still use the hammocks if permitted to return into the wild country far from the white man's roads, down toward Shark River, Jimmie Tiger repeated what he had said earlier. "A lot of Indians, they would go back down there if they could." He kept on nodding. "I was raised down there, you know. That is my territory." He gazed down toward the south. "You people call it the Shark River, but we called it Hatchee Chokti, the Long River, because it goes so far."

Jimmie turned to look at me again, not in a staring way,

holding my eye, for Indians consider that bad manners, but briefly, to fix my attention to what he intended to say.

"When the Breathmaker put breath inside us, He told the people, This dirt, this clay, this earth—this is your body! Never forget this! Take good care of it, and hold it as long as you live! And my great-great-grandfather, he warned us long ago: some day somebody will come along, show you a paper, try to take this land away. Do not make your sign on that paper: if you give this land away, it will be like cutting off your arm. That is the reason why Miccosukee people have to keep this little land that there is left; it is our body, our free country, where everything that lives here, the snake and the bird, is natural and free, just the way that God created it, a country where everything is free. Indians want to live in that free way, too. And so we want the land *the way it is*, we do not want to change anything, because it is very nice to be here."

How just, how *right* it would be, I thought, to restore to the Miccosukee of all factions their traditional use of Pa-hay-okee. Excepting the main access route far to the south, the Everglades National Park is almost roadless; in the region of the Long River where the Miccosukee lived before, there are no roads at all. Plenty of territory exists for the few families who might wish to return to traditional life: the tourists would never see them, never hear them. For the rest, the knowledge that there was a homeland for their children to return to would suffice. Meanwhile, Indians might be trained to replace some of the white National Park personnel, and take over the Park services and concessions. If the system worked, then the "Americans" might right the balance even further: since no white people use this north half of the park, and since it is legally Indian land, why not restore it to the Indians? This is their country, and the Indians would certainly observe the restrictions necessary to protect rare plants and animals; they have done so forever, needing no laws, out of reverence for their native earth and sacred homeland. The Indians' trust and friendship could be gained by a simple and far-sighted act that would benefit the Everglades as well. And yet this idea that would benefit *everyone* would be called "naive," especially by that "higher order of men" who sought "to exercise dominion over the land, sea, and air above us."

Off to the west, over the cypress, an orange sun of early March sank down into pink-grays of the low cumulus, and strings of ibis, three gaunt wood storks, and a solitary duck hurried down the turning sky to twilight destinations, over clean water glinting black with the loss of light. "I guess it's time we headed back," Jimmie Tiger said. Off to the north the silhouette of a large hardwood hammock of big trees rose in the dusk; I was surprised that such a hammock still existed. "Johnny Buck's Island," Jimmie Tiger said, answering my unspoken question. "He was my uncle. Lived out here in the Glades alone when almost all the other people had moved down to the Trail. Johnny Buck killed himself out there about 1964; that's where we found him." The old man shrugged. "I guess he just did not want to come in."

. . .

In early January of 1983, the state of Florida granted Buffalo Tiger's Miccosukee Tribe its long-sought lease on 189,000 acres of the FCD's Conservation Area No. 3, together with $975,000 for "economic development." In the opinion of the Osceola family, the lease contract is a government payoff to a "puppet Indian." As Homer Osceola told a reporter for the Miami Herald *on January 9, 1983, "He's not doing things the Indian way at all. He can't live like the old Indians used to live. . . . If the Indian people are going to change, let nature change them, not some money-hungry guy telling them what to do. Far as we're concerned, Florida is not part of the United States in the first place, because we've never been conquered. . . . How can the white man give it to us when we already own it?*

To this, Buffalo Tiger retorted, "Just because their last name is Osceola, they still think they're great leaders like Chief Osceola, but they're wrong. The man died long, long ago. These people better wake up and be like everybody else." Hearing that he had been criticized for driving a "1983 gold-colored Cadillac," he said, "It's only an '82, but it runs pretty good."

In recognizing Tiger's disputed right to speak for all his Miccosukee people, the U.S. government and the state of Florida tried to extinguish all future treaty claims by Florida Indians, and President

Reagan, who signed the agreement into law, promptly received an angry letter protesting the unlawful sale of "our Everglades homeland" by "Mr. Tiger and his fake tribe." The letter was written on ancient stationery that still carried the name of Buffalo Tiger, who had resigned from the General Council in 1961; it was signed by Homer, Howard, Bill, John, Leroy, and William Osceola, together with a nephew, Rainey Jim.

· 3 ·

MESAS

At The Gap trading post, we bought a few supplies and continued south. It was very cold, with a cold rain, and in the ditch lay a drunken Navajo, unconscious. Craig Carpenter had a set look on his face; he did not wish to pick him up, although it seemed to me that the man might die there of exposure. Craig shook his head. "He won't die; you don't know Indians. When he gets cold enough, he'll come to, and go on home." As an Indian who has dedicated his life to what he calls "the Indian rebirth movement," Craig disliked the sentimental idea that his people drink to blot out the grief, anger, and frustration caused by the loss of Indian country and the death of their culture. "That is also the cop-out of the drunken Indian. The Indian drinks because he *likes* to drink, and he can't handle it because all his traditions go the other way."

In the rearview mirror I could scarcely see the body in the ditch. Wherever home was, it was a long way off; on this road that ran south from The Gap into the strange colors of the Painted Desert there were only a very few lone shacks, and here and there a traditional Navajo hogan with the entrance faced toward the sunrise, and the wind and the cold.

From the Painted Desert, we turned east again, to Moenkopi, a Hopi farming colony, now increasingly settled, that lies forty miles west of the Hopi mesas. A sign alerted us that we were now under the jurisdiction of the Hopi police, and that no firearms or spirits were permitted on the reservation. Craig was contemptuous of the Hopi police and of their sign; they were only bullies for the Hopi Tribal Council, which took its orders from the Bureau of Indian Affairs. Hunched into the cowl of his dark hood, with his hawk nose and turquoise earrings, this Mohawk had the fierce, grim profile of Savonarola. On the grounds that the Indian Nation should not be subject to federal or state laws, Craig refuses to earn enough to pay taxes (he barters his labor) or obtain a driver's license, or otherwise appear in the white man's records, and once went to jail rather than participate in the white man's wars. For many years he had been a Hopi "messenger," entrusted with the correct oral presentation of the Hopi prophecies and teachings to which many traditional Indians around the country look today for spiritual guidance: the Hopi prophecy, which takes many hours to relate, must be presented without the smallest error or alteration or omission. "It is best to hear the Hopi message face-to-face from

the proper leaders and spokesmen until one thoroughly understands it from the Hopi viewpoint," Craig had told me. "I want
you to approach Hopi in a proper traditional way. . . ."

In the somber southern sky of desert winter, the San Francisco Peaks were low on the horizon. This landscape of the Colorado Plateau is ruled by dark ancient volcanos, among which four
are known to the Hopi as "sacred breathing mountains" where
high lightning activity and electric energy patterns (recognized by
scientists as well as Indians) bring about "an endless oscillating
movement of air, water, breath, and spirit"* that maintains not
only a healthful climate but a natural harmony of land and life:
"the whole universe is given the same breath," the Hopi say,
"rocks, trees, grass, earth, animals, and men." These days, the San
Francisco Peaks, one of the four mountains sacred to the Hopi
and Navajo, were often shrouded in dull smog from the great
power plants that produced the unnatural energy of the white
man, and its high green slopes were scarred by logging roads and
trails. All this change distressed the Hopi, who had wandered a
clear desert land for perhaps ten thousand years. Once their domain had extended over much of northern Arizona, from the
Grand Canyon south one hundred miles or more to the San Francisco Peaks and the plateaus beyond; the ruined village of Wupatki
lies near Flagstaff, sixty miles from the Hopi settlements of the
present day. In a region of faulted sedimentary rocks, eroded and
wind-worn into stark, dramatic cliffs and mesas, split apart into
buttes, rock ridges, spires by the myriad canyons that flow out in
broad dry washes onto the deserts, the road followed the southern
rim of a steep-walled plateau about 5,500 feet in altitude, from
which Navajo Mountain rises up another mile or more. The tableland, known as Black Mesa, is a sacred female mountain of the
Navajo as well as the Hopi, whose village-states are located on
three finger-mesas that protrude from this southern escarpment.

Along the road, in little hollows where thin topsoil has collected, the Hopi have made tiny orchards of apricot, peach, and
apple, sometimes no more than a single tree. To plant corn in
semidesert country, one must use the same earth only every other
year, and sometimes the holes in which kernels are sown must be
very deep, in order to reach moisture. Like the ancestral Anasazi,

*Joan Price, "The Earth Is Alive," *East-West Journal*, September 1979.

the Hopi are expert at "dry farming" with no irrigation and a minimum of rain—an estimated eight to fifteen inches a year. Therefore, life depends on the pure aquifers of fossil water hidden deep beneath the Black Mesa, and the precious rains brought by the kachinas, or "rain power beings." Through ceremony and prayer, the Hopi pay reverence to Mother Earth, which is the true heart of their culture, as well as to all forms of life upon it. The land is the foundation of the Hopi life way, or "Hopi way," which is based in turn on natural law. To live this way is to live morally according to the Life Plan of the Creator, who long ago guided the Hopi ancestors to Maasa'u, the great spirit of Techqua Ikachi, "Land and Life," to receive their prophecies and sacred instructions; only if the Life Plan is followed will sufficient rains come to this near-desert to support the grazing pasture and the crops. As with other Indians, the land is not owned nor can it be sold, since it belongs to the Creator. For this reason, the traditional Hopi are mortally offended by the strip mining of Black Mesa that has taken place in recent years, which they see as a desecration of sacred ground. However, the "progressive" Hopi no longer abide by the Creator's Life Plan, and more and more of them have let their gardens go, counting on mining leases, federal jobs, and federal assistance for their support. Although Hopi numbers have increased three times since the first appearance of white Americans in the 1870's, the land that is actually cultivated has decreased from five thousand acres to little more than half that number.

It was winter and the windblown dust on the plateau was biting. The world was stark and beautiful and gloomy: we stopped to inspect some dinosaur prints on the mesa rim. At twilight we passed Hotevilla, and came down to the head of the Third Mesa. Craig showed me some gigantic footprints made near the old path along which Indians once ran to their gardens at Moenkopi, forty miles away. Some say that these footprints were made by a giant Chemehuevi Indian, but others know that this was the Big Man whose form is sometimes taken by Maasa'u; as the spirit of Death as well as Life, Maasa'u is feared as a dangerous moral force.

There was no light from the wood stoves of Oraibi, and its old worn silhouette was low along the rim at the mesa's edge. Off to the east was a large rock on which was etched a pictograph of the Hopi Life Plan that warns the people against straying from Hopi way: those who have taken the wrong road seem to be wandering off into oblivion, while the figure on the true path of peace is harvesting corn as the people have done from the beginning. We stood before it in the wind as Craig transcribed it for me in the strong voice that has made him so effective as a Hopi messenger, carrying the Hopi prophecies to Indian people all over America. In recent years, progressive Hopi have made a garbage dump of the area behind the Life Plan Rock.

Because Craig was leery of the Tribal Council police, we made camp here, out of sight of the main road. In the night it snowed, with a hard wind, and the next morning the sacred ground was strewn with blowing litter. Before departing, we cleaned up the refuse that the wind had scattered.

In bleak daybreak light Oraibi looked abandoned, a cluster of stone ruins among stones. Oraibi is the oldest settlement in North America that has been continuously inhabited; some of its house beams have been dated to 1150 A.D., in a period when wandering bands of Anasazi settled here in response to instructions given them by Maasa'u. Here they were to await their True White Brother, who would return as a purifier to correct wrongdoers, carrying a stone tablet that would match the one given to the first people at Oraibi; and here a *hopi* culture was developed— for "Hopi," from *Hopitu*, the "Peaceful Ones," refers not to an ethnic group but to an attitude. They are the descendants of the Anasazi—the "Old Ones" of the Navajo, or more precisely, "Those-Who-Were-Here-Before-Us."

· · ·

The history of the Hopi encounter with the white man* began in 1540, when the Spanish appeared out of the south: at first the Hopi took them for the True White Brother, but instead of a stone tablet, they bore a cross. Finding no gold, nor even a good soil, the *conquistadores* condemned these Indians to the mercies of their savage friars. Here at Oraibi, the Hopi were compelled to build a Catholic church, where a century later, according to Spanish

---

*Background material on the Hopi is mostly drawn from Richard O. Clemmer, *Continuities of Hopi Culture Change* (Ramona, Calif.: Acoma Books, 1978), perhaps the clearest and most concise account of this people's modern history that is now available.

records, a hooded monk would beat one Indian until he was "bathed in blood," then douse him with boiling tar and set him afire as a means of casting him into perdition. All over the Pueblo world, the Franciscan priests burned the people's sacred masks to express their contempt for a faith different from their own, and the years of drought and famine in the middle of the seventeenth century were seen by the Indian religious leaders as an inevitable consequence of such disrespect for their Creator, which had caused this imbalance in the harmony of land and life. In 1680, in what is sometimes called the Pueblo Revolt, the Indians all over the Southwest united to drive the Spaniards south into present-day Mexico, and the Hopi, at least, never let them return. The priests were hurled down from the cliffs here at Third Mesa, the Catholic church was utterly destroyed, and twenty years later, when the easternmost village of Awatovi tried to welcome the Spanish back, it was obliterated—according to white historians—by Hopi led by vengeful people from Oraibi and Second Mesa.

In the next centuries, the villages were afflicted by drought, famine, and epidemic, and also by raiding parties of Ute and Navajo, who had acquired horses from the Spanish. At one time, the Hopi were apparently reduced to a few hundred survivors, as the nomadic Navajo moved into all the empty lands around the villages. Then, in the middle of the nineteenth century, bands of white men appeared for the second time, mostly trappers and Mormon missionaries from Deseret. When the Mormons began to homestead near the Moenkopi gardens, their aggressive tactics were bitterly resented, and although these homesteaders were removed in 1900 with the creation of the West Navajo Reservation, the Hopi have been beset by Mormons ever since.

For many years the United States, which acquired this region from Mexico by the 1848 Treaty of Guadalupe Hidalgo, showed little interest in the Moqui, as the rightful inhabitants were officially known until 1922. Not until 1874, when a Moqui Pueblo Agency and a schoolhouse were established eleven miles east of First Mesa, handy to the trading post of Thomas Keam, did the white economy become a fact of Hopi life.

As the village farthest from Keams Canyon—and because the *kikmongwi*, or village leader, Loloma, resisted any contact with the white man—Oraibi maintained its ancient way until the 1880's, when Loloma was persuaded to join leaders of other villages in a conference in Washington to discuss Navajo encroachment on their land. In 1882, President Arthur established the Moqui Indian Reservation, an arbitrary rectangle that left the farming colony at Moenkopi about fifteen miles outside the boundary. In return, the Indians were asked to allow missionary societies to establish themselves, one for each mesa, and Loloma chose the Mennonites, apparently under the impression that they meant to construct a school for his people. For this he was repudiated by the other leaders of Oraibi, in particular Yukiuma of the Fire Clan, who was to lead Hopi resistance to Washington interference for the next forty years. Defying an agreement made by Loloma, he refused to send the village children to the new school at Keams Canyon, and encouraged the people to pull out the survey stakes marking the land officially allotted to each Hopi family under the terms of the General Allotment Act (the Dawes Act) of 1887; this law they deemed a sacrilege, since all land had already been apportioned to the clans according to instructions from Maasa'u. In 1891, a small cavalry troop arriving in Oraibi to make arrests was met by a large group of "Hostiles" brandishing rifles as well as bows and arrows; they were led by masked figures including Maasa'u, the Creator's guardian of Life and Death. The cavalry withdrew, returning a month later with reinforcements to make their arrests; they returned again three times in the next four years to capture children and take them away to boarding school, where they might be kept for several years without any communication with their homes. By 1889, there were government schools at Moenkopi and on all three mesas.

The Santa Fe Railroad soon brought tourists into Hopi Land, and most early pictures of the Hopi dances are cluttered with people setting up their tripods in the very midst of the most sacred ceremonies. One of the worst offenders in this regard was the Mennonite missionary, H. R. Voth, whose school turned out to be a big church built with Hopi labor, like the Spanish church of the slain priests three centuries before. Voth is still hated in Oraibi, and no one attended his church, which had to be struck three times by lightning, Craig says, before the stubborn Voth gave up and went away. Since 1903, the church has been a ruin, a gaunt and broken monument to white intrusion, set apart on the south rim of Third Mesa, on the desert sky.

At Loloma's death in 1901, his nephew, Tewaquaptewa, became kikmongwi, inheriting the opposition of the faction led by Yukiuma, who brought in thirty men from Shungopovi to uphold his stand against white influence. In 1906, Tewaquaptewa ordered them to leave his village, and in the shoving match that followed, Yukiuma's son, Katchongva, was nearly killed. That afternoon, the Fire Clan chief and his followers were driven out of Oraibi. Carrying what they could take away on their backs, Yukiuma's band moved into the sand country four miles westward, which would become the settlement called Hotevilla. Because winter was coming on, they were desperate for food and shelter, and the history books tell us that the U.S. Cavalry, taking pity on these people, forced Tewaquaptewa to permit them to return for their belongings. Katchongva and others have denied this.

For resisting the government, Yukiuma and some of his men were sent to prison, and others were sent to the Carlisle Indian School in Pennsylvania. To avoid this fate, some of the Hostiles tried to go back to Oraibi, but so coldly were they received by Tewaquaptewa and his people that they departed a second time, and with government help constructed another new village near Hotevilla called Bacabi. But the Hotevilla people received no help whatever, and their pitiful situation was made worse by the imprisonment of their best men. By the time Yukiuma was released, in the spring of 1907, his alienation from the U.S. government was complete. To compound the problem, the Indian Bureau decided that Tewaquaptewa, too, needed reforming if he was to be a good American, and he and his family were sent away to Indian school in Riverside, California, for this instruction, which has been compared to forcing a Chinese to become a German. By the time he returned in 1910, he was as embittered as Yukiuma, and directed so much of this resentment toward Oraibi people who had cooperated with the white man and become Christians that these "progressives" felt obliged to move down to the bottom of the Third Mesa, near the site of an ancient village called Kiakhotsmovi, where yet another government settlement was established. Kiakhotsmovi, which has never had a kikmongwi, was the logical place for a U.S. Post Office, white trading posts and churches and, some years later, the imposing headquarters of the Hopi Tribal Council; it is known today as New Oraibi. In 1920, deciding that these people had been lost forever to the white society, Tewaquaptewa cut all ceremonial ties with them; having separated from the traditional societies and clan lineages early in the century, the Christian converts became logical candidates for the Tribal Council hierarchies of today. But Tewaquaptewa would not make common cause with Hotevilla. Although both he and Yukiuma (who was sent repeatedly to prison) continued to fight off interference from the U.S. government and the thriving missions, the villages of Oraibi and Hotevilla have maintained their differences from the great split in 1906 until the present.

The Indian agents had joined hands with the missionaries to suppress not only Indian religion but culture, language, and dignity as well (they felt entitled, for example, to seize Hopi people of both sexes and dip them forcibly into sheep pesticides in order to rid them of suspected lice). Many Oraibi people moved away to Moenkopi, and the decline of Oraibi was completed by the influenza epidemic of 1918, which killed so many residents so quickly that the ones digging the graves could not keep up. A village which, at the turn of the century, had been the largest settlement in all Hopi, with perhaps a thousand inhabitants, was reduced to a crumbling stone ruin that sheltered about one hundred people, most of them old. As for Hotevilla, it was despised by the progressives for being so conservative, so "backward," although everyone knew that if the government subsidies were withdrawn, or the tribe terminated, the Hotevilla people would be the last Hopi on earth because they were holding fast to Hopi way. And it is to Oraibi and Hotevilla and Shungopovi that Indians of North America now look for spiritual guidance; the traditional Hopi leaders of these villages have never signed a treaty with the U.S. government, and are probably the least compromised of any Indian leadership on the whole continent.

· · ·

Craig Carpenter had brought me to Hopi to introduce me to Sackmasa, chief of the the Coyote Clan, the man who had started the Hopi Rebirth Movement in 1947. But in working with traditional peoples, he said, it was important to observe the "proper traditional way." We would start off at the First Mesa villages, which are the farthest east and therefore closest in all ways to the white world at Keams Canyon, then return westward to Mishongnovi and Shungopovi, on Second Mesa, where Sackmasa and most of the Coyote Clan leaders are found. Not until we had made good contact with these leaders, and been accepted by them, would we go on to Oraibi and Hotevilla, on Third Mesa, where Hopi way has been maintained in its purest form.

Polacca, a new settlement of government housing between First Mesa and the state road, is nondescript, depressing, like any barren outskirts in America, and Craig, hunched up in his hood against the cold, jerked his stubbled chin at it. "Government Indians don't know how to live together any more—see how scattered out those houses are?" But Walpi, far out on the long narrow escarpment of First Mesa, where sheer cliffs fall down on three sides to the desert floor, is probably the most picturesque Hopi village; its inhabitants include the descendants of a Tewa Pueblo people who took refuge here from Spanish harassment about 1700. Because it lacks modern conveniences, few people live there any more, and the stone houses seemed frozen in a desolate north wind off Black Mesa. Excepting one disheartened dog, there was no sign of life, only the sour smell of longtime human habitation, and the glint of tin and bright, bad chemical colors that littered the rocks below. People have been dumping refuse off these cliffs for centuries—old bones, husks, baskets, broken implements of wood—but only in very recent times has the refuse turned into inorganic and unsightly garbage. Craig pointed with disgust at the steel reinforcing cables, glass windows, and cinder-block additions of the Tribal Council's federally funded Walpi Restoration Project, intended to make this place and its inhabitants an attraction for tourists, who come here in great numbers every summer. In a grim way, he was amused by the locks on all the outhouse doors, there to keep witches from stealing feces of their proposed victims. Witches are still feared at Walpi, despite the presence here of a Christian missionary.

A man emerged, a little groggy, from a kiva, or underground ceremonial chamber, near the cliff edge; he was surprised to see us, and not friendly. Craig demanded to know why the main kiva had a padlock on it, "like the outhouses! I never heard of *that*!" he said. The man acknowledged that the large kiva wasn't used much any more, and Craig shook his head, upset. To make the man feel better, he said, "Well, I'm glad *some*body's using *some* kiva around here." To me, he said with a pained grin, "At least the dogs are friendly."

Descending the steep road around the cliff, we gave a lift to an old man on his way down to Polacca, and Craig asked him about Ned Nayatewa, the kikmongwi of Walpi, who had fought the recent construction of the Mormon church here at Polacca— the first new church in Hopi in twenty-five years—and resisted the Tribal Council by refusing to certify council representatives from First Mesa. The old man was noncommittal and uncomfortable. "He's ashamed of himself," Craig said, after the man got out, "and he should be."

We returned to the paved road and started west again. At the Second Mesa trading post, where we stopped for gas, a young Indian woman was signing over her welfare check, to pay for her food, and the Indian women present were all laughing. "Big check," they kept saying. "The *big* check!" One woman clowned and swaggered a little, puffing herself up, saying, "Take the big check up to town. . . ." I came out laughing and related the episode to Craig, who has a good sense of humor when he chooses. He was not amused.

We went next to Second Mesa in search of the leader of the Coyote Clan. Since Craig's last visit, Sackmasa had died, but his brother, Chief Guy Kolchaftewa, who had been sent to the Carlisle Indian School in Pennsylvania and who used to perform Hopi dances all over the country, was now kikmongwi, and welcomed us into his house. In August 1971, in a last protest against the disruption of his village, Chief Guy had ordered the white people removed from the sixteen-day Snake Dance ceremonies here in Mishongnovi, but he had been unable to prevent the installation of electricity and the increasing dependence on white goods and services that had followed. Because he is old and deaf, he suggested that we come back after sunset, when his nephew would be present. Chief Guy, a leader of the Coyote Clan and head priest of the Antelope Society (the societies, unlike the clans, are confined to autonomous villages; there are no tribal societies and no "Hopi tribe"), is responsible for the correct perpetuation of tradition, but he says that his authority is increasingly undermined by the Tribal Council, which has taken away the spirit of the Hopi life. "I go to the kiva still," he said, "but I do nothing."

When we returned to Mishongnovi in the late afternoon, Chief Guy sent us down the hill to see his nephew, Douglas Lomayaktewa, who professed ignorance of what we wanted. He fed us a fine piece of apple pie and suggested a return visit. Craig referred to this as "stalling," a procedure to test our sincerity: to wait several days and return several times would be evidence that we were serious, and not in a rude hurry like the white men.

•   •   •

The establishment of tribal councils, now widespread among the Indian nations, began with the BIA administration of John Collier, the man identified with the "Indian New Deal"—the Indian Reorganization Act of 1934. The IRA set out to reverse the repressive policies of the Indian agencies which ruled the reservations assigned to the defeated Indian nations in the nineteenth century. It was the anthropologist Oliver La Farge who, as adviser to Collier, wrote the constitution and by-laws of the Hopi tribe, Arizona (and thereby created "the Hopi Tribe, a union of self-governing villages" as well as its tribal council); this constitution was apparently approved by the Hopi people in October 1936. However, a strong argument has been made that by putting out misconceptions about the vote and other devices, Collier rigged a landslide in favor of his theoretical ideas, which were designed to bring about the worthy principle of self-determination. As other anthropologists had warned from the beginning, the IRA "tribal councils" would accomplish exactly the opposite, laying the groundwork for the coercion of the majority of the people by a privileged minority backed by the money of the white man's church and state; like the discredited agency system, the tribal councils strongly favored those Indians who were willing to become Christians and consumers. Far from affirming the traditional forms of Indian government, honed by the patience of many centuries, the constitution imposed a new form from outside that could never find any justification in the Creator's Life Plan, and was therefore anathema to traditional people who still wished to live according to the Hopi way.

In regard to the Hopi Tribal Council, the constitution specifies that the kikmongwi of each village is to be regarded as its leader, and in villages where a kikmongwi exists, representatives on the Tribal Council must be certified by him. This condition has been regularly flouted or ignored. At the start, all the villages except Hotevilla and Oraibi–Lower Moenkopi sent representatives, but a year later, the Second Mesa villages (Mishongnovi,

Shungopovi, Sipalovi) withdrew their representatives because Tribal Council programs threatened village sovereignty. The Tribal Council, they said, was only a front for the BIA and had already broken its own charter by its consistent failure to consult with the kik-mongwis on important issues: this general complaint has been heard ever since. In 1940, the BIA withdrew support from its stumbling puppet, and the Council collapsed in 1943, not to be propped up again until eight years later.

In the late forties, the long Hopi resistance to encroachment by the Americans became organized. In 1947, Chief Sackmasa of the Coyote Clan decided to reveal to the leaders in his kiva certain teachings and prophecies that he had been instructed to keep secret "until a gourd of ashes fell from the sky," boiling water, burning the land, and leaving ashes where nothing would grow for years to come; this gourd of ashes would be a sign to the Hopi to declare their prophecy and message to the world before it was too late. Then another man stood up and said he had been told to speak "when the Coyote spoke." Other leaders of other clans had similar instructions, and all of them agreed with Sackmasa that "the gourd of ashes" could only be the terrible atomic bombs that the white man had dropped two years before at Alamogordo, New Mexico, three hundred miles away, and later at Hiroshima and Nagasaki. In subsequent councils, they, too, revealed their teachings, and eventually, the spiritual leaders of all villages were invited to take part in a meeting at Shungopovi that occurred in 1948. This meeting was the beginning of the Indian rebirth movement that was to spread all over North America. The meanings and proper presentation of Hopi prophecy and ideology were agreed upon, and the participants took upon themselves the obligation to fulfill the duties of transmitting the teachings to non-Hopi people, thereby restoring abundant life to the modern world. ("For the first time in history," Craig says, "the secret clan prophecies were brought together, and they were sending out prayers for help. And this was just about the time I started getting zingy about Hopi! Hopi! back in the East.") Spokesmen for the village chiefs were chosen, and also four interpreters who were to carry the Hopi message to the outside world in language and political action that the *bahana*—the "white man"—could understand. One of these men would also be a special interpreter for all Hopi, and the one chosen for the job was a disciple of Dan Katchongva, son of Yukiuma, who had become the leader of Hotevilla. Though not initiated into the men's societies, this man, Thomas Banyacya, was exceptionally well-versed in Hopi traditions, spoke good English, and was a member of the Water-Coyote Clan, with the obligation as well as the power to fulfill his duties in a Coyote way—"keep eyes and ears open, know what is going on, learn to operate along the periphery of the white man's world, present Hopi prophecy and teachings in regard to changing events, warn of danger." (It was Thomas Banyacya, in Los Angeles in 1975, who had first invited me to Hopi.)

A year later, Hopi resistance was formalized in a letter from these leaders to President Truman, which read in part:

> This land is a sacred home of the Hopi people and all the Indian Race in this land. It was given to the Hopi people the task to guard this land not by force of arms, not by killing, not by confiscating of properties of others, but by humble prayers, by obedience to our traditional and religious instructions and by being faithful to our Great Spirit, Maasa'u. We are still a sovereign nation. . . . We've been self-governing people long before any white man came to our shores. What the Great Spirit made and planned no power on earth can change.
>
> The boundaries of our Empire were established permanently and . . . written upon Stone Tablets which are still with us. Another was given to his white brother who after emerging of the first people to this new land went east with the understanding that he will return with his Stone Tablet to the Hopis. These Stone Tablets when put together and if they agree will prove to the whole world that this land truly belongs to the Hopi people and that they are true brothers. Then the white brother will restore order and judge all people here who have been unfaithful to their traditional and religious principles and who have mistreated his people. . . .
>
> Today we are being asked to file our land claims in the Land Claims Commission in Washington, D.C. We, as hereditary Chieftains of the Hopi Tribe, can not and will not file any claims. . . . We will not ask a white man, who came to us recently, for a piece of land that is already ours.
>
> Neither will we lease any part of our land for oil development at this time. This land is not for leasing or for sale. This is our sacred soil. . . .

This letter and another in 1950 repudiated the Indian Claims Commission and the Indian Reorganization Act, the Bureau of Indian Affairs and its Tribal Council, the Hoover Commission proposal to "convert the country's 400,000 Indians to full, taxpaying citizens" (what is now called "termination"), the proposed leasing of land for oil development, the North Atlantic Treaty Organization and U.S. wars in general, the drafting of Hopi youth for the armed services under laws made against their will, and related matters. The second letter also warned that these complaints would be taken before the United Nations, and both letters set the tone and general content for a whole series of sharply worded statements that were to be sent out for the next thirty years. The guiding voices behind most of the letters belonged to Andrew Heremequaftewa, chief of the Bluebird Clan at Shungopovi and spokesman for its kikmongwi, and Dan Katchongva, Sun Clan chief at Hotevilla, who spoke little English but made himself heard through the dedicated voice of Thomas Banyacya.

The Tribal Council had been resurrected in 1951 when certain Hopi, seeking access to more Hopi land outside the so-called Hopi Grazing District, got word from Washington that their only hope lay in the Tribal Council, which had been moribund for the last eight years. The prospect of an exhumed council was rejected out of hand by Oraibi, Hotevilla, and Shungopovi, but a quorum of representatives, legally certified and otherwise, was patched together from the other villages with the support of the BIA; and this new council, claiming a majority, submitted a land claim against the Navajo to the Indian Claims Commission that same year. None of the council representatives were hereditary chieftains, and since most belonged to the Church of Jesus Christ of Latter-day Saints, they hired a Mormon lawyer named John Boyden, who paid a ceremonious visit to all villages, escorted by BIA personnel as well as the Tribal Council. Unimpressed, Hotevilla, the Second Mesa villages, and Lower Moenkopi refused to recognize Boyden as their representative, and old Chief Tewaquaptewa of Oraibi refused to speak with him at all. Boyden was forced to negotiate separate contracts with the progressive villages and could not claim to represent "the Hopi Tribe" until 1955, when, after sixteen days of BIA hearings in all villages except Oraibi (in which most of the testimony repudiated the programs of the BIA and especially the activities of its Tribal Council), it was decreed that, like it or not, the Hopi Tribal Council was the only representative of the Hopi people that would be recognized henceforth by the U.S. government. Even for Oliver La Farge, this outrage was too much; in a letter to Thomas Banyacya that same year, he rejected this monster of his own creation as "an unlawful organization called together by the superintendent of the BIA to further the will of the superintendent."

* * *

Such was the plight of the Hopi Nation when Craig Carpenter first came there in the early fifties. In the spring of 1952, on the banks of the Paria River, near Lees Ferry, Arizona, about seven miles upriver from Marble Canyon, Craig received a spirit message to go immediately to Hopi: "Stop what you're doing. Take a bath. Go to Shungopovi and ask the leader of the Bluebird Clan about the problems of his people." At first Craig tried to resist the message: "I didn't have my garden in, and I only had one buffalo nickel to my name." But the spirit voice assured him that the customary one meal a day would be provided, and that the message would be verified if he arrived at Shungopovi just at sunrise. He did so, and rested against a house which turned out to belong to the Bluebird leader.

On this first trip, this bright-eyed, intense young man was received coldly. His pale skin, long head, and hawk nose of the Iroquoian tribes did not fit the Hopi idea of an Indian; because his long hair was secured in a Navajo chignon, they called him Haymsom Bahana, "Chignon-White-Man." Unable to find a way to help, Craig returned to the Colorado River to begin a career as a river guide that would support him in the next few years. But eventually he was accepted by the leaders and sent for instruction to John and Mina Lansa at Oraibi. Before long, he became a messenger, entrusted with the correct presentation of the Hopi Message to other Indian nations and the outside world. Although John Lansa gave him suggestions, he was not under anybody's orders. "Among traditional people, once you understand what your duties are, you do them; it's no one's responsibility but your own. That's what the Hopi say: 'It's up to you.' "

The following year, Craig edited a partial transcript of the principles set out at the Meeting of Religious Peoples called at

Hotevilla (August 1956) by Katchongva; because this meeting was attended by other Indian nations and also whites, and because Craig's booklet, sent around the country, was the first widespread dissemination of the Hopi Prophecy and the first call to other Indian nations to return to the Great Spirit's Way, the Hotevilla meeting represented the evolution from a Hopi movement to what Craig speaks of as an "Indian Unity Movement" that would spread all over Indian country.

Craig spent the winter of 1955–1956 seeking ways of drawing attention to Hopi difficulties, and the following winter he went to Los Angeles, where he would be based until 1969. The better to broadcast the Hopi message, he taught himself offset printing and made contacts with people in radio and film.

From the beginning, Craig worked closely with Thomas Banyacya, the special interpreter for the Hopi, trying to bring influential people out to Hopi and spreading the word to the few traditional Indians still left; it was these two men, most traditionals agree, who heralded the Indian Unity Movement that was born of the Hopi meetings. This growing movement would develop in the sixties into numerous protest groups, including the National Indian Youth Council (which supported the Indian fishing-rights fight in the Pacific Northwest in the early sixties), United Indians of All Tribes (which led the symbolic occupation of Alcatraz Island in 1969), and the American Indian Movement (AIM), an organization of young militants who were to engage in armed confrontations with state and federal governments in the early 1970's. Meanwhile, Craig encouraged such Indian spokesmen as Mad Bear Anderson (see Chapter 2), the Cherokee medicine man Rolling Thunder, and the Chumash medicine man Semu Huaute to lend their backing to organizational meetings that took place at Hopi between 1955 and 1966.

A passage in the Hopi teachings speaks of help that would come from white people who shared certain characteristics of traditional peoples everywhere, such as long hair, their own style of clothing and language, a holistic sense of identity with nature, and —because of peaceful attitudes—a name similar to Hopi. As a general account, this well described the disaffected young who were hostile to the establishment and sympathetic to minority causes, but who had not yet found a way to act on constructive alternatives. These people, being "hip" to the injustice in America, were already calling themselves "hippies," and one of their cult books was *Black Elk Speaks*, the teachings of the Oglala Lakota prophet. The four messengers sent out to help form and guide this "Hipi Nation" into useful ways were Rolling Thunder, Semu, Craig Carpenter, and Craig's teacher, the Hawaiian *kahuna** David Bray. All four were articulate and charismatic, and largely as a consequence of their efforts, the fad for long hair, leather clothes, beads, and headbands matured, during the sixties, into widespread support of Indian causes among young white Americans; much more important, it brought thousands of young Indians out of hiding. "The hippies were the first ones to respond to us," Craig said. "It took those Agency Indians and city Indians, all those powwow Indians, a hell of a lot longer." Then as now, Los Angeles had the largest urban population of American Indians in the world, but most were slow to stand up and be counted.

In those days, the Los Angeles Indian Center was being run by Stevie Standing Bear, the daughter-in-law of Luther Standing Bear, a Lakota chief who was one of the first real Indians in the movies and also the author, with help from his niece, Warcaziwin (Sunflower), of books such as *The Land of the Spotted Eagle,* one of the first books ever written from the traditional Indian point of view. Stevie Standing Bear knew a producer who wanted to make a film on the Painted Desert region and needed to talk to someone who knew it well; she recommended Craig Carpenter, who seized this opportunity to persuade the producer to dramatize the Hopi story. The producer agreed readily enough, but the conservative Hopi leaders, as Craig knew, would strongly resist. They were suspicious of any communication that was not orally transmitted, face to face, although their hereditary instructions seemed to make allowance for the written word ("marks-on-corn-husks") and even telephone and radio. As he had anticipated, they rejected the film idea in a meeting in David Monongye's kiva at Hotevilla. But Craig had come prepared with a ball of twine, the tip of which he had dropped into black ink. This $3/16$ of an inch, he told them, represented the number of people he was reaching with his mailing list, while the rest of the ball represented the estimated twenty million that might be reached by the proposed film. Then he rolled the ball, which went down the length of the

---

*Medicine man and/or shaman.

whole kiva and bounced off the wall without losing any noticeable bulk. The leaders sighed, very much impressed, and Craig was impressed, as well as frustrated, when they rejected the film idea a second time.

In his red wind band and long dark hair, and the turquoise earrings given him by a Hopi silversmith, Craig would become a well-known figure at the pop concerts, festivals, and rallies of the sixties, putting up tepees and speaking to thousands of young people in his strong, messianic voice. It was largely due to his colorful and commanding presence that those he calls "good-hearted people" banded together in the late sixties to form the Traditional Indian Land and Life Committee, which held annual forums in the Los Angeles area and guided such groups as Friends of the Hopi. His efforts came into full flower at the Hollywood Easter Love-In and the Monterey Pop Festival of 1967; for the first time, these young people had been organized, and some had enough sense of their own power to apply it to such causes as civil rights, the struggle of the farmworkers, and opposition to the Vietnam War.

· · ·

We had made our camp below the cliffs under Shungopovi (pronounced Chumopovi), among the ruined walls of a government school that had mysteriously burned down; the ruin stands in a pretty grove of cottonwoods, looking out over the Painted Desert, but paper litter from Shungopovi, on the cliffs above, was scattered everywhere, whirling on the wind through the dry trees. Craig, who grows all of his own food, refusing to eat white-man food or meat, had brought a variety of dried fruit and vegetables in cardboard cartons from his garden in northern California, and now he prepared some buckwheat bread, oka or sunflower potatoes (Jerusalem artichokes), and various kinds of beans. Skillfully, he built a fire in the wind, in a narrow slot between two stones, and baked the buckwheat on a grill.

On a clear, cold morning of late March, the dawn sky was a transparent yellow-blue. On a steep hill to the east of our camp, I found some shards of ancient pottery and wondered if they might have come from ancient Shungopovi, which after 1540 A.D. was moved from its first site in this vicinity up onto the cliffs as a defense against the Spanish troops of Coronado.

The rising sun touched the Corn Rocks Pinnacle under Mishongnovi. At this early hour, one could stare straight at the sun, imagining it as the translucent hole at the far end of a silver tunnel leading straight out into the universe. In a bright wind, the desert shone, and robins and juncos and horned larks came to the cottonwoods. We drove out on the rough track that winds around the base of Second Mesa, and followed the paved road uphill past the spring toward the village.

The day before, we had made a tobacco offering at this small cliffside pool that is a source of spiritual life for the "mother village" of Shungopovi. In these dark days, even the sacred spring is littered with spent containers and bottles that no one has bothered to clean up; they lie in the water and among the paho sticks with attached feathers, used for prayer, that had been stuck into the sacred ground. On the way down from the spring to the road, I picked up a paho that had toppled over, and Craig, as upset as I was by all the litter, snapped, "You know better than to pick up that stuff!" I said lamely that it had fallen over, but he did not answer; since our arrival, he had been alert for harassment by the Tribal Council or the Hopi police, and in a wary way he was watching a pickup truck that came down the hill and pulled up behind our own. Then he relaxed and went forward with a smile. Among the Hopi in the truck was his friend Herbert Talahaftewa, medicine man of Shungopovi and son of its kikmongwi; Talahaftewa had been one of the four Hopi interpreters appointed by the elders in March 1948 to represent the Hopi Nation to the outside world. Although glad to see Craig again, he did not wish to talk; he was busy preparing for the first kachina dance of spring, and suggested that we visit him next morning.

Shungopovi perches on the outer rim of Second Mesa, much as Oraibi perches on the Third, and the old stone dwellings roughly enclose a broad, open square; it is the only Hopi village in which the traditional village organization and all the religious societies are still intact. Despite a new kiva of cinder block that has a glass window built into the roof, it has retained its venerable appearance; but in recent years, its spiritual leaders have lost the fight to keep out electricity and running water.

Herbert Talahaftewa's house next morning was full of relatives and visitors whom, out of courtesy, he had to feed, and because our presence could only be an extra burden, we accepted a cup of coffee and took our leave. We were made welcome at the house of the kikmongwi, Chief Claude Kewanyama, and shared his family's feast-day mutton and beans, peppers, Hopi bread, and coffee, our first home-cooked meal in several days. However, Chief Claude did not ask us to stay for the kachina dances. Doubtless Craig would have been expected had he not been accompanied by a strange white man, and doubtless we could have invited ourselves, had we wished to do so.

Leaving Chief Claude's house at mid-morning, we returned to camp. The day was sunny, with a faint breath of spring warmth in the shifting weather over the mountain desert. On the high rocks overhead, at Shungopovi, the kachina dances—the first outside dances of the year—had begun. But all one could see from the foot of the cliffs were the high rocks on the blue sky; the ghostly drums of invisible men seemed to come from the earth itself, as if rocks and sky had taken up the chanting. The drums proclaimed the arrival of the kachinas (from the Hopi word *k'acinna*), the name given by all Pueblo peoples to the Rain Power or Cloud Beings who bring the rain needed to support life, and who are embodied by masked dancers in ceremonies that take place in spring and summer.

Toward noon, I walked out onto the desert. The wind had backed around from the north to the southwest, blowing down from the kachinas' home in the bright snows of the San Francisco Peaks; the snow shone on the horizon. To the north rose the pink-buff turrets of Second Mesa, and across the wind, on the blue sky, came the thump of drums, as steady as a pulsing of the universe. At first I thought it was my step on the dusty earth, for it was precisely the rhythm of my walking.

. . .

A night of rain, and a morning of cold wind and dust-shrouded sun. In a strange light, we returned to Mishongnovi, where Douglas Lomayaktewa stalled us once again—"They are still testing our sincerity," Craig said—by inviting us to come back that evening. Since we had visited three times, Craig felt that correct protocol had been observed, and contact made, and that a meeting would take place that evening. Therefore, we were free to pay our respects at Oraibi, on Third Mesa, while awaiting the meeting with leaders of the Second Mesa Coyote Clan. As Craig had written to me before our trip, "The people to talk with in Oraibi are, of course, the kikmongwi, Mina Lansa, and her husband John. The Lansas are almost the only ones among the leaders who have never made any mistakes, or at least not any that I know about; and Mina is the most articulate and convincing Hopi leader now speaking to the outside world."

Mina Lansa was the daughter of fierce old Tewaquaptewa, and apparently John Lansa's grandfather had made the original etching on the Life Plan Rock; his clan traces its origin to a people older than the Anasazi, who lived ten centuries ago in the cliff dwellings at Mesa Verde in Colorado. John Lansa is the chief of the Badger Clan and the head of the Powamu men's society which holds the Bean Dance every February; in that ceremony, young Hopi initiates are exhorted to follow the tradition of Techqua Ikachi, Land and Life, as set down by Maasa'u; to attend with respect to the gardens and the ceremonies, to follow "the way of the corn pollen," and thereby live out the harmonious long life of Hopi way.

Since Tewaquaptewa's death in 1960, Mina Lansa had acted as kikmongwi and was represented by her husband in the few ceremonies in which women are not allowed; she was the first woman kikmongwi in Hopi history. "That shows how desperate things are getting," Craig said sadly. But she was a strong and remarkable woman, as he is the first to admit: although in her seventies, she fought the strip mining of Hopi land harder than anyone, seeking out personal confrontations with Peabody Coal Company officials on Black Mesa and in their city offices as well. As kikmongwi, Mina Lansa was entrusted with the sacred stone tablet referred to in the traditionals' letter to the President in 1949, the companion of which will be brought back to Hopi land someday by the True White Brother.

Apparently Tewaquaptewa had been dissatisfied with his sons, Myron and Stanley, the first of whom moved down to New Oraibi and the second to Los Angeles, but recently, Myron had appointed himself Oraibi's representative to the Tribal Council without bothering about the kikmongwi's certification, and had put up council signs welcoming tourists to Oraibi, which Mina systematically took down. In 1973, after nearly a century of rude tourist intrusions (not only into the village but into houses), she put up her own sign, which read as follows:

WARNING   WARNING
NO OUTSIDE WHITE VISITORS
ALLOWED BECAUSE OF YOUR
FAILURE TO OBEY THE LAWS
OF OUR TRIBE AS WELL AS THE
LAWS OF YOUR OWN. THIS
VILLAGE IS HEREBY CLOSED.

Because I was with Craig, I was permitted into the village, and we went straight to the Lansas' house. These white-haired, handsome people met Craig warmly, without exclamation, moving to greet him with soft murmuring and smiles. Mina served us a good noon meal at which we were joined by Jacob and Thomas, the sons of Mina's sister and therefore Parrot Clan, like Mina herself; a green parrot, stuffed, sat in a hoop suspended from the ceiling. Jacob Bahnimtewa, who had been a little boy when Craig first came to Hopi, cried out, "I remember you! Always walking the road between the towns!" During lunch, a white man turned up at the door, saying he had been sent by mutual friends, whom he identified, and asking for permission to enter Oraibi. Very politely, very firmly, Mina Lansa said, "I'm very sorry, I have closed my village." To his credit, the man did not protest but simply said good-by.

The Lansas were upset about a recent documentary film made for British television that had not been shown to the traditional leaders before release, despite prior agreement that this would be done. Among other mistakes, the film perpetuated a white historian's account suggesting that people from Oraibi and Second Mesa had wiped out the degraded village of Awatovi, which had welcomed the return of the Spanish twenty years after the Pueblo Revolt. The elders say that this deed was done by a "new people," living at the edge of Hopi, who had not yet been accepted into the Hopi community, and who were afterward rejected, since Maasa'u had decreed that to be a Hopi one must be a peaceful person; as Craig likes to point out, the Hopi *never* fought the U.S. government, nor violently resisted its way west; all they ever wanted was to be left alone. Even worse, the film contained footage taken by a Hotevilla man of kachina dancers in full regalia and masks; such photography has been forbidden ever since 1906 because of repeated abuses of the sacred ceremonies. (For many years, white businessmen in Prescott, Arizona, have dressed up as kachinas and charged admission to their powwow concept of the dancing; for traditional Hopi, to accept money for the sacred dances, or even for "God's food" such as Hopi corn, is sacrilege.) "Because of this film," Jacob remarked, "the traditional people will never tell anything again." Mina Lansa bitterly regretted her cooperation with the filmmakers, which had been refused by David Monongye and other spiritual leaders of Hotevilla and also by the leaders at Shungopovi.

Spokesmen for other clans and villages came and went all day, including Otis Polelonema, Snow Clan chief and spokesman for Chief Claude of Shungopovi, and Will Mase, son of the late Chief Sackmasa, who started the Hopi Rebirth Movement in 1947. In the afternoon, the Lansas received a Navajo rancher and his wife who had come to seek advice on the trouble that had recently flared up between Hopi and Navajo, mainly because of the Tribal Council's belligerent stance against Navajo herdsmen whose animals stray onto Hopi territory. Many of this man's cattle had been impounded by the armed rangers sent out by the Tribal Council, which was pursuing the land policies first initiated in 1951, and was now erecting fences on an open range where no fences have ever been before. At one point, a man had been seized, jailed overnight, and fined $160—about one fifth of Navajo per-capita annual income—for watering his livestock at a spring that he had used for sixty years. The culprit was ninety-eight years old.

The Navajo, a tall, stolid man, had despaired of understanding from the Tribal Council and had come to ask traditional leaders for their help. "We hear about all this fighting between Navajo and Hopi," he said. "I never seen it. It is the white man who wants that, who says that. In the old days, maybe it was true, but now the Navajo just wants to live in peace." The Lansas nodded solemnly in agreement. From earliest times the aggressive Navajo had raided and harassed the Hopi, but the ancient trade between these peoples—mostly Navajo wool and mutton for Hopi corn, fruit, woven belts, and baskets—had led eventually to friendly intermingling. As an Indian agent reported in 1884, "trifling quarrels" between individuals are "usually caused by careless herding of the young Navajos, who allow their herds to overrun these outlying Hopi gardens. The Navajo are almost invariably the aggressors." But, he said, "these are the most serious difficulties these two tribes have had for years. . . . The best of good feeling generally exists. . . . they constantly mingle together at festivals, dances, feasts."* In the century since, Navajo encroachment on Hopi territory, while a serious problem, has never seriously interfered with trade and exchange and intermarriage between two peoples who, despite very different origins and ways of life, have come to share related cultures of masked dancing, song, and art.

Unfortunately, the Navajo population has increased from an estimated 12,000 in 1880 to more than 170,000 today (the Navajo tribe is much the largest in North America) and their sheep herds have overgrazed the range, while the Hopi, whose petitions to Washington date back to Loloma's trip in the 1880's, found themselves effectively restricted to what had become known as the Hopi Grazing District (District Six), created in 1943, a mere corner of the 2.5 million acres awarded to the Moqui by President Arthur, and a tiny fraction of their aboriginal domain; also, the government itself had come to regard District Six as effectively identical with the Hopi reservation, to judge from the fact that activities carried out beyond its borders had been turned over to Navajo agencies. Most Hopi still wished to discuss the matter peaceably, and as early as 1960, traditional leaders led by Dan Katchongva had notified the Navajo of their strong opposition to actions initiated by the "so-called Hopi Tribal Council," in collaboration with their Mormon attorney, to settle a "so-called Hopi–Navajo land dispute" in federal court; they had also appealed to the Ninth Circuit Court in San Francisco to reverse any legal decisions based on this "dispute," which they perceived as commercial collusion by the Tribal Council, the Church of Jesus Christ of Latter-day Saints, and the energy corporations, notably Peabody Coal, in which the Mormon Church now had an interest. Then in 1962, a substantial part of the original Hopi reservation was decreed a "Joint Use Area" in which the Navajo share equal rights, including a share of the strip-mine leases on Black Mesa, and inevitably pressure arose for a partition. By 1972, Mina Lansa was

---

*Cited in Jerry Kammer, *The Second Long Walk* (Albuquerque: University of New Mexico Press, 1980).

testifying before a congressional subcommittee against a bill to partition the Joint Use Area, declaring that the real purpose of the bill was to split Indian resistance and open up more Indian land to the energy leases desired by the Hopi Tribal Council, much against the will of traditional leaders in both tribes. For the Hopi, partition implies a prior Navajo right to this Hopi land, while certain Navajo—and especially those in the region of Big Mountain—felt threatened by eviction from land they have regarded as their home for more than one hundred years. Eventually the crisis at Big Mountain (see Chapter 12) would become one of the most volatile in Indian country.

The partition bill became federal law in 1974, and already the Hopi Tribal Council was vigorously policing its 911,000 acres, going out of its way to intensify bad feeling. In its campaign to recapture territory from the Navajo through eviction of Navajo herders and their animals from the Hopi section of the Joint Use Area, the Tribal Council sought legitimacy within the Hopi Life Plan by exploiting an historic "enmity" between these peoples. As a result, those Navajo who came commonly to Hopi festivals and were welcomed into Hopi houses no longer feel welcome here, and do not come. The Tribal Councils of both peoples are officially and legally opposed over the matter of land and grazing rights, with the BIA, not so mysteriously, supporting both: it is in the interests of the multinational concerns seeking leases on Indian land that these two peoples should be set against each other.

Will Mase, a big man of strong presence, assured us that the conflict was a very recent one and was not of the Indians' making— not unless one counted the Hopi tribal chairman, who had dutifully testified to an ancient enmity between these peoples. "In my youngerhood," Will Mase said, "I used to go out eagle hunting about this time of year, and around those buttes"—he waved his hand toward the strange mountains that rise from the mesa off to the southeast—"you'd never see no Navajos—just once in a while, around the trading posts. We never had no trouble until this joint-use thing was set up by the BIA. Now the Navajo sayin' they own everything out there! If anybody wants to live here, he has to become a Hopi—that's what the Prophecy said. Our shrines have been set up out there for a long time, and the Navajo know it." But like other traditionals, Will Mase is against the eviction of Navajo herders from the Hopi section of the Joint Use Area; the only Hopi who are eager to see this done are the few who run large herds of cattle, such as Tribal Council Chairman Abbot Sekaquaptewa, whose family owns one of the largest herds of all. Though Will agrees that overgrazing is a problem, and that the enforced reduction of Navajo herds (started in the 1930's under Indian Commissioner John Collier) is perhaps necessary, he feels that the people could work the problem out among themselves, in a peaceable Hopi way, were it not for all this outside interference.

The Tribal Council continues to erode Hopi traditions without a legitimate mandate from the villages. Its prospering bureaucracy, which now employs more than one hundred people, has no significant income apart from the mineral leases, which are needed to justify its salaries and functions, indeed its very existence. In 1977, the Hopi were asked to accept a government payment of five million dollars as recompense for all the land effectively taken from them—that is, every acre outside the Hopi Grazing District. The council tried hard to persuade the people that this payment was simply a gesture of regret over past wrongs, neglecting to mention that acceptance of this sum would clear the way for leasing of the land to the energy interests that their lawyer's firm had been dealing with for fifteen years. The absurd payment—from sixty cents to two dollars an acre, depending on the location of the acreage, and based on land prices when the land was "taken" in the 1800's—worked out to less than one thousand dollars per Hopi, as compared to the five hundred thousand dollars worked out as a fee for Boyden, who attributed his bloated compensation to the extra work caused by lack of cooperation from his clients. And this fee had the approval of the BIA, the government agency charged with protecting the interests of the Indians, since "the choice of lawyers and fixing fees" (Article VI, Section 1-b of the Hopi Constitution) must be approved by the Secretary of the Interior.

As a rule, the Hopi and Navajo tribal councils implement the land-use policies of the BIA, which are mainly directed by corporate interests through connections in the Department of the Interior; that five million dollar "recompense" from the U.S. government in the guise of the Indian Claims Commission was obviously a device for eliminating any land claims by the Indians before the profits started to roll in. Acceptance of this money meant tacit acceptance of the loss of ancestral land that was without price in its true worth to the Hopi people. "My father told me we should stand firm on the land," Mina said. "That is all we have. When the land is gone, we will walk away from our homes with our beds upon our backs."

Sitting on a straight chair against the wall, John Lansa nodded; he is one of the few adult Hopi who have never worked for the white man in any capacity, who have persevered in Hopi way throughout their lives. "We are getting older now," he said. "We wonder what our children will do with us. It is up to them." Sadly, the Lansas agreed that the younger people were no longer interested in Hopi way; like so many of their parents, they had been seduced by Tribal Council promises of automobiles and electrical appliances. "All we care about is money," Mina Lansa said. "It is our own fault. There is no longer love between people now, and everything is drying up."

When we returned a few days later, Mina Lansa was away; I would not see her again. In less than a year, worn out by distress as much as by disease, this woman revered by Indian leaders all over America, whom Craig had called "the most articulate and convincing Hopi leader speaking to the outside world," would be dead of cancer. (And also of other causes, Craig believes. "The job of kikmongwi is always dangerous," he says, "and in cooperating with that white film crew, Mina made her first serious mistake.")

. . .

Chief Sackmasa's son, Will Mase, appeared again at the Coyote Clan meeting at Mishongnovi, where we went after an early supper with the Lansas. Also present, besides Chief Guy Kolchaftewa and Douglas Lomayaktewa, were Harold Koruh, One-Horn Priest and protector of the kikmongwi at Shungopovi, and several others. The men sat at the big table that took up much of the one-room house, while Douglas's wife and grandchild and another woman sat in the corner. All these people were very concerned about the Tribal Council's role in the vote on the five-million-dollar government offer to recompense the Hopi for inequities of the past.

The vote had been held on the day of the Basket Dance at Shungopovi, Harold Koruh said, when most Hopi were up on Second Mesa. "And Hopi system is, if you don't want something, you don't go." Although less than three hundred people, out of more than six thousand, voted to accept the money, they were identified as the majority in a dismal turnout, and the vote was approved.

Like the Lansas and other traditional leaders, the Coyote Clan feared that the very heart of Hopi life was threatened: everyone agreed that the Tribal Council sits illegally and does many illegal things. The Tribal Council representative from Sipalovi (the village west of Mishongnovi) is self-appointed, without legitimate authority; he was contemptuously upbraided by a young girl in the street when he gave permission for unwanted telephone poles to be brought in. A very old woman had followed the telephone crew around, filling in the holes as fast as they were dug.

The men said that the Reverend Caleb Johnson, a Christian Hopi who is spokesman for the traditional kikmongwis, had been trying to attract public attention to the excesses of the Tribal Council, citing especially the policy—which is called "Washington policy" or "Goldwater policy"—of setting Hopi and Navajo against each other by fencing off land and impounding Navajo stock; one man spoke bitterly about poor Old Man Harris, whose burros had been impounded by the rangers: "They charged him forty dollars that he didn't have to let them out!" In this matter, as in all others, the Tribal Council paid no attention to the traditional leaders. Since 1971, Chief Guy had been trying to stop new urban housing of the sort seen in Polacca. "The Tribal Council ignores us. They put what they call a 'lagoon' in a sacred area. The lagoon is a cesspool." Sacred land of the Strap Clan (so-called because they used a bearskin tumpline in the old migrations) was defiled when the Tribal Council gave permission to the Second Mesa Trading Post to build there. In Shungopovi, sacred ground had been usurped for water and sewage lines for a housing development. At a village meeting at the house of Otis Polelonema, the developer said that the Tribal Council had given him the authority to dig this water line. Otis inquired how this could be done without the prior authority of the kikmongwi. The answer was that the kikmongwi was only a religious leader, with no political authority—in itself a flouting of tradition, since by Hopi custom, political and religious offices have always been the same. But this was sacred ground,

Otis insisted, upon which he was asked who paid for his dentistry and eyeglasses—an insinuation that he shouldn't resist the Tribal Council after accepting medical help from the BIA.

After a while, Harold Koruh said quietly that a thorough investigation of council abuses was required: "They are the source of all the trouble here." Will Mase nodded sadly. "Yeah. We sure need help here." There was some talk of suing the Tribal Council, but most of the men shook their heads. "We have learned that we will never win anything important in a U.S. court," said Harold Koruh.

In the winter of 1979, Harold Koruh and other clan leaders of Second Mesa would send a new letter to President Jimmy Carter, which read in part:

> As a result of the "Hopi Constitution," a "Hopi Tribal Council" was created. . . . Their attorney and main adviser, since 1951, has been Mr. John S. Boyden, whose contract has never been authorized by the Kikmongwis. In all actions, legal and political, that the council has undertaken in the name of the Hopi Tribe they have not had the authorization of the true and rightful Hopi leaders. It is now clear to us that the Tribal Council, in concert with Boyden, have conspired to divide, fence, and sell this land, our birthright, and to profit thereby. To us, it is unthinkable to give up control over our sacred lands. We have no way to express exchange of sacred lands for money. . . . We ask that you deal honorably with us and see that justice is done. The hour is very late.

In Hotevilla, where Craig wished to bring news to his own leaders, we made our base at the house of James Kootschongsie, or "Koots." James Koots had the flu and sat hunched before the stove, attended to by his wife, Helen, and son, Dennis; under his Indian name, Danagyumptewa, he is the translator of the great last statement of the teachings, history, and prophecies of the Hopi people made by Dan Katchongva before his death in 1972, and he is also editor of *Techqua Ikachi*, the small newsletter of the traditionals. Koots is very articulate, though he tends to communicate with wry laconic comments and ironic gestures. Wearily, he waved us to his table, in a manner suggesting that he himself might perish of the flu before we had finished eating up his food.

At a good meal of bean soup, blue-corn chips, tamales, frijoles, and Indian tea, James Koots and Craig discussed various Indian problems, and especially the friction between AIM militants and the traditional Indians that has developed since the rebirth movement began. The two agreed that most of the militants were urban Indians, and Koots was amused by the confusion of these people who had lost all touch with the old ways and were now trying to reclaim them, especially when so many of them had no idea which Indians they were. Helen Koots and her daughter were winnowing a basket of blue Hopi corn, and Mrs. Koots smiled. "What is that tribe they all call themselves?" she said. "Cherokee?" Everybody laughed. Yet Indians look to the enterprising Cherokee for leadership in activities all around the country. "They're the only Indians I know," Craig said, "who can leave their homeland and still retain the strength of their traditions. Most of the other Indians who were moved out west are shot." And the others nodded.

Craig repaid the Kootses' hospitality by suggesting that my truck be used to fetch a load of household coal from the mine site on Black Mesa. The job would be a dirty one, for the mine was fifty miles away over rough roads, and the coal would be piled inside the camper on the truck bed. But Craig had made an offer I could not refuse, and off I went with Dennis Koots, careening along rough dusty tracks on a bare tableland of sage, piñon, and juniper. We passed the trading post at Dinnebito ("Navajo-Our-Water"), then Big Mountain: this high tableland, like a truncated mountain, is inhabited by the traditional Big Mountain people, who will be evicted if implementation of the Joint Use Area partition is carried out. Lone Navajo hogans, a few ponies, distant sheep—in the cold light, the only birds were larks and mountain bluebirds, in a hard land between low dark ridges of yellow pine and oak. The boy, who was about sixteen, was taut and still, keeping his answers to my questions as short as possible, so that we made the hundred-mile round trip mostly in silence. When I asked him if he regarded himself as a traditional, he thought about his answer for so long that it seemed he was simply oblivious of the question. Then he said shortly, "I don't know yet. I just live up there, try to help out."

On the outskirts of the huge strip-mine operation is a pile of scrap coal that may be scavenged by the Indians. We opened the rear door of the truck and pitched in a load of coal in silence, our bare, blackened hands stiff and glazed in the raw wind. Below lay the gigantesque, strange edifices of the largest strip mine in the world, rising like an evil city from the landscape, but stern signs warned us against going closer. Like all strip miners, the Peabody Coal Company has had a lot of bad publicity and is anxious to hide its ugly and exceptionally destructive operation from the public. "They don't like people lookin'," Dennis said. "You go down there, they chase you off."

In 1964, mining permits were encouraged by the BIA and granted in secret by the Hopi and Navajo councils, and in 1970, to the astonishment of the shocked traditionals, Black Mesa was splayed open by Peabody's enormous operation. (Peabody, which made such a mess of Appalachia, was the largest coal company in the world, yet until recently, it was only a tentacle of Kennecott Copper; in Arizona, it was involved with a consortium of twenty-three power companies, called W.E.S.T. Associates, which planned to turn Black Mesa coal into electric energy for Phoenix, Las Vegas, and Los Angeles.) Extending over 26,000 acres, the strip mine has swollen to include innumerable drilling rigs, a railroad, power stations, and deep wells that are sucking up the pure, precious water of the desert aquifers in order to wash the "slurry" of particulate coal to the Mojave power plant in Nevada. The coal also goes, by rail, 275 miles to the Page, Arizona, power plant that is now polluting "beautiful Lake Powell," where the Colorado is backed up behind Glen Canyon Dam. The stacks of the Navajo Plant are seventy-five stories high, and this plant alone casts tons of dangerous pollutants into the clear desert atmosphere each day.

The Bureau of Reclamation, which owns and uses much of the power generated by the Navajo Plant at Page, is part of the hydra-headed Interior Department; so is the Bureau of Indian Affairs. By encouraging Tribal Council leases on Black Mesa that are absurdly disadvantageous to the Indians, adding economic insult to grievous spiritual and environmental injury, the BIA has seriously betrayed its trust.

The largest strip mine in the world seems to sprawl over an entire valley on this high plateau, and the gigantesque earth-eating machinery, the towering cranes and ugly structures, the enormous hills of coal and overburden, were leaving scars and toxic wastes that could never be removed, despite the smooth assurances to the contrary in Peabody Coal Company's contracts with the Tribal

Councils. (In this barren region of low rainfall, it is "virtually impossible" to reclaim strip-mined land, according to the National Academy of Sciences, which concludes that these arid plateaus must be left intact or written off as "National Sacrifice Areas"; here as elsewhere on the Great Plains, the "sacrifice areas" turn out to be on Indian lands.) And what may be the most deadly blight of all was nowhere visible—the depletion and pollution of the pure fossil water of the deep aquifers, by no means inexhaustible, that are being sucked up from two wells 3,500 feet deep at the rate of 2,300 gallons per minute. Before being scooped, the subsurface coal is broken by underground explosions that pose a serious threat to the scarce and precious water: should the poisoned groundwater drain through a man-made fissure into the deep aquifers, the Indian way of life, for both Hopi and Navajo, would come to an end.*

A Hopi group (which included a good number from the government villages) brought suit in 1971 against the Secretary of the Interior as well as Peabody, protesting the exploitation of the sacred center of the earth (the Four Corners region, called Tukunavi) and stating in part that "by caring for these lands in the Hopi Way, in accordance with instructions from the Great Spirit, we keep the rest of the world in balance. . . . The land is sacred and if the land is abused, the sacredness of Hopi life will disappear and all other life as well." Four years later, when Peabody was in full operation, this suit was dismissed by the U.S. Supreme Court without a hearing, and a belated attempt to void the Peabody leases by the kikmongwis of eight villages failed also, permitting Peabody to proceed apace with the ugliest ecological disaster of our time.

For many Navajo, whose estimated annual $900-per-capita income and high infant mortality rate are symptomatic of their desperate condition, the destruction of Black Mesa comes as a necessary evil. Except for the traditional people at Big Mountain, most Navajo do not revere Black Mesa as the Hopi do; it wasn't their land in the first place, and about three hundred Navajo (with only a few Hopi) have found employment at the mine. But the tribe as a whole is taken aback by the extent of the destruction.

*Groundwater is already scarce in Arizona, where the Papago, the Ak-chin, and the Indian bands along the Colorado were all fighting to preserve their water from outright usurpation by developers and large agricultural interests.

A year after the strip mining had started, a Navajo living on Black Mesa told the photo-journalist Dan Budnik, "I think as I walk this earth, what will next summer bring? Since the company started their work, people began to change. The air began to change. The plants seem to have no life. When the wind blows our way, the dust covers the whole ground—the food, the animals, the hogans, the water." Meanwhile, the Indians have become ever more dependent on money. By century's end, the coal will be gone, the money spent, and the land contaminated forever. Nevertheless, the Hopi Tribal Council was permitting its lawyer, Mr. Boyden, to negotiate new mineral leases which, to judge from the experience with Peabody, will be chiefly profitable to Boyden's law firm and the corporations. As on many other reservations, Indian leasing policies encouraged by the BIA are much more profitable to the non-Indians involved than to the Indians themselves. By one estimate, Peabody's income for the thirty-five years its mines are expected to produce coal is $750 million, over fifty times what the Hopi can expect to receive in royalties over the same period. After that, the company will vanish, leaving behind vast tracts of ruined landscape that can never be restored. More serious still, Peabody will have pumped billions of gallons of water from the desert aquifer to carry coal slurry, more than can be replaced in many centuries by the minimal rains that fall in this semiarid region.

In order to justify the original lease, the former chairman of the Hopi Tribal Council authorized the Salt Lake City agency representing the consortium of coal-buying power companies to issue a press release attacking a protest against the strip mining signed by seven traditional leaders; in this release, he went on to state that "our Elders have told us that the Creator has placed valuable resources for us in the ground and that it is our obligation to discover those resources and to use them for the benefit of man. And this is exactly what we are doing . . . we are not a self-sufficient island set out here in the great southwestern desert. We need cars from Detroit and manufactured goods from southern California. We must have something to sell them in exchange. . . ." Similarly, his successor, Abbott Sekaquaptewa, had publicly identified the return of the True White Brother with the appearance of the white Americans out of the East. In this expedient interpretation of the Hopi Prophecy, the Hopi chairman had confused the True White Brother with the Great White Father, who is not known to possess the missing companion of the Stone Tablet held by Mina Lansa in Oraibi.

. . .

On raw, graded tracks that wind like scars on the thin hide of the plateau, Dennis Koots and I returned south fifty miles to the paved road. There we turned eastward, climbing a long rise toward Hotevilla, which, unlike the ancient villages of Oraibi and Walpi and Shungopovi, as closely knit as forts on their rock rims, is scattered wide across the barrens, as it must have been in the autumn of 1906, when Yukiuma and his people found such shelter as they could in these windy dunes. But when Yukiuma died in 1929, Hotevilla had already established almost all the traditional societies and ceremonies, and effective leadership had been assumed by his son, Dan Katchongva, who had been too old in 1906 to be taken away to school and so had never learned to read and write. By 1947, when the Hopi rebirth movement got under way, Katchongva was already an old man, yet he saw to it that his forceful and articulate ideas were heard by having his disciple, Thomas Banyacya, made interpreter to the outside world for the Hopi Nation. In addition, this old chief of the Sun Clan dictated many letters to the white authorities and made excursions into the white world; in 1968, already more than one hundred years old, he appeared with Marlon Brando on a television show in a successful effort to muster public support for a confrontation then taking place in Hotevilla between traditionals and an Arizona Public Service crew invited in by the progressives to install utility poles for electricity.

This running battle over the installation of electricity, already lost in almost all the other villages, is symbolic of the fight between the Hopi factions. Electricity was certainly to be desired, yet this intrusion of unsightly poles and wires without formal village approval was not only a breach of Hopi sovereignty, but an inducement to buy the expensive appliances—refrigerators, dishwashers, TV—that a village struggling to stay independent could not afford. Electricity was the key to the door that led to increasing dependence on the white man for goods and services, and laid open the Hopi world to the material temptations and corruption that have been warned of in their Prophecy.

The traditionals have always been wary of the white man's consumer mentality, and now they were worried about what could happen when the Black Mesa mine was dead, when a dependent and poverty-stricken people, having been left with waste and desecration where a sacred mountain had once stood, found themselves forced to accept more leases and more desolation. This threat was increased by the prospect of legal "termination," or dissolution of a people as a cultural unit, with which Indians are threatened every other year. Termination legislation, which had already wiped out a number of small tribes, not only withdraws all federal aid, but turns the Indians over to the mercies of state jurisdiction and property taxation, forcing a people with no other recourse to put their last resource—land—upon the market. ("That is all we have. When the land is gone, we will walk away from our homes with our beds upon our backs.") By eliminating an Indian nation, termination quiets Indian claims to tribal lands that were never ceded to the U.S. government by treaty, which happens to describe almost all the "federal" land in the Far West; instead, the people must accept whatever monetary settlement has been bestowed upon them by the Court of Claims, which was set up not to administer justice but to expedite adjudication of land titles and head off any future claims that Indians might make on lands already coveted by the white economy.

The Hopi chairman's brother, Wayne, a prosperous Mormon, proprietor of a thriving Hopi craft shop, with holdings in the family ranch and a construction company, complains in his progressive newspaper, *Qua Toqti*, of the poor attitude of the traditionals toward "their fellow tribesmen in business," and criticizes white supporters of the traditionals for "wanting to keep us in our 'primitive' state." He has declared, "We will never go back to our cornfields and orchards unless we are forced to." In another column in the newspaper, Wayne Sekaquaptewa inquires, "When will someone come along to convince us that we are squabbling like untrained children over everything in the name of our useless religion?" (Sekaquaptewa believes that the true story of the Hopi may be found in the Book of Mormon.) Not surprisingly, *Qua Toqti* vociferously supports the eviction of the "enemy Navajo" from Hopi land.

The progressives feel that there is no place for old, slow Hopi ways in a world that is going on without them; they look down on the traditionals, with their wood stoves and kerosene lamps and outhouses, their "useless religion." (I notice, however, that outhouses in Oraibi and Hotevilla are not locked to keep out witches, as are the Christian outhouses of Walpi.) The traditionals know that those who follow the lead of the progressives will be assimilated—that is, swept away into a competitive economy for which they have no training. So long as the Hopi hold their land, those still able to make corn grow in the slow, patient techniques of dry farming will survive even when all help has been taken away, proceeding as best as they can according to their sacred instructions until the Day of Purification restores harmony and balance to all land and life, until the bad road taken by the white man comes to its inevitable end, as foretold in the stark etching on the Life Plan Rock.

Toward noonday, we said good-by to the Koots family and headed eastward, stopping off at Oraibi for a last visit with the Lansas. Carrying a hoe, John Lansa was standing all alone in the windy street, as if awaiting us. He was on his way to break the winter soil in his clan gardens; he grows corn and beans, peppers and apricots, peaches and apples. A young boy came out and stood beside him in the bare spring light. "Perhaps he will go with me," John Lansa said, and the boy followed him as he started down the street, on the way out of the village. The tall old man stopped a last time, turning back toward us, but pointing in the direction he was going. "That is *my* security," he called. "I always have my orchard and my field." John Lansa is one of the last great Hopi runners; as a young man he would go, from time to time, to work his garden, then at Moenkopi, and return the same day to Oraibi, a round trip of ninety miles along the high rimrock of Black Mesa.

· 4 ·

LOST ELOHEH LAND

In the late nineteenth century, a remnant band of Cherokee—descendants of those who had hidden in the Great Smokies in the 1830's when the rest of the tribe was "removed" on the Trail of Tears to Oklahoma—came down from the North Carolina mountains to a ceremonial place overlooking the valley of the Cherokee River. There an old prophet, climbing onto a high stump and gazing out over the traditional heartland of his people, received a vision of a dreadful day still several generations in the future when this valley would be flooded over, and the faces of countless buried ancestors would glimmer upward through the unnatural waters as through a floor of glass. Tearful and frightened, the old man told his people that they must resist the projects of the white men, "who didn't know what they were doing"; when the river no longer ran free through the sacred valley, the Ani Yunwiyah—"the Principal People"—would be destroyed forever as a tribe. The recent damming of the Cherokee River, now known as the Little Tennessee, fulfills this prophecy and affirms an older one that anticipated the white man's disturbance of the earth's natural balance, with calamitous consequences for mankind.

Although the Tennessee Valley Authority's Tellico Dam project had been repudiated for a decade in Congress and the courts as uneconomical, unlawful, and unnecessary, it finally achieved through procedural tricks and political blackmail what it had never been able to win in a fair hearing. In June 1979, a last-minute amendment insinuated into an energy and water appropriations bill authorized the TVA to complete the Tellico Dam "notwithstanding the Endangered Species Act or any other law"; this high-handed and very dangerous precedent is thought to be the first such rider ever to put an unfinished project beyond legal restraint. On September 25, President Carter, expressing "regret," failed to veto H.R. #4388, and on November 29, when the flood gates were lowered, a small perch called the snail darter, whose only known natural habitat was the last free-flowing stretch of the Little Tennessee River, became the earth's first living creature ever delivered willfully into oblivion.

Though only one of many urgent reasons why the Tellico Dam should never have been started, this little fish was taken up by the news media to the virtual exclusion of more fundamental issues such as the transgression of Cherokee sacred ground. Even defenders of the darter became troubled by the trivialized controversy as set out by the dam's advocates and parroted in newspapers and on TV: did the perpetuation of a "useless" three-inch "minnow" justify the waste and critical energy loss of a nearly completed $110 million hydroelectric dam? As I discovered in early November 1979, when I went down to the Little Tennessee River to have a look at the historic valley before it disappeared, this presentation of the case was false from beginning to end.*

The TVA and its long-time supporters, led by local politicians and developers, big business, and big labor—all the old familiar well-fed faces—claimed that Tellico Lake was needed for recreation, improved navigation, and flood control; that much of the shoreline of the lake would be used for industrial development, providing jobs in this depressed pocket of western Appalachia; and that the dam would make a vital contribution to hydroelectric energy production in the region. In fact, twenty-four major dams and lakes already exist within sixty miles of Tellico, and most of them have large areas of undeveloped shores. The recreation, navigation, and flood control claims have no merit whatever, and as for the energy contribution, this dam contains no generator of any kind: its token contribution of twenty-three megawatts (out of a current TVA regional capacity of 27,000) will be produced by a diversion canal through the nearly adjoining Fort Loudoun Dam on the Tennessee River.

How many Americans, I wonder, are even aware that the Tellico is a small dam in a 38,000-acre project and that most of that "wasted" $110 million was actually spent on speculative acquisition and road development of twenty-two thousand acres that were never intended to be flooded. Land appreciation of the proposed lakeside properties has long ago offset the twenty-two million dollars in materials and labor (exactly one fifth of the figure used for public consumption) that is the true cost of the dam and its embankments. And often these properties were taken by right of eminent domain with little or no concern for the rights of the

---

*Statements by traditional Cherokee people in what follows are taken mostly from affidavits supplied by their attorney, Ben Bridgers, of Sylva, North Carolina; Jimmie Durham's statements were provided by Mr. Durham himself. Environmental background material was furnished by environmental attorney Zygmunt Plater, and local residents Roy Warren and Janet Thiessen offered much incidental information.

legal owners. In a typical case, the TVA condemned the ninety-acre farm of an elderly widow, Mrs. Nell McCall, even though less than two acres were to be flooded. ("I offered to give them that for nothing," Mrs. McCall said, "but they said everybody had to go.") Under the circumstances, the 341 families evicted from their hard-won homesteads to make room for speculators in lakeside lots may be forgiven for calling the whole ruthless enterprise "a land grab."

In the Depression, when the Tellico was first conceived, the claims made for it by the TVA may have seemed valid: after all, the TVA had been set up to help the threadbare regional economy. Since then, it has ossified into a huge autonomous bureaucracy, influenced by special interest groups and "pork-barrel claques" tied to federal agencies. Grown immense at the bulging pork barrel of highway, dam, and waterway construction, it requires increasingly vast projects and appropriations merely to justify its girth—hence, the oppressive grid of steel and concrete that has locked up the rivers of this region into a chain of stagnant ponds descending from the mountains all the way west to the Mississippi.

The Tellico, which proposed to throttle the last wild stretch of the Little Tennessee, seemed like one dam too many even to the U.S. Congress, where it had been debated annually for the past fifteen years. Throughout this period, the proposed dam was protested by the Cherokee, who went unheard. TVA—or someone in Tennessee—wanted this dam badly, and the state's politicians, notably Senator Howard Baker, were encouraged to persist far beyond the call of duty. Funds for the dam were finally appropriated in 1966, but construction, started the next year, was halted in 1971 by a coalition of local people and environmentalists, who were able to demonstrate in court that the project flouted the National Environmental Policy Act. Thus, the shortcomings of Tellico were obvious well before the summer day in 1973 when an ichthyologist named David Etnier discovered a small, pretty, banded perch, unknown to science, at Coytee Springs, the historic site where British troops in 1756 made their first treaty with the Indians.

Biologists concluded that the original range of *Percina tanasi*—which needs a clear, cool flow of water to oxygenate its clean, pebble-bottom spawning beds—included most of the Tennessee River drainage; it was only after the TVA had killed 2,500 miles of river that this species was apparently confined to the Little Tennessee. A volunteer lawyer, Zygmunt Plater, who has fought for six years against the Tellico, recalls the meeting when the Valley farmers agreed to file a suit on behalf of the darter under the Endangered Species Act of 1973: "I lived on this river all my life and I never heard of it," said Asa McCall (who died during the struggle, and whose widow, Nell, now seventy-five, was one of the last hold-outs against TVA seizure). "But if this little fish can help us lick this thing, then I'm all for it."

Almost overnight, this obscure perch (together with a reticent Maine weed called the furbish lousewort) became a kind of wry national joke. The joke was hammered by Tellico's proponents, who saw that the public would soon lose sympathy for a "useless minnow," and eventually this ridiculed small creature, used originally as a delaying action, was doing the cause a lot more harm than good, despite all efforts to point out its role as an indicator of human and economic values. It was also claimed that the fish had been transferred successfully into nearby streams: the truth was that two of the three transplanted populations had died out, and the third was threatened by the acid spills and other pollutants in the Hiwassee River.

Meanwhile the TVA had acquired a new board of directors, and with it a strange ambivalence in its own attitudes. In a letter to Secretary of the Interior Cecil Andrus, in April 1978, TVA chairman David Freeman conceded that "Contrary to TVA position, forming a permanent lake is not vital to the Tellico Project and may not even be the option with the greatest public benefits." Subsequently, a 258-page TVA document, "Alternatives for Completing the Tellico Project," acknowledged that income from the valuable farmland to be flooded would probably exceed the "projected benefits" of the new lake by nearly a million dollars per annum;* that fourteen million dollars in additional construction would be needed before the dam could pass safety requirements; that annual dam maintenance would substantially exceed its income; that local job opportunities created by the dam were out-

---

*TVA's candor about "projected benefits" would be more impressive in the absence of a congressional study made by the General Accounting Office in 1977, which concluded not only that the dam was uneconomic but that all but about one percent of TVA's dam benefit claims were unreliable.

numbered by those that would be lost; and that aside from the Endangered Species Act, the dam was in legal difficulties on numerous counts, including the Historic Preservation Act, the Environmental Policy Act, the Rivers and Harbors Act, the Clean Water Act, the Fish and Wildlife Coordination Act, and the Executive Order on Floodplain Management, none of which the TVA had complied with. ("TVA does not argue the law," says Ben Bridgers, attorney for the Cherokee. "They argue that they are *above* the law.")

Even the TVA, in short, had now concluded that its dam made no practical sense at all. From other points of view—moral, aesthetic, and environmental—it was what the Philadelphia *Inquirer* called "an abomination of irresponsibility . . . a towering symbol of almost everything that is rotten in the District of Columbia." A beautiful river known affectionately throughout the state as the "Little T" has been stopped up like a clogged pork barrel to create a muddy artificial lake, and silted beneath this superfluous lake will lie not only the drowned homesteads of hundreds of defenseless people but also sixteen thousand acres of some of the richest river-bottom farmland in the United States, and an historical treasure perhaps as important as all these other losses put together: the hundreds of archeological sites in the Little Tennessee Valley include not only ancient mounds but the buried ruins of the Seven Towns that two centuries ago were the sacred center of the Cherokee Nation. (Most Eastern Cherokee now live on the Qualla Boundary reservation in the Blue Ridge Mountains, just across the North Carolina border, but the Little Tennessee remains the spiritual homeland.) A report prepared for the TVA by Interior Department archeologists—dated May 24, 1979, but mysteriously withheld until after the final Tellico appropriations were signed into law by President Carter on September 25— ascribes "world-wide significance" to these sites, declaring that "the physical records of American prehistory present in Tellico cannot be matched in any other area this size in the continent."*

Why were the great historical values of this river, not to speak of its sacred importance to the Indians, given virtually no mention in the national debate on the Tellico Dam? For it seems clear that

*Cultural Resources of the Tellico Project (TV-50461A), Department of the Interior, Interagency Archeological Services.

if the public had been fairly informed as to the true nature of what was being perpetrated at Tellico, the public servants could not have got away with it.

. . .

I had not expected that the place would be so lovely. In the sad, soft light of early November, the muted fire colors of the fall, moss-green faces of the rock walls at the river bends were reflected like memories of other centuries in the clear, swift water rolling down from the blue ridges of the Great Smoky Mountains, to the east. The day was filled with drifting leaves, the rich mineral smell of humus, a wistful resonance that echoed in the autumn calls of birds. "You don't have to be a Cherokee to feel the spiritual power here," murmured Roy Warren, a local environmentalist and amateur archeologist who had fought for years against the loss of "the Little T," and who had kindly volunteered to share his knowledge. Warren had met me at Fort Loudoun, site of the first British outpost west of the Appalachians, and from where we stood, just upriver from the mouth of the stream known to the Indians as "Tellico," we could see the tattered cornfield that marks the buried town known as Tuskegee, birthplace of Sequoyah, the great Cherokee teacher whose name has been commemorated in a national park as well as a mighty tree. The Indians planted corn, beans, peas, potatoes, pumpkins, cabbages, melons, and tobacco. Gerhard de Brahm, the surveyor-general who built Fort Loudoun in 1756, recognized the superb quality of the topsoil in this "American Canaan," which he deemed "equal to manure itself"; yet the white men had to be restrained by the Indians from building their fort right on top of the rich gardens.

In the eighteenth century, the domain of the powerful Ani Yunwiyah—the largest Indian nation in the South—extended into what are now eight states, and protected the beleaguered British of the Middle Atlantic states from French-led Indians to westward (the safety of the colonists "does under God depend on the friendship of the Cherokees," according to a declaration of the Carolina General Assembly in 1730). Yet four years after it was built, Fort Loudoun was destroyed by an embittered Ostenaco, who had once sent warriors to help George Washington and the Virginia Militia in the Big Sandy Expedition against the Shawnee; the Fort's only

survivor was saved by Chief Attakullakulla, who had been painted
by Hogarth in London in 1730 (Ostenaco himself was painted at
a later date by Sir Joshua Reynolds) and who would say before
his death, "I pity the white people, but the white people do not
pity me." By the time Independence was declared, in 1776, the
Cherokee and the colonists were mortal enemies, and the following year, the proud "Principal People" were defeated. Even so,
Old Tassel refused the white men's demand for all land north of
the Cherokee River, which would have put the white man's farms
within sight of Chota:

> It is surprising that when we enter into treaties with our
> fathers the white people, their whole cry is more land. . . . It
> has seemed a formality with them to demand what they know
> we dare not refuse. . . . Much has been said of the want of
> what you term "Civilization" among the Indians. Many pro-
> posals have been made to us to adopt your laws, your religion,
> your manners, and your customs. . . . We should be better
> pleased with beholding the good effects of these doctrines in
> your own practices than in hearing you talk about them.*

A rabble of "American" settlers was already coveting the
Valley, and pieces of its land began to go. In 1814, still trying
hard to accommodate and even emulate the white men, the Cherokee set Andrew Jackson on the road to the White House by
turning the tide in the Battle of Horseshoe Bend against the Creek,
an act of friendship which was promptly repaid by a final rush
upon their lands in Tennessee. In 1828, gold was discovered on
Cherokee lands in Georgia, and the following year President Jackson recommended that his old allies—most of them Christians—
be sent away to Indian Territory west of the Mississippi, where a
number of displaced Indians had gone as early as 1817. The Removal Act passed by a single vote in 1830; it was fought by such
distinguished Americans as Henry Clay, Daniel Boone, and Daniel
Webster, and was also repudiated by Chief Supreme Court Justice
John Marshall. (But Marshall did Indians a fatal disservice by declaring them "domestic dependent nations" of the American re-
public, and this at a time when many of these nations were still

*Alberta and Carson Brewer, "Valley So Wild: A Folk History" (Knoxville: East
Tennessee Historical Society, 1975).

uncontacted, far less conquered; this opinion by a great jurist "friendly" to the Indians has been cited ever since as an argument against Indian claims to sovereignty.) The Cherokee were banished to present-day Oklahoma, together with the Choctaw, Chickasaw, and Seminole, as well as their old enemies the Creek, and the cost of the Removal was deducted from the $4.5 million awarded them in compensation for the loss of most of the southeastern United States. "Their calamities were of ancient date, and they knew them to be irremediable," de Tocqueville wrote of the passing bands of stoic, ragged Choctaw. The exodus culminated in 1838, when almost all the Cherokee remaining were rounded up by General Winfield Scott and "removed" westward: this was the infamous Trail of Tears, which at least four thousand Indians did not survive. "The Cherokee Removal was the cruelest work I ever saw," said one of Scott's own soldiers.

. . .

Driving farther up the Valley, we left the main road and crossed old fields, now condemned, that according to Warren had been farmed by the same family ever since the Cherokee were driven out. (The Indians' rights to their own land have been ignored since their first land claims in 1820.) A sharp-shinned hawk darted back and forth, once, twice, three times, over the hedgerows, in apparent pursuit of small foraging parties of titmice and chickadees, and a marsh hawk tilted at slow speed over the dun and wheat and gold of the river bottom. On high ground overlooking the broad valley, where sparrows flicked and twitched through the yellowed leaves, stood huge red and black oaks that had served as shade trees for a farmstead that had come and gone, leaving an emptiness in the old grove that was somehow deepened by the autumn clamor of the jays and crows. The farmstead overlooked the sites of Tommotley (Hewed-Timber Town) and Toqua, named for a great mythic fish which inhabits the river at this place. Toqua was a Mound-Builder site before the coming of the Cherokee, and throughout the Valley the buried evidence of Stone Age man and the mysterious Mound-Builders—some of the sites are thought to be eight thousand years old—is scarcely touched, despite the crude and hasty digs that the threat of flooding has inspired. In 1967, archeologists of the University of Tennessee were invited by the TVA to investigate these sites as well as others, which they did on an emergency "salvage" basis, using TVA's backhoes and bulldozers. Though later work was more responsible, the early "digs" were crude and greedy. "It was infuriating," said Roy Warren, an amateur archeologist who located the old gate of Fort Loudoun about six years ago. "Those so-called archeologists went ripping into one of the most beautiful Indian mounds in the whole country, and when they were finished, there was nothing but a pile of dirt criss-crossed with ditches." He showed me ugly photographs that he had taken of the damage done at Toqua and the other villages, the exposed skeletons in the broken graves, the ornaments, pottery, axe heads, and other artifacts that lay hidden in such profusion here beneath our feet, the gangs of unsupervised looters—or "grave poachers," as the Indians call them—who descended on the place: 634 graves were excavated at the Toqua site alone. "It was quite a while before TVA got around to putting in that fence," Warren said, pointing at a rectangular enclosure with a sign that read "Archeological Site—Property of the U.S. Government." For some reason, the bureaucrats had kept the patch inside the wire carefully mowed, and the spot of caged lawn looked lonely in the autumnal colors of the valley, like an unused cemetery for dogs. "Yessir," Warren said, disgusted still. "That's what those people call the Chota Mound. It isn't Chota and it isn't a mound, not any more."

As he spoke, he turned his head toward the sound of a fast-moving car: a white van was howling down upon us with undue speed, considering the fact that we were parked in a dead-end turnoff. "They're pouncing on us even before we *do* anything!" Roy complained, mildly amused. As the van wheeled to a halt, I could see that the uniformed guard inside was holding a microphone to his mouth, as if summoning assistance; recognizing Warren, he relaxed his vigilance only slightly. "Back again, huh?" he said. "We never give up," Warren said affably. The guard, heavyset with slicked black hair, in crisp khaki and a bright white T-shirt, looked me over; he asked Warren my identity, which he wrote down. Aggravated by the way he did this, I made a show of reading his badge and taking down *his* identity, then inquired if this wasn't public land. "Feder'l land!" he said. "That's not public?" I asked. He eyed me narrowly, to show me he had me spotted as a troublemaker, and certainly, he was equipped for trouble: besides the handgun on his hip, he had an Ithaca .37 riot gun mounted upright beside him and a carbine rifle ready on the back seat. "What are you guarding?" I inquired, jerking my chin at all the shooting irons. "Berl grounds," he said, " 'n' looters." Warren sighed. "Won't need to guard them much longer, I guess," he said pleasantly. "Okay if we look around a little?"

We continued eastward up the Valley, on the new road along the wood edge bulldozed up out of the "borra pits" and bulwarked by stone riprap wall; when all this bottomland is flooded, this road will be the lakeside drive for the new shorefront owners on Tellico Lake. The fallow bottomlands were set about with gentle wooded hills, in the last oak reds and sweet-gum purples and hickory yellows of the autumn, and here and there a gold leaf-burst of sassafras, in one of the loveliest prospects of river and mountains I have ever seen. In this broad and harmonious bend on the south side of what was once known as the Cherokee River were the sites of Tennasee, or Old Town, for which the state was named, and Chota, the Council Town, the secular and ceremonial center of the Cherokee Nation. Like Toqua, Tanasi and Chota had been grievously assaulted by the emergency archeology demanded by the TVA: when Roy Warren had first come here, four years earlier, the old lady whose family had lived here since the nineteenth century burst into tears as she described to him the desecrations that had taken place. Warren pointed out a three-acre riprapped elevation that is soon to be an island: "They bulldozed that thing up and named it Chota," he said, "as a consolation to the Indians."

Here at Chota in 1797, the future French king Louis Philippe fell off his horse in the furor of an Indian ball game, and later slept in the place of honor between the chief's grandmother and great-aunt; Warren pointed out the flat where it is thought the ball field was located. And here at Chota, just two weeks ago, the Cherokee and a number of white sympathizers, undeterred by nails strewn across the access road and some sticks of dynamite— apparently planted by those local people whose property near the new lake has soared in value—had held a cheerful rally by the river. That day, Roy Warren had made friends from the Cherokee reservation on the Qualla Boundary, fifty miles eastward in the North Carolina mountains, where the remnant Cherokee had hidden when their kinsmen were rounded up and driven off to Oklahoma.

At Chota, the river flowed between grassy meadow banks and beautiful white rock, and Warren searched the sandy riffles, hoping to show me one of the big fish that have made this the finest brown trout stream in the East. "There's trout in here up to thirty pounds," he told me, "and the fishermen bring a million dollars every year to local business; nobody talks much about the trout, but they're going to go, too." There were still two ancient Indian fish traps in this part of the river, stone walls that supported weirs of sticks, with a wicker basket net at the point of the V where the walls met, downstream. But today the clear river ran too deep, too swift, and like the doomed trout, the ancient fish traps remained hidden.

Roy Warren waved an arm at the empty woods and the blue mountains rising beyond. "They even claimed they wanted to 'improve navigation'! What're they gonna do, run up a barge load of garbage for the possums?!"

The easternmost of the Seven Towns (seven is a sacred number to the Cherokee) was Tseetaco, "Good Fishing Place," located between two hills, for at this place the Valley had already begun to narrow, and the strange steep ridges known to the Cherokee as "the Enemy Mountains"—home of the dread ogress known as Spear-Finger—loomed high over the river in the northeast. At Tseetaco, in 1788, in the course of the last resistance to white encroachment, a Cherokee war party surprised and killed a detachment of militia raiding the Indian orchards, in what became known as the Battle of the Peaches. Warren wonders if Tseetaco might not have been the oldest and the largest town of all: in just one and one-half acres of excavated ground, he said, there was evidence of 234 burials. As at the other sites, the Indian remains, together with ceremonial artifacts of burial, were made off with by the white people, despite the distress and protest of the Cherokee, and he suspected that most of them wound up in labeled boxes in the McClung Museum at the University of Tennessee. Some 1,140 Indian remains are known to have been taken, and Indian requests for reinterment have been ignored, whereas the graves in the white cemeteries in the Valley have been carefully relocated elsewhere. The Indians, profoundly upset by the disturbance of sacred burial grounds and ancestral spirits, would prefer that the graves were damaged by the rising water rather than have the bones picked over by the curious fingers of the white man; nevertheless, they dread the artificial flood, which they perceive as an unnatural inversion that forces man out of harmony with his surroundings. "If the homeland of our fathers is covered with this water," an old medicine man named Lloyd Sequoyah has said, "it will cover the medicine and spiritual strength of our people because this is the place from which the Cherokee people came. When this is destroyed, the Cherokee people cease to exist. . . . Then all of the peoples of the earth cease to exist."

A few miles above Tseetaco is Chilhowee Dam, named for another Cherokee town submerged above it. Warren asked if I wished to see this dam, and I said no. On the way back down the Valley, in the sharp shadow lines of autumn dusk, we passed the parked van of the guard. "Next time we see you," Roy Warren called out to him, "I guess we'll be riding in a boat."

. . .

How amazing it seemed that in this state, where the economy is based in tourism and agriculture, its congressmen would sacrifice a lovely, historic valley in the face of so much well-informed opinion that for more than a decade has dismissed Tellico as a bad idea. Yet in 1978, Senator Howard Baker, sensing that hard times had diverted public sympathy from that pesky "minnow" to all those "wasted" megawatts and millions, cosponsored a Cabinet-level review committee (including the Secretaries of Interior, Agriculture, and Army) whose first business was to decide if Tellico should be exempted from the provisions of the Endangered Species Act. To his dismay, this imposing group agreed unanimously that Tellico was economically unsound (as the Chairman of the Council of Economic Advisers, Charles L. Schultze, pointed out, the total projected benefits of the dam amounted to less than the cost of completing the damned thing, let alone building it) and therefore did not deserve exemption: after more than a decade of court and congressional hearings, the Tellico pork barrel was sealed. But on June 18, 1979, in a nearly empty House, Baker's confederate, Republican Representative John Duncan, flouting House Rule No. 21 that forbids using appropriations bills to change existing laws, used a whole bag of procedural tricks to sneak an unseen, unread, undescribed, and undebated amendment past his unsuspecting colleagues in just forty-three seconds. One of the victims, Representative Paul McCloskey (Democrat from California), warned the House that its integrity had been undermined, that the public would condemn Congress for adopting without reading "an amendment of this degree of controversy."

On its first test, the amendment was repudiated by the Senate, but on September 10, Senator Baker made last-minute deals with (let us name these heroes) Senators Danforth, Dole, Domenici, Gravel, and Wallop, to win by just four votes, declaring untruthfully to the end that the dam represented vital energy and that the future of the transplanted darter was assured. Baker may have suspected that President Carter, in his eagerness for re-election, did not have character enough to veto a whole "energy" bill merely to eliminate a dishonest amendment, although Secretary Andrus urged the veto ("I hate to see the snail darter get credit for stopping a project that was ill-conceived and uneconomic in the first place"); if so, his instinct was correct: "with regret" the President signed into law an amendment designed to frustrate the will of the American people as expressed in Congress and the courts. (The day after President Carter signed the fatal amendment, he telephoned environmental lawyer Zygmunt Plater from the presidential airplane, asking Plater, in effect, to tell him that what he had done was for the best. "He seemed to be whimpering for forgiveness," recalls Plater, who told the President that no conservationist in the country could conceivably support what he had done.) In cynical ambition—to embarrass Carter, to assist a crony, or perhaps just to please those local politicians who had invested in lakeview properties back home—Baker had sabotaged the unanimous findings of the responsible review committee sponsored by himself, thereby damaging not only the integrity of Congress but the long-term welfare of the nation that he claimed, every four years, to be fit to lead.

The day after Carter's cave-in, the TVA rushed in its machines to complete the dam. But on October 12, the Eastern Cherokee, citing the American Indian Religious Freedom Act of 1978, appealed to the U.S. District Court in Knoxville for an injunction against the flooding, pending a hearing on their claim that the Duncan Amendment was unconstitutional: the destruction of their spiritual homeland, which many still visited regularly, they said, would deny religious rights that were guaranteed by the free-exercise clause of the First Amendment.

The TVA attorneys, calling the Cherokee appeal "unfair," pretended that the religious issue had been brought up too late, even though the Indians (who had no constitutional right to sue until the federal government acquired ownership of the land) have been protesting the wholesale desecration of their sacred burial grounds and ceremonial sites since 1967. The TVA made much of the fact that Ross Swimmer, Chief of the Cherokee Nation in Oklahoma, expressing gratitude to the TVA for having located Chota for the Indians, had belittled the idea that Chota was a sacred site; his view was repudiated by the traditional Ketooah Band on his own reservation, who strongly support the position of the Eastern Cherokee. Chief Swimmer, a well-to-do bank president and tribal attorney (and protégé of the larcenous "principal chief," W. W. Keeler), had recently declared himself a Republican candidate for Senator from Oklahoma, an ambition in which, interestingly enough, he had the pledged support of Senator Howard Baker of Tennessee.

On the morning of the day that I visited Chota, the Cherokee appeal for a temporary injunction against the flooding was turned down by the U.S. District Court in Knoxville on the grounds that ownership of the property involved was a prior condition of a First Amendment claim. Subsequently it was dismissed by the Sixth Circuit Court of Appeals in Cincinnati, and by Justices Stewart and Brennan of the Supreme Court, who simply scribbled on the appeal the word "Denied." The judiciary, it appeared, was weary of the fight, and anxious to bury the whole smelly mess as soon as possible. As the Cherokee's lawyer told me, "We've been overwhelmed by the past, not by the merits of the case; all we're asking for is a chance to appeal the merits. The judges are reading their newspapers, not the Constitution." In questions of First Amendment rights, the government must demonstrate a "compelling state interest" before a Constitutional protection can be overruled; "compelling state interest" scarcely describes the ambiguous situation acknowledged in the TVA's own big book of "Alternatives."

* * *

On November 3, a bright blue mountain day, I drove eastward up the Pigeon River into the Great Smoky Mountains; in the fall breeze, the red dogwood leaves and berries seemed to flutter in the cold sun-sparkle of the stream. Crossing the North Carolina line, I arrived soon afterward at the town of Cherokee, where I was met by a pretty young woman named Myrtle Driver. Ms. Driver, who helps the elderly people of the community as an interpreter in their dealings with white people and who served as a tribal interpreter in court depositions having to do with the Tellico Dam, led me to an out-of-the-way community back in the mountains known to the Indians as Raven's Ford, called commonly "Big Cove," where I hoped to talk to two elderly medicine people, Ammoneeta and his brother Lloyd Sequoyah, about the Cherokee's continued interest in the valley. But Ammoneeta was in the hospital and Lloyd could not be found; instead we visited Myrtle's father, a traditional healer named Charlie Johnson, who said that when his great-great-grandmother visited Chota as a little girl, crossing the mountains on a walk that required several days, there were a few old Indians living there still. "That place was sacred to us," he said, "and it was also the capital of our nation, the way you people think of Washington, D.C." Not until these years of struggle to save the sacred valley, Myrtle said, had she realized how much her heritage still meant to her. In the words of Jimmie Durham, a Western Cherokee who had testified against the dam in 1978, in a Congressional hearing,

> Is there a human being who does not revere his homeland, even though he may not return? . . . In our own history, we teach that we were created there, which is truer than anthropological truth because it was there that we were given our vision as the Cherokee people. . . . In the language of my people . . . there is a word for land: Eloheh. This same word also means history, culture, and religion. We cannot separate our place on earth from our lives on the earth nor from our vision nor our meaning as a people. We are taught from childhood that the animals and even the trees and plants that we share a place with are our brothers and sisters. So when we speak of land, we are not speaking of property, territory, or even a piece of ground upon which our houses sit and our crops are grown. We are speaking of something truly sacred.

Myrtle's aunt, Emmaline Sequoyah Driver, who lives deeper in the mountains, up the Straight Fork of the Oconaluftee, had made a recent pilgrimage to the sacred Eloheh Land, where she had visited the place where the old seer "made his last prophecy" upon the stump: she is a full-blood Cherokee who prefers to speak in her own tongue, and so is her brother Ammoneeta, who had lived for five years in an abandoned cabin at Chota and still makes regular journeys there to gather medicinal herbs, chant *idi-gawe-sti*, or sacred incantations, and perform the going-to-water purification (the bather dips seven times into the flowing river, facing the rising sun). "We have always been told that that Valley was the Center, that's where we began," Myrtle Driver said. "We don't have to live there. Just knowing it is there makes us feel better."

Like her brothers, Emmaline Driver had given a deposition against the dam on religious grounds, but now she shrugged. "White people mostly don't care what we think, we're just Indians. They say, Sorry, we can't help you," the old lady said.

"No, they *won't* help you, just *because* you're an Indian!" Myrtle Driver exclaimed, relating the trouble she had had in getting anyone to pay attention after her brother had been shot by a white man. "Had to have his leg amputated. Wouldn't give us a court hearing until I said I was friends with the U.S. marshal over in Asheville, and when they *had* the hearing, they wouldn't let us know the day, so because my brother wasn't there, they threw his case out!" I nodded unhappily: from travels among Indians elsewhere in the country, I knew there was nothing unusual about this sort of justice.

The Eastern Cherokee of the Qualla Boundary are among the few Indian peoples east of the Mississippi still living in their original homeland, but these mountains were not the "Center" of their nation. "In talking to these elders," Myrtle said later, "it seems that a lot of our words and traditions and legends began down there at Chota: this place up here in the mountains came much later. Seems like that place is the source of almost all the myths of the Cherokee people. Like Dakwa, the big fish—that's Toqua—well, the snail darter became 'a big fish' to the Cherokee people when it stopped the flooding. TVA tried to say we weren't aware of that place—it isn't true. In our own family, people always went over there. That chief out in Oklahoma, Ross Swimmer, he sold us out, and he ought to be hung; he actually *thanked* the TVA for letting us know where our own place was!" The Indians are under no illusion about the real purpose of the Tellico, which in the words of an old man named Goliath George, is there to "fatten someone's hip pocket"; and this, too, he says, fulfills a prophecy, for "Tellico" is the white man's distortion of the Cherokee *ade la eqwa*, or "big money." "Even if they didn't respect us living Indians, they should at least respect our dead Indians," Goliath George said in an affidavit. "Since I have heard about this dam, I have been on my knees about these things many times."

The next day, I telephoned Lewis Gwin, a TVA spokesman for the Tellico, who said that no definite date had been set for the closing of the dam; the last crops in the Valley, grown under lease, had not been harvested, and there were still a few people, including Mrs. McCall, who had not moved out of their homes as they were told. Mr. Gwin seemed anxious to point out that the present Board of Directors was not originally responsible for this project, and had sponsored the candid "Alternatives" report in order that Congress might make the proper choice. True, Congress had decided against the dam three times, but once Congress had ordered the TVA to proceed "notwithstanding the Endangered Species Act or any other law," the TVA had no choice—"Our hands are tied," Mr. Gwin told me. As for the Cherokee appeal, he acknowledged that they had protested the dam for fifteen years, but he could not comment on the validity of their claim while the case was in litigation.

After talking to Gwin, I drove over to Tellico on the highway that crosses the huge old Atomic Energy Commission (now the Nuclear Regulatory Commission) reservation in Oak Ridge. Off to the west, I could see the huge strip-mine scars along the high slopes of the Cumberlands, commemorating the days when this country had been stripped of its virgin forests. When the day of gigantic hydroelectric and nuclear power schemes arrived, the poverty-stricken people of Appalachia said very little; dependent on the timber and coal companies, then big government, they were evicted from their homes over and over to clear the way for dams and lakes and AEC reservations.

In this sinister forest, unsettling signs directed the authorized traveler to such destinations as the Weapons (Y-12) and Gas Diffusion (K-24) Plants; other signs read "Bear Creek Road—Closed to Public"; "Experimental Area—Trespassers Will Be Prosecuted"; "No Swimming or Fishing"; "Water Unfit for Human Consumption." Here and there, bright yellow warnings read "Radiation Hazard—Keep Out." Although it was Sunday, a line of military tanks clanked down the highway, escorted by the pervasive security vehicles, and both tanks and police seemed to intensify an oppressive atmosphere of man at war with his own habitat, of a blind few imposing their will upon the many. However, public relations are still important: the TVA's nuclear reactor in Chattanooga has been made part of the "American heritage" by being named after the great Sequoyah,* and in this region big green signs do their best to persuade the casual observer that the TVA's Tellico Project is "Building a Better Environment."

Where the highway crosses the huge Fort Loudoun Dam across the Tennessee River, one can see the small Tellico Dam where it blocks the mouth of the Little T downriver: the lakes behind these dams will be less than a half mile apart, and largely devoid of the local recreationists for whom they were constructed, to judge from the sterile emptiness of Fort Loudoun Lake on a sunny, warm, and windless Sunday morning. Finding the Tellico heavily fenced against the taxpayers, with a gate that brandished warning signs as well as chains, I drove down to a parking lot under the Fort Loudoun Dam, then walked downriver, passing without difficulty through a fence in the river woods and moving inland through the fields at the mouth of the Little T to the long embankment for impounding water that leads out to the dam itself. Climbing the embankment, I could see far up into sun-misted distances of the lovely valley; in the softened autumn light of the river bottom, a lonely farmer was working on Sunday to harvest the last crop from this "American Canaan" that has fed man bountifully for perhaps three thousand years. The sight of that lone, hastening figure, working against time and greed and folly, brought on a wave of melancholy and profound anger.

At both ends of the embankment stood large herds of huge yellow earth-moving machines. Because it was Sunday, these dinosaurs were still, but at the sight of a loose citizen, a security vehicle came in a great hurry down the road. "Ain't supposed to *be* in here!" the guard exclaimed, instructing me to get into the

*In 1981, the Sequoyah Plant led the nation with 238 potentially dangerous "incidents"; it operated only eleven percent of the year. TVA's controversial Clinch River nuclear breeder reactor in the same region is named for Colonel Douglas Clinch (see Chapter 2), who led a detachment of Tennessee Cavalry to "chastise" the Seminole in 1813.

back. I could truthfully say that I had seen no signs to that effect down by the river, and he seemed happy to accept my alibi. "They knock 'em all down!" he said, perplexed. "Can't keep a sign up for two days!" He drove me out to the chained gate where another guard in big black shades, thumbs hooked into his holster belt, awaited us: this one's manner suggested that I was getting off too easy. When I asked him why the Tellico needed so much security, he said they had had a bomb threat just four days ago. Both guards blamed the destruction of the signs on "environmentalists," probably "them ones that had planted that dynamite up there at the Chota Mound two weeks ago, and strewn them nails on the road while they were at it."

The first guard, going off duty, was kind enough to offer me a lift back down to the "T." He was an older man, born up the Little T in the region of the Indian villages, and he admitted that the dam was a poor idea, but like most Americans, he had come to accept the version of the controversy drilled into all of us by the news media, and felt that not to finish the job now would be an unacceptable waste of money. Anyway, he said, there were no snail darters left in the Little T; they had all been transplanted out of Coytee Springs and other places. The old man pointed at the mud-gray Tennessee. "Hell," he said, "they's a big sandy bar down here on the T, they doin' better there than they *ever* done up the Little T! Why, right out here where we're lookin' at, they's so many of them darters, the fishermen been dippin' 'em right with the minnas, usin'em for bait!"

He granted that the Cherokee had a case. "Hell, they's Injuns buried all over the place up here, and U.T. [the University of Tennessee] has people all over, diggin' up graves." He shook his head in disapproval, then jerked his head in the direction of what I took to be a certain grave he knew in some town on the far side of the river. "I don't blame them Cherokees for bein' so upset. Anybody tried to dig up *my* son, I mean, I'd *do* sump'n about it!" I nodded. How would a white community react if more than a thousand of its forebears had been excavated without ceremony and heaped up in a museum basement?

The following week, official vehicles descended upon the last hold-outs in the Valley, Mrs. Nell McCall and Thomas Moser, who were evicted from their homes by federal marshals. Mrs. McCall had been promised that her belongings would be spared, including her mother's china, but when she returned that afternoon, her house had been burned down, china and all. Mr. Moser's house, also destroyed, was the house where he was born. In the words of Mrs. McCall's daughter, in a letter sent me a few days after the eviction, "The 'horrors' that happened on November 13 are not easily forgotten or forgiven."

On the morning of November 29, without waiting for the Indians' court hearing, the TVA closed the Tellico Dam, and the clear waters of the Little T backed up behind it; in a few weeks, the darter's spawning beds would be silted over. The twenty-fifth artificial lake within sixty miles rose to flood the Seven Towns, as the Cherokee (supported now by the ACLU and the National Council of Churches) kept on fighting for a hearing in the courts. The Indians believe that wave action from the rising water will erode the ancestral graves that escaped the backhoes of the archeologists; they also believe that the Little T will return into its bed and that the sacred valley will restore itself if the dam is opened by court order in the next few years.

Having made four desperate appeals to the White House in the final months without receiving so much as an acknowledgment, the Eastern Cherokee had abandoned any hope of honest dealing with the TVA, for reasons made plain in a letter from John Crowe, Principal Chief of the Eastern Cherokee, to Chairman Freeman:

> The Cherokee people are well aware of the fact that white graves in the Tellico project area were removed and reinterred with all due respect to the law and religious beliefs. They are also aware that TVA did not treat their ancestors with the same respect and regards for religious beliefs but chose to sack up their bones and toss them into a basement at the University of Tennessee.
>
> TVA is guilty of the most flagrant racial and religious discrimination by its actions and this has been made clear by your refusal to honor our request. I cannot find words strong enough to convey my contempt for the lack of honor to be found among TVA and federal officials.

The Tellico Dam is a transgression against whites as well as Indians; much that is vital to our national well-being will be lost forever under the dead waters of Big Money Lake. Let them dynamite the dam and drain the valley. Let the concrete ruin stand as a monument, not to short-sightedness and greed but to the wise redress of a national calamity; as a symbol and a deterrent, the ruin would more than justify the wasted money. A beautiful river can be restored, invaluable farmland and historic sites can be recovered without undue damage, and perhaps one day the farmers, too, will have their day in court. Only a small pretty gleam of river life called the snail darter will be gone, like the old way of the Cherokee before it.

A Cherokee has said, "We want our universe, our Eloheh Land, with all of its fish and all of its life to continue. And we are sure that this *cannot* be against the interests and wishes of the American people." If the Cherokee River is not restored, the "strong water" will be transformed into *ama huli wotshi*, or "dead water," the floor of glass of the old prophecy through which the faces of the ancestors will appear, like pale dead leaves seen dimly through black ice.

· · ·

In November 1980, the snail darter was "rediscovered" about eighty miles south of the dam site; since then, it has turned up at three other locations (in Alabama and Georgia as well as Tennessee) and is no longer considered an endangered species.

Three years after its gates were closed, the TVA itself acknowledges that the Tellico Dam Project is a failure. Not a single industry has located there, and much of the land around the lake is on the market. Yet previous owners of this land are denied the right to buy back their property, about half of which was transferred in November 1982 to a "nonprofit development agency," composed, predictably, of Tennessee politicians and local bankers, presumably for future speculation. "I'm not a defender of the Tellico," former chairman David Freeman says today, taking refuge behind the congressional order to complete it. "I don't think there's any way the Cherokee are ever going to feel good about the

Tellico project. It's flooded out their ancestral homelands.... Every displaced landowner is going to be bitter the rest of his life."

Ammoneeta Sequoyah once observed that with the destruction of Eloheh Land the life of the Cherokee people and his own would come to an end. Both Ammoneeta and his brother Lloyd died in 1981, the last Cherokee medicine men to be born into their ancient tradition.

· 5 ·

AKWESASNE

In recent years, a very dangerous confrontation between armed Mohawk factions on a small and remote reservation on the St. Lawrence River was all but ignored by the news media, which mostly contented themselves with the official interpretation put out by New York State authorities. This ongoing crisis, the state said, was a struggle for power between supporters of the state-sponsored elective system, or "Tribal Council," on the St. Regis reservation and those who call the reservation "Akwesasne Territory" and follow traditional Mohawk Way; the two factions were protected from each other by the benign intercession of the state police. But in fact, the state police role was so ambiguous as to warrant an investigation—on June 13, 1980, or so it appears, the police were on the point of joining "the tribals" in an assault on the armed camp of "the traditionals," which had been in a state of siege ever since the previous August—and New York State itself was a very interested third party, whose efforts to circumvent the traditional Indians of the Six Nations or "Iroquois" (Mohawk, Seneca, Onondaga, Oneida, Cayuga, and Tuscarora) and their claims to sovereignty over vast areas of the state have been the source of trouble for two hundred years. In addition to the Mohawk, the Oneida and Cayuga nations have filed land claims, refusing to be bought off with money settlements, and one very large Oneida claim is thought to be one of the strongest of the many Indian treaty claims in process all around the country.

The traditional Indians believe that the state encouraged the dispute to keep the Mohawks from uniting in a common cause, but because their camp was blockaded by police, few observers made any attempt to visit the traditionals and hear their views. According to Oren Lyons, a traditional Onondaga chief and a spokesman for the Six Nations, who first alerted me to the crisis, it was important that their side of the story be told as soon as possible, before people were killed.*

On Friday June 13, 1980, I telephoned Chief Lyons to find out how I might reach the besieged camp. That very day, as it turned out, hundreds of armed tribals ("the Concerned Citizens of St. Regis") erected a barricade at the head of Racquette Point

*Much of the background material for this chapter was provided by Chief Oren Lyons and Mad Bear Anderson, by Howard Berman of the Indian Law Resource Center, and by *Akwesasne Notes*.

Road, threatening to storm the well-armed camp of the traditionals with the stated purpose of protecting "the tax-paying and law-abiding citizens of the reservation, and to show support for the state and local police." To the police, the crowd declared, "If you don't go in there and clean 'em out, we will," whereupon a messenger was sent into the camp with an ultimatum: unless certain Indians under indictment were delivered to the police, and all "outsiders," Indian or otherwise, were removed from Racquette Point, action would be taken in two hours. When the police made no effort to disarm the crowd, despite its disruption of highway traffic, the besieged traditionals had to assume that New York State supported the proposed assault.

Remembering previous threats of police action (at Onondaga in 1971, where Indians refused "to give up one inch to the state" when New York proposed to widen Highway 81 through the reservation; and at Moss Lake, called Ganienkeh, where Mohawk traditionals occupied an unused piece of their former territory in 1974 as a sovereign Indian nation, not subject to state laws or the U.S. government), the people besieged on Racquette Point were apprehensive; that large police force at Onondaga, called away at the last minute, had taken part in the deadly assault on the prisoners at Attica Penitentiary. On June 13, when it was discovered that their telephone lines had all been cut, fears of another Attica increased. An emergency system using CB radios and a contact phone on the Canadian side of the reservation sent out protests to the governor's office and the media, and someone got hold of Oren Lyons, who happened to be in New York City. Lyons and his brother Lee went straight to the law offices of Raymond Harding, the governor's special assistant for military and Indian affairs, who had the authority to stop a police assault, but by this time Harding had alerted others that the state police, in order to avert a bloody action by the "Concerned Citizens," were preparing to carry out an assault of their own, and "might have to move within the hour."

The ultimatums, threats, and preparations did not really subside until late next day. "Friday was a situation that almost exploded," Oren Lyons told me when I caught up with him by telephone a few days later, "and it could go bad again at any time." There was no doubt in his mind that the phone lines had been cut at the instigation of the state police, presumably to keep the

Indians from attracting the attention of the outside world. "They want to put us under state jurisdiction, right down to the county level, and the feds are standing by to back them up. When this crisis came down, the Onondaga and the Tuscarora issued warnings to all the power companies, the police, the hospitals, that if the state troopers invaded Akwesasne, we would cut all the power lines and gas lines that cross our reservations. Last Friday, the authorities understood for the first time that the Six Nations are really united; if they attack the Mohawks, they attack us all. Even the Christian Mohawks began to understand the real intentions of the state when they saw their council house being occupied by state police. It's like Pine Ridge before Wounded Knee, back in 1973, when the BIA building was headquarters for the FBI and the U.S. marshals as well as the BIA police; the government agency that supposedly represented Indians was the focus of all the police activity against them. The Christian Mohawks were angry that their leaders had called in the state police and had threatened to use the national guard against their own relatives. After years and years of animosity, the Christians and traditionals are really getting together now as the Mohawk people, and that is what the state is most afraid of."

Chief Lyons said that he would get word to the Akwesasne camp that I was coming, and gave me a contact number but no name. "Just let them know when you arrive," he said, "and they'll take you in."

On Saturday, June 20, a young Mohawk named Francis Boots met me at Massena, New York, the site of Alcoa and Reynolds Metals, a General Motors foundry, the Robert Moses Dam, and two locks of the St. Lawrence Seaway, all of them located on the original Mohawk land claim, which has never been invalidated by the courts. Leaving the airport, Boots took a back road along the Racquette River ("Polluted," he said. "All the rivers around here are polluted.") because Highway 37 had been blocked off by a series of police barricades. We drove over the Seaway International Bridge and through the U.S. and Canadian Customs, which are located on the Canadian side of the reservation, on Cornwall Island; Canada considers Cornwall Island part of Ontario, while the Indians consider it part of the Akwesasne Territory of the Mohawk Nation. A section of "the Res" also extends into Quebec, and there are other small reserves and reservations in Quebec and

Ontario; altogether, perhaps twenty-five thousand people consider themselves members of the Mohawk Nation.

On Cornwall Island, Francis Boots turned off on a dirt road that led to a bluff edge overlooking the St. Lawrence. "He'll take you over," he said, indicating a young Indian in an outboard skiff at the river landing below. I descended the bank and got into the skiff, which set off across the swift broad river toward Racquette Point. The besieged camp of the traditionals lay just below the locks, bridge, power project, and Long Sault Dam that contains Lake St. Lawrence, one of the largest artificial lakes on earth.

On this first day of summer, in a light warm haze of fluoride effluvium from the Reynolds plant, gulls lifted and settled, lifted again, picking at the scraps of eels killed in the locks, and a big freighter, rusty black with a white superstructure, churned upstream on the gray surface of the river. Looming over Racquette Point, the General Motors foundry sat on the bank like an unnatural gray city; beyond, above the Seaway Bridge, rose the high stacks of Reynolds and Alcoa. Across the river in Cornwall, Ontario, was the Domtar pulp mill, a division of Reed International; this company had been sued by the Anishinabe, or "Ojibwa," of the White Dog and Grassy Narrows Reserves of western Ontario for massive mercury pollution of their water, which had led to a kind of "Minamata disease" among the inhabitants. (When it was no longer possible to pretend that the blurred people were just falling-down-drunk, the Canadian government recommended to the Anishinabe that they eat less fish.) Since then, fish in the St. Lawrence were also found to be toxic, and the Mohawk, for whom fish have always been a staple, were told not to eat the few survivors in this part of the river. Mercury, Mirex, and PCBs are only a few of the deadly poisons from the industries and municipal outlets that line the banks of the St. Lawrence, all the way upstream to dead Lake Erie. Because of the massive contamination of the region, the near-obliterated landscape of a once beautiful country of great hardwood forests, lakes, rivers, and mountains, immensely bountiful in fish and game, appeared almost sinister in the summer haze.

In terms of landmarks of the present day, the original homeland of the Six Nations, which included all the northern and western regions of what is now called New York State, is roughly bounded by a line drawn through the industrial conglomeration on the St. Lawrence and Lake Ontario, west to the nuclear waste dump at West Lake and the chemical quagmire at Love Canal, then south into Pennsylvania to the approximate location of Three Mile Island. Its sphere of influence extended from the Atlantic to the Mississippi and from the St. Lawrence southward to the Ohio River, Tennessee, and North Carolina, from where, about 1710, the Tuscarora tribe, beset by the early colonists, made its way north to become the sixth nation of the Confederacy.

To its own members, the Six Nations Confederacy is known as Hodenausaunee, usually translated as "People of the Longhouse"; the Longhouse, or council building, with its sacred fire is still the center of traditional culture. Whichever their nation, the people know themselves as Onkwehonweh, the Real or Pure People, those who still live according to a set of principles transmitted from the Great Mysterious (*la Grande Mystère* in French, changed by English Christians to "Great Spirit") to the Huron Deganawidah and his spokesman, Hiawatha. The Mohawks were the first to endorse it, and the confederacy known as "the Great Peace" was founded at Onondaga about 1450, according to anthropologists, and much earlier than that according to the Indians themselves.

In the great colonial tradition of adopting the derogatory name given to a people by their enemies (Cheyenne, Sioux, and Eskimo are other examples), the white men called this people "Iroquois," a French rendition of an Algonkin word for "rattlesnake" or "adder." Yet their government was much respected by Dutch, French, and British alike; the Dutch, whose Two-Row Wampum Agreement with the Longhouse People in the early seventeenth century was the basis for all treaties with the Europeans that came after, were the first to recognize in writing the sovereignty of these strong nations, which sent raiding parties as far west as the Mississippi and all but destroyed the Huron of Ontario, who were allies of the French. In the eighteenth century, the Six Nations contested the French for control of the lower Great Lakes and upper St. Lawrence; though officially neutral in the American Revolution, they were later subjected to the punitive campaigns of General John Sullivan. In 1779, when Sullivan did his utmost to destroy the Iroquois, fish were still so plentiful in Indian country that according to Sullivan's soldiers the bottoms of the clean, clear streams could not be seen.

The political reality of the Six Nations was recognized in the

Treaties of Fort Stanwix (1784) and again at Canandaigua (1794), mainly because President Washington realized that his new country was not yet strong enough to wipe this people out. But directly after Fort Stanwix, which affirmed Indian boundaries, New York State instituted a policy of ignoring the Longhouse Council of Chiefs—the traditional authority of the Six Nations—and dealing separately with individuals or groups who could be bribed, swindled, or coerced into signing away the tribal lands. This policy is active to the present day. Most of the Oneida lands were annexed by the state as early as 1785, and additional Oneida and Onondaga land was taken three years later. But with the adoption of the Constitution in 1789, the federal government took over all responsibility for Indian affairs, and one of the first pieces of congressional legislation was the Non-Intercourse Act of 1790, largely designed to placate the angry Iroquois—so dangerously situated on the frontier with the British—over the loss of ancestral lands to New York State. The 1790 Act was very specific: "That no sale of lands made by any Indians, or any nation or tribe of Indians within the United States, shall be valid to any person or persons, or to any state, whether having the right of preemption to such lands or not, unless the same shall be made and duly executed at some public treaty, held under the authority of the United States."

Although Governor Clinton of New York wrote to the Secretary of War the following year, urging support of New York's policy of encouraging divisions among the Six Nations, President Washington was intent on calming the northern frontier. In regard to the Non-Intercourse Act, he told the Seneca, "Here then is the security for the remainder of your lands. No state, no person, can purchase your lands, unless at some public treaty held under the authority of the United States. The General Government will never consent to your being defrauded, but it will protect you in all your just rights. . . . You possess the right to sell your lands . . . but . . . when you find it for your interest to sell any part of your lands, the United States must and will be your security that you shall not be defrauded in the bargain you make."

Government negotiations culminated in the Treaty of Canandaigua of 1794, which reaffirmed the sovereignty of the Six Nations and recognized its general boundaries. New York State, ignoring the treaties as well as the Non-Intercourse Act (the basis for many if not most of the eastern Indian land claims of recent

years, notably the Penobscot—Passamaquoddy case in the state of
Maine) continued to deal with manipulable Indians for the next
half century, annexing almost all of the Six Nations territory without the consent of the traditional chiefs of the Longhouse Council.
The United States had grown stronger as the Six Nations became
weakened, and the few eastern Indians not banished to the west
(after the Removal Act of 1830) were confined to such small
reservations as Akwesasne.

In order to expedite acquisition of territories from the unwilling Indians, New York State, in 1802, had appointed three
"head men" for the Mohawks who were authorized to transfer
land out of Mohawk Nation title. By this time, Jesuit missionaries
had been working in this region for more than two hundred years,
and "head men" were usually chosen from those Mohawk families
converted to the Catholic religion and therefore hostile to "the
Longhouse People" who sought to perpetuate traditional Indian
way. Although the authority of the head men has never been
recognized by the Longhouse Council, nor approved by the Mohawk people, the system was codified by New York State law in
1892 and persists today. The state-sponsored elective system, with
its three "elected chiefs," is commonly referred to as "the Tribal
Council," and corresponds closely in function and intent to the
tribal councils set up in 1934 under the auspices of the federal
Indian Reorganization Act administered by the Bureau of Indian
Affairs. (The Mohawk Nation overwhelmingly rejected the IRA
in a referendum held in 1935, and tried in vain to dump the
"elective system" as well.) Since 1971, when the "electeds" were
recognized by the BIA, they have controlled some five million
dollars annually in federal funding; thus the Tribal Council creates
and dispenses almost all jobs on the reservation, and does not
hesitate to use this power for political purposes, and abuse it, too,
according to allegations made by Christian Indians as well as the
traditionals. The Tribal Council was supported by the Akwesasne
police, or "Indian police," a few of whom had been deputized by
the Franklin County Sheriff's Department to keep law and order
on the reservation.

Despite relative poverty, the traditionals refused all federal
and state assistance, holding out for the principle of complete
independence and self-determination as a sovereign nation as set
out in the old treaties. In 1922, the Cayuga chief Deskaheh trav-

eled to the League of Nations in Geneva in a vain quest for international recognition of the Six Nations' sovereign rights. They refused the American citizenship offered to Indians by the Citizenship Act of 1924, and fought successfully against the induction of young Indians in the armed forces during World Wars I and II (many more volunteered than would have been inducted; but in the Korean and Vietnamese wars, which the clan mothers decided were not just, such volunteering was forbidden). Even so, encroachment on their lands continued. During the fifties, the disbelieving Seneca (who had issued a declaration of independence from New York State in 1939) fought in vain against the proposed construction by the Army Corps of Engineers of the Kinzua Dam and its Allegheny Reservoir, which was to inundate ten thousand acres of good farmland, together with houses, hunting and fishing places, and burial grounds (including the gravesite of their great chief Cornplanter) and all but obliterate their Allegheny reservation on the western New York–Pennsylvania line, in open violation of the Treaty of 1794. The Corps went about its gargantuan work in the same hard, heavy-handed way in which it destroyed so much Indian land with its huge Oahe and Fort Randall dams in the Dakotas, and the Garrison Dam that drowned the sacred town sites of the Mandan, most ancient of all the Great Plains nations; its tactics in regard to the Kinzua Dam embarrassed its own supporters in the U.S. Congress. ("Apparently you don't want to try to do anything for this Indian tribe!" cried Representative John Saylor. "Apparently you have become so calloused and so crass that the breaking of the oldest treaty that the United States has is a matter of little concern to you!")*

The tragedy suffered by the Seneca resounded all over Indian country, and fired the resolve of the Longhouse People, who in the "termination" atmosphere of the Eisenhower and Kennedy administrations found their lands assailed from all directions. In the late 1950's, led by the Tuscarora medicine man Wallace "Mad Bear" Anderson (who organized mass nonviolent resistance and even attempted a citizen's arrest on the Commissioner of Indian Affairs), the traditionals fought the wholesale construction of seaways, dams, bridges, power plants, and industries upon their lands,

*See Alvin M. Josephy, *Now That the Buffalo's Gone* (New York: Alfred A. Knopf, 1982), p. 143.

although the construction work furnished the many ironworking jobs on which the economy of the reservation became based. In recent decades, Mohawk ironworkers have been much sought after, due to their skill and balance on high structures (including the Verrazano Bridge between Brooklyn and Staten Island and the World Trade Center in Manhattan), and today they travel widely in the East, returning to Akwesasne on the weekends; the traditionals among them have been spared the extreme poverty of traditionals on most other reservations.

The Six Nations people do not think of themselves as "Americans" or "Canadians," nor would they recognize state jurisdiction over the small remnant of their territories that they still control. From the beginning, the elective system or Tribal Council found its main support among Christian Indians eager to adjust to the white economy and culture, but in the years after World War II, a wave of longing for traditional Indian way swept the depressed reservations from one end of the country to the other. In 1948 the Mohawks voted that the New York State elective system be abolished; that same year, a Franklin County judge decreed that the Mohawk Nation no longer existed, that these people were simply "St. Regis Mohawk Indians" whose lands and persons were subject to state laws. With the support of the state police, the elected chiefs were maintained in office until large infusions of state and federal monies restored their restless constituents to a position of economic dependence, and an uneasy peace prevailed once more until 1979.

· · ·

On the far bank, where the GM foundry looms over the western edge of Akwesasne, I was waved past by a security man with a pistol on his hip who had been alerted about my arrival from Cornwall Island; it was now eight days after the crisis of Friday the 13th, and the phone lines to the besieged camp were still unrepaired. Climbing the spill banks from the Seaway dredging, which like the locks and customs buildings and factories had been dumped onto Indian land, I entered a makeshift compound of makeshift buildings surrounded by three outhouses, a pigpen, a shed with a NO SMOKING sign, a vegetable garden, a few small tents, and two hay wagons carrying plywood siding to screen off the view of the Akwesasne camp from police "snipers" on the GM foundry roof. Behind the buildings, a bunker had been constructed near the Racquette Point Road, which led out to the main police barricade; the huge snowplows being used by the police to block road access to the camp made strange yellow blotches in the summer trees.

Because it was Saturday, a number of relatives and friends of the camp families had crossed over the river from Cornwall Island, bringing in food and medical supplies. Young children ran in all directions—one bespectacled kid had his head shaved in an "Iroquois" scalp lock—and boys lobbed balls back and forth with old lacrosse sticks. In the green-gold breeze, men and women sat talking at wood tables, as swallows coursed the river air through a blowing shimmer of milkweed silk and big pale shadflies. To the west, the sun was sinking toward the GM foundry, and a young Indian assigned to security let me look through his binoculars at the policemen posted on the roof; when I raised the binoculars, one of three men in gray uniforms raised binoculars of his own. "Usually five of 'em up there," the boy informed me.

A middle-aged Indian with rifle, cartridge belt, and a paper bag of food walked through the compound, headed for one of the outlying bunkers. "That's our oldest warrior," the young Indian said, laughing affectionately. (Every few hours, I would notice, men with rifles walked through camp as the shifts changed.) Most of the older men were in the Council House, a half-finished building, still unsided, striped with tar-paper sheathing between raw pine studs. On this hot afternoon, a consensus was being reached in the Indian way about what the spokesmen were to say at next week's meeting with the state authorities.

When the conference ended, I was introduced to Bear Clan Chief Tom Porter and Wolf Clan Chief Jake Swamp, and also Bear Clan subchief Loran Thompson, a good-looking young Indian with a baseball cap and a big smile who lives in one of the two permanent houses here on the riverbank. The besieged camp lies mostly on Thompson land, where in 1979 the episode occurred that was blown up into this confrontation a year later. That morning, May 22, 1979, Loran Thompson and his friend Joe Swamp found a work gang cutting down trees on family property; the woodcutters were members of the federally funded Young Adult Conservation Corps (YACC) engaged in a "boundary-delineation project" for a proposed fence around the reservation, and they had already cut a swath eighty feet long and two hundred feet wide by the time he arrived. Since any fence delimiting the reservation symbolically weakened Mohawk claims to their ancient territories, the traditionals were very much against it. " 'Maybe I ought to confiscate your chainsaws,' I told 'em; I didn't really know what I ought to do. I looked at Joe, and he just shrugged. 'Yeah,' I said, 'I think I better confiscate your equipment.' And those kids helped me put their stuff in the back of my truck!" Loran Thompson laughed, shaking his head, as if still marveling that this good-humored episode should have led to twenty-three indictments, an armed siege, and the expenditure of millions of dollars of public money.

Although the trespass and destruction of the trees ("There were some big sugar maples in there, too," Loran Thompson told me) were illegal under both New York State and Six Nations law, Thompson could not take his complaint to the police, since the traditionals do not recognize police jurisdiction on the reservation; nor could he expect any satisfaction from the Tribal Council, which had promoted the fence project in the first place. On the afternoon of the chainsaw confiscation, Akwesasne Police Chief Harris Cole and the YACC supervisor agreed that a meeting to settle the matter would be held a few days later, by which time Chief Thompson could have consulted with Chiefs Swamp and Porter and the other six members of the Mohawk Nation Council. Yet that same evening, although no violence or threat of violence had occurred, nor any damage except to the Thompson land, Chief Cole, accompanied by a Bureau of Criminal Investigation officer and several state troopers, returned with a warrant for Thompson's arrest; why the authorities had chosen to escalate the episode was not yet clear. Thompson informed them that he was not subject to New York State law while on Mohawk territory, which is not a part of Franklin County; it was therefore his duty as a leader of the Mohawk Nation to refuse arrest. Massive reinforcements arrived quickly, and Thompson was subdued and seized in a brief skirmish with twelve policemen in front of his frightened children; a seventy-three-year-old neighbor, Mary Tebo, knocked down by one of the police, had to be hospitalized. Taken under heavy police escort to Malone, New York, the man whose person, property, and household had suffered the damage was arraigned like a common criminal and jailed.

Even more serious, a matter that should have been settled by the Indians themselves had been turned over to "foreign" jurisdiction. By refusing to negotiate, the Tribal Council had subjected a traditional chief of the Mohawk Nation to illegal forcible arrest on sovereign Mohawk territory, and also to the criminal justice system of New York, which took quick advantage of this opportunity to act on the 1948 finding by the Franklin County court that the lands and persons of "St. Regis Mohawk Indians" were subject to state laws.

That the Mohawks still held legal title to 7.5 million acres in this region (which cannot be claimed until the people are united) suggests that New York's intrusion into the case had more to do with jurisdiction over Mohawks than with the alleged "theft"; it also suggests why the state might favor the ongoing dispute. Inevitably the state endorsed the faction led by the elected chiefs, and continued to encourage the Tribal Council's negotiations under the Non-Intercourse Act of 1790 for fourteen thousand acres of state forest in exchange for certain tracts of ancestral land. The traditionals repudiated these negotiations; like other Indians all over the country, they were applying to international tribunals for affirmation of their treaties and the principle of sovereignty as well as the return of sufficient former territory to establish an economic base and a real homeland. Oren Lyons, Francis Boots, and others had gone to the United Nations Human Rights Commission in Geneva the previous March, and Chief Porter told me that there was strong European support for traditional Indians; the Six Nations people had a pact of mutual assistance with traditional Hopi, Miccosukee Seminole, Lakota, Cree, and Western Shoshone which "we consider the basis for the Indian Movement in America, at least since Wounded Knee."

The day after Thompson's arrest, the Akwesasne police were informed by the Mohawk Nation Council that in attacking and arresting Loran Thompson, they had attacked the laws and sovereignty of the Hodenausaunee, and that their presence on Mohawk territory as agents of a foreign government could no longer be tolerated: they had twenty-four hours to resign and disband for the good of their people. When they refused, they were given the second of the traditional three warnings, on the assumption that they had not understood the serious implications of their actions. When the second warning was ignored, chiefs from all of the Six Nations convened here for an emergency meeting. On May 29, to the sound of drums, several hundred unarmed Indians walked in procession from the Akwesasne Longhouse in Hogansburg to police headquarters in the elective system's building, not far away, where five chiefs, including Porter, Swamp, and Thompson, asked the police for the last time if they meant to disband. When they refused, the chiefs informed them and their supporters that the matter was now in the hands of the Mohawk people, who rushed and disarmed them after several minutes of fighting, then took over the building. The state police made no attempt to intervene, despite an invitation to do so from their deposed colleagues. Later that evening, the traditionals abandoned the building to an armed crowd of tribals, who later accused them of minor thefts and damage.

The elected "chiefs" and their supporters were outraged by the ouster of their police and the occupation of Tribal Council headquarters, which they saw as a breakdown of law and order; refusing to negotiate with the traditionals, they demanded that the state carry out its laws. On June 20, although everyone knew that the chainsaws had been confiscated and not "stolen," Loran Thompson and Joe Swamp were indicted by a grand jury called by the Franklin County district attorney and charged with grand larceny in the third degree. Thompson, identified in the local papers as a tool thief, was also charged with resisting arrest. The Mohawk chiefs instructed Swamp and Thompson not to appear for their arraignment on July 5, or otherwise recognize the court's authority; as Chief Tom Porter told the court, "one of our chiefs will not be taken by another nation to be judged." The attorneys for the Mohawk Nation, acting on their instructions to defend the principle of Longhouse jurisdiction as well as the defense of Swamp and Thompson, argued the position that Mohawk sovereignty had been incontestably established in treaties between nations that took precedence over federal and state laws as the supreme law of the land; the unilateral abrogation of treaty obligations by legislative order, as practiced repeatedly by the United States, was illegal under international law. Because the treaties were still in effect, they had therefore been violated by the armed invasion of a foreign force that had carried out the arrest of Loran Thompson.

Persuaded that negotiation was still possible, the local judge rescheduled the arraignment for July 27, and meanwhile the Mohawk Nation issued a press release, which read in part: "We have a responsibility to seven generations in the future to guarantee to them a homeland and a Way of Life. We can never submit to the imposition of alien laws and the colonization of our territories and people."

"Alien law" was represented by New York State's criminal-court system in the person of Franklin County District Attorney Joseph Ryan, who had referred in court to the Mohawk traditionals who disarmed the police as a bunch of animals, and who seemed strangely eager to prosecute the case, despite the trivial nature of its circumstances. However, Judge Jan Plumadore granted the defense request that no arrest warrants be issued when Swamp and Thompson ignored the second arraignment on July 27; the Department of the Interior and even the White House, the defense said, might intervene. On July 30 an agreement was reached whereby the Department of the Interior would request the state to drop the charges against Swamp and Thompson, would replace the destroyed trees, and would apologize to the people of the Mohawk Nation, once the two saws and the bush hog were returned. This sensible solution did not satisfy the district attorney, who declared he would press the resisting-arrest charge even if the theft charge was withdrawn; unless his intransigence had been encouraged by the state, he seemed to harbor an unusual vindictiveness toward the Mohawk, who get their land, so he complained, courtesy of the U.S. government—the same government they blame for their troubles. On August 2, after the federal agencies had failed to act on the agreement, Ryan prevailed upon Judge Plumadore to sign arrest warrants, whereupon he announced that he would also prosecute certain unnamed participants in the occupation of the Community Building two months before. On August 13, twenty-one Indians were named in sealed indictments, which made the defendants subject to arrest without their knowledge, and those who suspected that they might be on the list began to gather with their families in a defensive camp centered around the house of Loran Thompson. Tribal Council Head Chief Rudy Hart now "deputized" forty supporters and threatened to arm them if the state police did not execute its warrants, while the state police said they would not serve the warrants until the strong emotions on the reservation had calmed down. The state itself, apparently content with the zealous attitude of the Franklin County D.A., refused to discuss the political issues behind his rickety indictments (not one of which was ever destined to stand up in court) or anything at all, in fact, except the terms of the arraignments; instead, it accused the Mohawk Nation of being unwilling to negotiate.

Increasingly uneasy, and anxious that the outside world remain aware of what was going on, the Mohawk Nation put out another press release on August 10:

> Ever since our first contact with Europeans we have worked to maintain our sovereignty and independence as a distinct people. Our history is filled with treaties that recognize this position, and are worded to enforce this reality.
>
> The stand we take today is not a new one, but one that we have maintained for hundreds of years. We perceive ourselves to be members of the world community, and have turned to the world community to ask assistance. . . .
>
> These events will not go by without international attention, and our stand, here today, will be known throughout the world.

The first meeting between the Mohawk Nation and the state of New York took place in Massena on August 27, 1979, over three months after the small episode that fired the jurisdictional dispute; besides Chiefs Tom Porter and Jake Swamp, the Indian negotiation team included four Mohawk people and two editors of the Indian newspaper *Akwesasne Notes*, which has its office on Thompson property. Lawyer Raymond Harding, a lieutenant colonel in the New York National Guard and special consultant to Governor Hugh Carey on military matters and Indian affairs, declared that "the court mandate will be enforced. . . . the time has come where we have made a judgment to minimize, to mitigate loss of life, the letting of blood; it is more responsible, it is in the long run less painful for the State to execute these warrants rather than to stand by and let others do it. . . ." The "others" referred to by Harding were the so-called "vigilantes" organized and armed by the elected chiefs in support of the Akwesasne police. Harding seemed to be acknowledging that although its very jurisdiction here was in dispute, the state preferred to risk a little blood-letting than to reason with an obscure county D.A.; this vigilante group would not be disarmed by the state troopers, merely replaced by them. When the traditionals responded that any attempt to execute the warrants on Akwesasne territory could endanger the lives of state policemen as well as the defenders of the camp, Harding insisted that the state law must be carried out and that the decision to enforce the warrants had been made. The following morning at five o'clock, the state police invaded the reservation, accompanied by the Akwesasne police, and supported by a police airplane and by paramilitary special weapons and tactics (SWAT) units that surrounded the camp; they burst into houses, and they marched Chief Swamp's wife around in her nightgown as they searched the premises for her husband. A frantic telephone campaign directed at Governor Carey's office alerted the outside world to what was happening, and for this reason, perhaps, the police stopped short of a bloody assault on the inner enclave; they withdrew about midafternoon, taking along three of the indicted Indians whom they had found in the outlying houses. Meanwhile, they sealed off all the roads, placing the camp effectively in a state of siege.

After the dawn raid at Akwesasne, the tension between Mohawk factions was too rigid to dissolve through negotiations. Within a few weeks the state police had withdrawn their large force from the perimeter of the Thompson property, but because District Attorney Ryan had insisted upon sealed indictments, those people who thought they might be prosecuted did not dare leave the camp. With the roads blockaded, Akwesasne was supplied by small boats crossing the St. Lawrence from Cornwall Island, and meanwhile emergency housing and defense bunkers were constructed to protect the inhabitants during the winter. Before long the emplaced traditionals were as well-armed as all those Christians who wished to throw them out, and a December meeting with Raymond Harding did nothing to resolve the crisis.

As the siege continued through the long winter months of cold and privation, a number of "tribal" Indians felt increasingly uncomfortable about their embattled relatives and former friends, and increasingly they criticized the elected chiefs. While some still complained that non-Mohawks and non-Indians had brought most of the trouble to the reservation, and that a nest of armed resistance to authority had encouraged a general atmosphere of lawlessness which increased every day that the state police failed to execute warrants, they nonetheless resented the fact that the "electeds" had invited state troopers onto Mohawk ground, and that fathers and uncles and cousins and brothers (and mothers, aunts, daughters, and children, too) might be killed at any time because of a minor political dispute that had justified neither the August raid nor the heavy police presence ever since. This feeling found dramatic expression in a spontaneous "unity march" on April 19, 1980—the strongest expression of Mohawk unity since 1948, when the nation attempted to vote out the elective system. That day, people from every faction were welcomed into the Thompson camp for feasting and dancing.

"The government has always used divide-and-conquer tactics from the very beginning of its dealing with the Indians, and they encouraged the missionaries, who pitted Christian Indians against the traditional Mohawks," Chief Tom Porter says. "They would even divide our delegations to Washington, on religious grounds, although we did not feel divided. That Unity March on April 19, there were over one thousand people; relatives came here from as far as four hundred miles away! And the majority were Christians! And there was a traditional, Ira Benedict, ninety-four years old, who walked all the way from Hogansburg! Oh, the *feeling* here! I cried, it was so powerful! Such a powerful demonstration of what our people are just beginning to do, for the first time in maybe 250 years."

Jake Swamp agrees. "When it comes to uniting the Mohawks, more has been accomplished in the past year than in the previous ten." In its efforts to promote disunity among the Mohawks, as recommended by Governor Clinton nearly two hundred years ago, the state had gone too far; the dangerous crisis had drawn the Indians closer together.

The increasing unity of the Mohawk people was a threat to the authorities, and on June 5, a new element in the explosive mix, State Police Major Robert Schneeman, appeared at the gate to Racquette Point Road, where he warned the traditional chiefs and their supporters of the possibility of a state-police assault upon the camp. Two days later, Dr. Solomon Cook (a former elective-system man whose nontraditional supporters got more than one thousand signatures on a petition requesting the D.A. to drop all charges against the traditionals in the name of a peaceful solution) was elected to the Tribal Council, replacing Head Chief Rudy Hart; Dr. Cook's election was seen by both sides as a sign that Mohawk sympathy was flowing hard in the direction of the traditionals. On June 9, after an outbreak of lawless incidents in the community, the traditionals issued a public warning that an assault on the camp appeared imminent, and the next day, sixty-one women met with Major Schneeman; describing thirty years of harassment, violence (including the fatal beating of an Indian man), and sexual abuse from his state troopers, they pleaded with him not to launch an attack on Akwesasne. The next day and the next, Schneeman allegedly held meetings with the "Concerned Citizens," and the following morning the telephone lines were cut and a big, angry crowd threw up the barrier across the road to the encampment that was later taken over by the state police.

"The tribal faction started to get nervous after April 19, and they began to reorganize," Tom Porter said. "We believe that the state police helped them to organize, that Major Schneeman suggested to them that state troopers would back them up, and that the state police would be backed up by the National Guard, if necessary. We think Schneeman is somewhat crazy, and maybe District Attorney Ryan and Harding, too; instead of talking reason, and finding a peaceful way, they always talk in terms of force."

· · ·

In New York City the day before, I had interviewed Mr. Harding, who was eager to lay out the state's version of the case and his own role in it. "I'm more than a consultant to the governor," said Harding, a big dark man with black straight hair and black-rimmed glasses, black pants, and the large damp-looking white shirt that one associates with politicians. "I am his special assistant on disaster-preparedness, military affairs, and Indian land claims"—Harding did not comment on the state's association of these three activities—"and I am his personal representative in all negotiations with the Indians." Harding presented me with four pages of mimeographed information on the history of Raymond B. Harding, then set forth at length his own perspective on the events since May 22, 1979.

"A guy by the name of Chief Thompson has a house on the St. Regis Reservation," he began, proceeding briskly from the matter of the chainsaws to the confrontation at the Community Building a week later, where the traditionals "bodily threw out the Indian police; it is alleged that they removed some foodstuffs of a certain value, and also some cash money. The Franklin County Indians registered a complaint, and a grand jury issued indictments—so far, New York State has nothing to do with it." When nobody responded to the indictments, Harding continued, the judge issued bench warrants that neither the state police nor the county sheriffs enforced. "Finally the 'electeds' told the state police, If you don't enforce these warrants, we will, through our own police, and since they are so few, we'll back them up. Since the state police knew through their informers that the traditionals were well-armed, they thought it unwise for the 'electeds' to take the law into their own hands and 'made a determination' to enforce the warrants on their own." In late August, Harding called the Massena hotel meeting, declaring a truce so that indicted people from the Racquette Point enclave could attend; at his meeting, Harding notified the traditionals that the state police intended to exercise the warrants—in effect, that the state claimed jurisdiction on Mohawk territory.

Harding explained that, to the police, warrants are warrants, however inconsequential they might appear to himself or to me; to enforce warrants was their duty as they saw it. Sure, the business over the chainsaws was "nonsense," but the D.A. would not dismiss any of the indictments until the revolvers taken from the Indian police had been returned. "Maybe they could be found under a bush by Lee Hunt," Harding suggested, referring to a BCI lieutenant who had been trying to work with both sides. "That would be helpful, and we think that all the charges would then be dismissed. But we can't tell the local D.A. to dismiss them if he sees prosecuting them to be his duty."

Since the previous August, he said, the state police, avoiding an armed invasion, had settled on the policy of executing warrants when and if they caught someone outside the camp; they were not eager to get people killed, Harding explained, police included. There matters had stood until early June 1980. "I wanted to stage another meeting on June 2 in Albany, using Howard Rowley as mediator, and the good offices of the chiefs at Onondaga. But the traditionals canceled the meeting, and on the thirteenth, all hell broke loose, because the other side had decided that the police weren't doing enough. All those barricades and guns were unbearable, and they wanted to throw the non-Mohawk people in that camp off the reservation; Friday morning, there were two hundred to two hundred fifty people, ready to storm the Thompson property.

"Around two-thirty Friday afternoon I was getting the impression that the state police might not be able to control the situation; there was a three o'clock ultimatum from the 'electeds.' I told Rowley and Coulter [the Mohawk Nation attorney] that all guarantees were off; I wasn't sure we could stop what was going on. Meanwhile, Chief Oren Lyons and his brother came here, and for the rest of the afternoon, over the phone, they tried to ease things through their channels while I did the same through mine."

I asked Harding about Major Schneeman, whom Oren Lyons had described to me as "an emotionally involved individual with Custer tendencies" and whom Tim Coulter had blamed for inciting the tribals in the days that led up to the crisis. Harding answered very carefully that the State Police Superintendent had persuaded him that the superintendent was on top of the situation at all times. When I suggested that Harding was evading my question, he repeated what he had just said, but with more emphasis, peering at me over his black glasses to make sure I understood. (A few days after this conversation, Major Schneeman was replaced by someone less likely to present Governor Carey with another Attica in an election year.) He went on to say that the Police Superintendent had informed the governor's office by 2:45 that no directive had been issued for police participation and that none would be.

By this time, Harding and I were beginning to communicate; he was no longer responding to tough questions by telling me that my head was screwed on wrong. But other tough questions occurred to me after I left. Why had the police made no attempt to disarm an angry and dangerous crowd? Why hadn't Harding told me (or denied) that for a brief period, at least, the troopers were preparing to accompany, and perhaps lead, the assault on the camp? And why was the governor's office, in an election year, being so delicate about the prerogatives of a county D.A. whose vindictive zeal and sealed indictments had caused much of the trouble that the state said it wished to avoid?

"It so happens that in terms of the current situation since last Friday [June 13]," Harding concluded, "it is my best opinion that if the state police were withdrawn from the reservation totally, within a very short period there would be a civil war, with many people killed or injured, and the state police would have to return, to put down massive violence. Their continued presence there serves to keep peace, in the best sense of the word."

Escorting me out to the elevator, Harding said, "The Indians think Ray Harding is a prick, but they trust his word: 'Ray Harding-he-talk-truth," he added, giving me his idea of Indian speech. Unhappily, he was mistaken; the traditional Indians, at least, did not trust him at all. This does not mean that Harding is a liar. Throughout our interview, I had the impression that he was telling me the truth as he perceived it; and Howard Rowley, whom the Indians *do* trust, and who has been an independent mediator in Indian dealings with the state since shortly after the Ganienkeh crisis in May 1974, said, "I'm not sure that tact and diplomacy are part of his game plan, but Ray Harding has always been honest and forthright with me. He was straight with us throughout the negotiations over Ganienkeh, and he contributed a lot to that solution. I was in Massena last August 27 when the negotiations broke down: Harding warned the traditionals that his truce period would be over in two hours, after which all guarantees were off, and he told them that police action would take place. He didn't say when, of course, and I guess I was a little surprised when it took place the very next day. Last Friday morning, he took the trouble to alert me that the state might have to move within the hour. In my opinion, Harding has been straight with the Indians, too, and I have told them so, but I can understand why they don't agree."

"This Harding who speaks for the governor," Oren Lyons told me, "is a very hard man, and he's holding a very hard line; he's not on their negotiations team for nothing. The Indians don't want to deal with him, but he is the one they sent us."

"The press was given the impression that the police were there simply to keep order between two Indian factions," Tim Coulter said, "so this is what everyone believed. Harding was pretending that the state police could not disperse that mob; we don't believe it. When I spoke to Harding about two-thirty, he said [here Coulter left the phone to get the exact quote] 'You've got to tell them that the state troopers are going in at three o'clock with the electeds.' When I protested that the troopers had no authority on the reservation and would be legally liable, he told me I was just complicating matters. Anyway, the crucial question is, Who issued the original authorization for the state police to enter Akwesasne with the mob, and why was this authorization covered up? And who countermanded that order? Because sure as hell, something in the plan broke down between two o'clock and four on Friday afternoon, when they realized that things were no longer in control, and tried to pull the fat out of the fire."

For one reason or another, Major Schneeman was not available when I tried to reach him for a comment, but Lieutenant Lee Hunt furnished the police perspective on the crisis of Friday, June 13. Rumors of impending trouble had started to come in by Thursday evening, and Hunt, a local man on a cordial basis with many of the Indians, was in charge of about eighteen troopers assigned to the Racquette Point area, where he arrived at 5:30 or 6 on Friday morning. By 10 a.m., he said, a crowd of perhaps one hundred sixty tribals had assembled. They were not "vigilantes," Hunt assured me earnestly—that was only what the traditionals called them—but supporters of "Concerned Citizens of St. Regis." Actually, the "vigilantes" used this name themselves; what the traditionals called them was "the mob." By whatever name, this herd of people came well-armed; there were even women there with bats and clubs. ("When we seen *that*," a young traditional named Marge Marquis told me, "we women started hunting for something that we could use on *them*.") By this time, someone had seen to it that the traditionals had no telephone to the outside world.

When I asked Lee Hunt who cut the lines, he said, "Traditionals or electeds, you mean? I just don't know." Subsequently, Lieutenant Hunt, a mild-spoken, courteous man who was doing his best to be helpful, acknowledged that the traditionals did not have much reason to cut off their own lifeline, and that he had "a pretty good idea" who had actually done it. The line break was on traditional territory, he said, and the lines had not been restored because telephone line men, unlike the police, were not paid to risk their necks by venturing into a hotbed of armed Indians. Hunt expected service to be restored next day, June 24. (It was not restored until early July, and was cut off again for an extended period soon thereafter.)

For lack of a phone, the tribals sent their ultimatum to the traditional camp by messenger, demanding that the indicted people be turned over to the police and that all outsiders, Indian or otherwise, be removed from the reservation. Apparently the armed crowd was surprised when word came back that the heavily out-numbered traditionals would not comply; in any case, the ulti-matum was deferred, and deferred again. "They didn't have the heart to go in without police support," Oren Lyons said, but Lee Hunt was not so sure. "They were pretty well-disciplined, and I never thought they would suddenly go in without consulting, but it was always a possibility. And if they had decided to go in there, we would have had no choice but to go, too." Yet asked if the police could not have prevented an assault by the Concerned Citizens, Lee Hunt said, "No."

I asked Hunt the question I had neglected to ask Harding: if the state was really interested in seeing to it that nobody got hurt, if all those state troopers, as stated to the press, were only there to serve as a buffer between hostile factions, then why hadn't the police simply dispersed an armed and angry crowd that had forced them to blockade all the nearby roads and tie up traffic on Highway 37? "It's not against the law," said Lieutenant Hunt, "to walk around with a gun on New York State roads."

The traditionals say that as the day progressed, the Concerned Citizens fortified themselves with beer, and while Hunt admitted he had heard this, too, he said he saw no evidence of it himself. What *did* increase during the day, he declared, were the numbers of people, which reached between two hundred and two hundred fifty before noon and twice that number by the evening. (Ac-cording to the traditionals, these numbers—also used by Har-ding—were much inflated to excuse the failure of the police to disperse the crowd.) "You have to keep in mind," he said, "that twenty percent of the work force here are away on ironworking jobs at any one time, and many of 'em come back Friday night; we had word from our outside patrols that a lot of Indians were headed home. Another thing, when you're dealing with large groups, the beginning isn't so bad. But after a while, people get restless, impatient, they have to go to work, go home, and they want something to happen before they go. That night, when the crowd got big, that was the worst time; in my opinion, Friday night had the highest tension of all."

· · ·

A fortnight later, the tension was still high. I was riding in a pickup truck with a young Indian, on our way to the Massena State Police station in search of Major Schneeman, when one of five troopers in three blue-and-orange cars at the outer roadblock at Highway 37 and the Racquette River gave us the finger. I asked my uneasy companion to pull over, then walked back to inquire about this salutation. Although alone, and taking care to hold my hands well out to the sides, I was challenged while still at a distance, in a loud, aggressive way. When I stopped short and asked my question, the finger man drove off in his patrol car, after which an immense mustachioed trooper, speaking at all times in a shout, denied that anyone had given us the finger and informed me that if I wanted trouble, I should step over his way and he would give it to me, presumably with assistance from his associates. Then I identified myself as a reporter, and the trooper's snarl changed mysteriously to a dead smile.

The troopers at the Massena station were more pleasant, responding smoothly if not persuasively to all my questions. One of them tapped meaningfully on a cautionary booklet entitled "Red Indians," featuring pictures of AIM leaders Russell Means and Dennis Banks upon the front and evidence of dark Communist plots within: apparently the police share a general view among the tribals that the Mohawk traditionals are "Communist-inspired." As for the episode at the roadblock, the troopers explained that the men's nerves were shot from too much hot sun and too little time off in the past week. Subsequently I was told by Howard Rowley that a trooper had died on the reservation some years ago in an unsolved killing, and that policemen's memories are long; whatever the reason, I could testify that at least some of the troopers at the roadblocks were jumpy and aggressive, and very eager to act out their anger—just the sort, in other words, to precipitate the bloodbath that the state had risked and was now trying to avoid.

Mohawk attorney Howard Berman is small, slight, self-effacing, and soft-spoken, yet in a quiet way, he seems to have as much self-confidence as the brash Harding. Asked about Harding's complaint that "outsiders—the wrong people" were speaking for the traditionals, notably Berman himself and two "loudmouth young Senecas," John Mohawk and Mike Myers, Berman explained that the best Mohawk speakers, such as Tom Porter and Jake Swamp, could not go to the meetings because they would be arrested, as Harding knew; and anyway, by Indian tradition, "the spokesmen

are not those who have led in the decisions, they are just spokesmen, appointed to that job."

John Mohawk agreed. A volatile, swift-speaking man, Mohawk is well-informed on all Indian matters and the editor of
Akwesasne Notes, the best-known Indian newspaper in America
since its inception in 1968; the paper had moved its offices to
Loran Thompson's place in 1978, and now occupied the second
floor of the kitchen building. "Harding likes to throw around big
words that you have to have three years of college to understand,"
John Mohawk said. "So the leaders say, You go over there because
you can understand him. So we go in, Harding calls us a bunch
of idiots, and things degenerate from there."

Mohawk laughed a peculiar laugh with little mirth in it, gazing
restlessly around the camp; we were sitting on the hay wagons
that do not really screen the camp activities from the binoculars
of the police on the GM roof. "It's in the interests of the state to
obscure the issue, reduce it to a conflict between Indian groups
struggling for power. But it isn't a struggle for power: the issue
is sovereignty. What would happen if they had to deal with a
united, sovereign Mohawk nation? The Indians might want clean
water out there, in that stretch of river that runs through their
territory, or clean air in that sky over that factory." He pointed
at the grainy sky over the GM foundry. "Akwesasne used to be
a fishing place, but all these locks and power dams cut off all
the anadromous fish and raised the water levels, which ruined the
trapping and fish spawning grounds and waterfowl nesting in the
marshes. There is no hunting or fishing any more. The flying ash
and fluoride from the Reynolds plant have ruined the dairy farming—the cattle's teeth grind down, they starve, they live four
years." In 1959, when Reynolds began its operation, there were
five times as many cow barns on Cornwall Island as there are now:
the Indians say that the starving cattle, disabled by bone afflictions,
lay down to graze, and crawled from one place to another. Meanwhile, a healthy high-protein diet of fish, meat, and corn has been
replaced by an unhealthy one of potatoes, macaroni, bread, and
gravies. The island's bees have vanished, wild game and home
gardens are drastically depleted, the conifer forests are dying away
from tip necrosis. "We think everybody here is being poisoned.
On Cornwall Island, which is downwind from Reynolds, skin le-
sions and nervous disorders began to occur simultaneously with

the fluoride pollution, but because the companies are on the U.S. side and the people are Indians, the Canadian government takes no interest in the problem."

John Mohawk gazed about him in the evening dusk. The smoke from the stacks of the GM foundry and the Reynolds plant behind it was beginning to turn color, and Mohawk said that although Reynolds had installed antipollution devices in 1973, these bypasses were opened up at night, when the poisonous smoke was less visible to the public. "In the twentieth century," Mohawk said, "we're going to see if 'a people' like the Mohawk people can survive; if they cannot, then 'people' cannot either. Our prophecies say that there will come a time when rivers will catch on fire and burning will be out of control—that already happened a few years ago, on the Cuyahoga River in Ohio—and that this would be a sign that the prophecies were about to come to pass, that the life-giving force was being withdrawn from the earth by the Creator; the big waters would breathe forth new organisms and new diseases, and the people would be unable to defend themselves."

"What impresses me," Tim Coulter says, "is that these people are fighting for *survival*, not just self-determination; they're just as threatened by that aluminum plant as they are by the guns of the police. The industries, the ships, the locks, part of the power plant, even the customs buildings are all trespassing on their territory every day. Land is also wanted for an aluminum reclamation plant which would create even more pollution than Reynolds, and the Tribal Council wants this dross plant because it would provide a few more jobs; all these industries support a way of life that supports the very existence of the elective system."

Attracted here in 1959 by cheap electric power from the huge Moses–Saunders Power Dam, Reynolds Metals sells aluminum to the General Motors foundry next door and would like to share this "dross" plant with Alcoa. Alcoa and Reynolds claim that they should not pay taxes, since their industries are located on Indian lands. (Ironically, this self-serving maneuver may benefit the traditional Indians, since it contests New York State jurisdiction on Mohawk territory.) Meanwhile, more nuclear power plants have been proposed for the St. Lawrence basin; 765-kilovolt power lines similar to those being fought by the embattled farmers' movement in Minnesota have been installed near Akwesasne; and the transport of nuclear wastes from Chalk River, Ontario, over the Seaway Bridge is now expected.

"To fight the money and power of the Tribal Council, the whole apparatus of the state, and the federal government behind it, is suicide," Coulter explains. "But for the traditional people, not to fight is also suicide. Exchanging the land, moving away may be the only solution, but they've been there for hundreds of years, it's a beautiful place, and they don't want to go; it's very painful for them."

Francis Boots had said that he might leave Cornwall Island. "When I was a kid, this island was a beautiful place, and all the families helped each other, worked together; now other people's ideas have been imposed upon us."

At dark, I accompanied John Mohawk into Loran Thompson's house on the river bluff, where we were joined after a while by Chiefs Porter, Swamp, and Thompson, and also Mike Myers, Howard Berman, and Ron LaFrance, a member of the Mohawk negotiating team who identified himself as the man I had first spoken to on the contact phone. LaFrance, who had been fired from his job at the Salmon River School for traditionalist sympathies, served as a messenger to the other side, with whom he maintained serviceable connections. The previous Friday evening, he had gone to the main roadblock at Highway 37, where on behalf of the traditionals he asked Major Schneeman to confirm the word received from Coulter and Rowley that under no circumstances would the state police be given the order to "go in." At this point in his account, LaFrance stood up and did a very comic imitation of Major Schneeman's consternation. "He was walking up and down like this, waving his arms," LaFrance declaimed, walking up and down the yellow kitchen, waving his arms, "just like Custer must have done while his men were being slaughtered. 'I don't know where you get your information!' he hollers. 'I'm about to start the first stage of my assault! Over there to my right, I have fifty men, ready to go in right now; over here to my left, I have fifty more who are ready to go too!' Well, Lee and Max [Lieutenants Lee and Max Hunt, not related] were right there, too, they were staring at Schneeman, and I'm telling you, those guys were scared shitless, I seen it in their eyes, and I don't blame 'em; he was scaring me, too!"

(Lee Hunt later confirmed that one hundred troopers had

been present, and he did not really deny LaFrance's story. Though in no way disloyal—"I can't really speak for the Major"—he was clearly uncomfortable, wandering off into generalities about the high tension of that evening. He did deny that Schneeman had encouraged an assault by the Concerned Citizens at several meetings in the days preceding.)

Loran Thompson shook his head. "How come the vigilantes never tried to come in before now? We've been here since last August!"

"Longest siege of Indians in history," Mike Myers said. "Wounded Knee was only seventy-two days."

When I asked for evidence that Schneeman had encouraged the crisis, Myers said, "Who can prove that Hitler knew all about Auschwitz?" Someone else said sharply, "You want proof that our phone line was cut off?" He held the phone out, and I listened dutifully to the dead silence, then put it back onto the hook. What about the repeated statement that if the police had not cut the lines themselves, they had at least suggested it to the tribals? "Diane Lazore over at *Notes* headquarters on Cornwall Island, she called the telephone company that morning and demanded that they restore service, and they told her that they could not do that without police approval," said Ron LaFrance.

"And not restoring the lines is even more serious than cutting them in the first place—it's nearly nine days now," Howard Berman said.

In reference to Harding's suggestion that the four handguns confiscated from the Akwesasne police be left under a bush where Lee Hunt might find them, after which all charges might be dropped, Loran Thompson said, "Sure, they would drop the chainsaw charges against me and Joe Swamp; we never heard that they would drop the others. That's only two indictments out of twenty-three, and if we accepted it, it would break the unity of our position and of this camp." Everyone nodded; this was the key point.

Chiefs Tom Porter and Jake Swamp listened in silence to the others. Both are gentle and soft-spoken men, still in their thirties, whose words are given much respect, and Porter was especially eloquent, even by the high standards of a people who prize eloquence as the great gift of the oral tradition.

Tom Porter said quietly, "Mohawks have been referred to as Rattlesnake People by the other tribes. But the rattlesnake is a very peaceful creature, raising its offspring on its own homeland; if its territory is large enough, it will run away. But if you persist, he warns you with his tail—please stay away! If you come closer, he warns you more loudly, and if finally you give him no choice, then he will strike you. We are called rattlesnakes because we have that character, and this is what Governor Carey and Mr. Harding are finding out in 1980. I've never met Governor Carey, so I have to reserve judgment, but I have met his representative and his police forces." Tom Porter sighed, then resumed mildly, "In the Six Nations, we always have a prayer before any meeting, so that we will be guided to a clear decision; when we meet with representatives of the state, that is always done. When a prayer was made at his meeting last August, Harding was so nervous, so disrespectful, that he just smoked and smirked and went in and out of the door."

Jake Swamp nodded. "There was a man from the federal government at that meeting. He was very embarrassed, and later he apologized to us."

"I can't say that Harding lies," Tom Porter said. "When he says that he will do something, he generally does it—"

"I say that he lies," John Mohawk said. "He lied for hours on Friday morning—either that, or he had no control over the situation. Either way, he can't be trusted. I think he was angry that we canceled his meeting—there was nothing but four-letter words out of his mouth for a whole week—and maybe he wanted Schneeman to teach us a lesson."

"No assault would have been permitted without the approval of the governor's office," Mike Myers said, "and that's Harding. I don't care what he says, they were still ready to assault on Friday evening."

"We're all ironworkers here," Jake Swamp said, after a pause. "The tribals, too—most of them are hard-working guys . . ." His voice trailed off, and he shrugged unhappily, as if upset all over again by the division in his people. "He's playing a chess game with our lives," Chief Swamp resumed forcefully, close to anger. "Because of the power that he has. He even tries to tell us who should negotiate for us, and when he doesn't get his way, he takes dangerous actions."

Loran Thompson said, "Maybe they were just trying to bluff us, and it didn't work. And now they've lost all their momentum, they're not psyched up any more, they've had time to think." John Mohawk nodded. "Even if they were bluffing, they could have gotten a lot of people killed; we weren't panicked that day, we were just outraged that it was so out of control."

Francis Boots had told me that more than half the vigilantes had been Quebec Catholics, organized around the Hogansburg Fire Department by former Head Chief Rudy Hart. "A lot of my cousins are from over there, and I asked them, How come you guys went up to Loran's with guns? And they were ashamed; they didn't even know why they went. And they admitted that a lot of their people were juiced up—it was Schneeman and alcohol. Apparently Rudy Hart told somebody, 'Give those guys two beers, and they'll do *anything*.'" Since the crisis, Francis said, his own community on Cornwall Island had been turning away from its Band Council leaders to the cause of the traditionals, and had just nominated a moderate named Ernie Benedict to represent them.

Ernie Benedict's son Lloyd, who had started a small newspaper named *The Rezz*, is doing his best to remain neutral, although he acknowledged that, whatever they might say publicly, everyone here had actually chosen one side or the other. "A lot of the people are starting to think, Hey, this isn't politics any more, it's a question of right and wrong. That's when they choose." Like every family on the reservation, the Benedict clan was painfully split by the whole controversy. Lloyd's cousin, Brian Cole, was a security "warrior" in the defense bunkers of the traditional camp. "My cousin carries a thirty-ought-six with heat-tempered bullets that supposedly can pierce a bullet-proof vest. When I reminded him that our Uncle Joe was over there with the vigilantes, he really started to sweat. 'A lot goes through your mind out there,' he told me. See, it's not a fight between political factions, it's between your uncles, your cousins, maybe even your brother!" Brian's brother Harris was the head of the Akwesasne police, the man who first attempted to arrest Chief Loran Thompson. The two have not spoken since last summer, and their mother blames what she regards as the unrealistic attitude of the traditionals, whom she belittles; all the real traditionals, she says, are long since gone.

Of the three elected chiefs who served on the Tribal Council before Dr. Cook replaced Rudy Hart, the most reasonable was said to be Leonard Garrow, who seemed disconcerted when I asked him about the bothersome discrepancy between the alleged offenses of the traditionals and the violent retribution that was being threatened by the Concerned Citizens. "They fail to tell you that theirs was the first offense—hell, we don't even know for sure that that was Loran's property, and anyway, I was born and raised here! Loran Thompson has no sugar maples down there!

"For a year, we've been trying to damp things down, and avoid shooting. The group that threw up the barricades, they went on their own. I didn't agree because I didn't want to see people killed, but I could see why they were just sick and tired of this damned thing, of a reservation without law and order.

"Coulter and Berman are the ones who are causing the real split here. They keep talking about sovereignty! How in the hell could we get sovereignty, unless Congress changes the law, which they're not going to do; we have to accept the law as it is written. Read the traditional news releases; it's all lawyer talk, it's not just plain folks talking to each other, trying to solve something. And Mohawk and Myers, they were run off their own reservation for being troublemakers! They're very streetwise, and they just go from one trouble spot to another—Alcatraz, Wounded Knee, Moss Lake [Ganienkeh], and now here—and they always get off scot-free, leaving the local people to clean up the trouble. Those people down there—I mean, those politically motivated Indians—those people are masters at getting out their story, they even have their own newspaper, *Akwesasne Notes.* They make it seem like they're surrounded, they put out land mines, they have AK-47s that must have come from Communist countries *some*where! Hell, we can't have *that!*"

I returned to my original question: even if all these points were valid, did the actions of the traditionals really justify an armed assault on an armed camp in which numbers of people, women and children included, might be killed? Again Garrow talked around the question: clearly he had not made his own peace with it, perhaps because he did not believe that New York State might have encouraged the dispute. "Any time you get a group of five hundred armed people saying, 'We're going to take action whether you like it or not,' what can you do? The crisis of Friday the thirteenth was very real, it could happen again."

· · ·

Toward midnight, I fell asleep on Loran Thompson's sofa, awakening about five-thirty next morning to the sound of chants and drums—the sunrise tobacco-burning ceremony in the Council House that takes place every day. The dawn was beautiful and cold and clear, with a northwest wind that quickened the dying river, and drinking coffee in the early sun, Chief Swamp told me that this land has been a hunting and fishing area of his people for many hundreds of years. "All Six Nations people call themselves Onk-wehonweh—the Real or Pure People—but the Mohawk are Ga-neinkehaga, the People of the Flint, because there were so many flintstones in our old homeland in the Mohawk Valley. 'Onondaga' means Of-the-Hills, and so forth. This place—Akwesasne—means Place-of-Partridge-Where-They-Drum."

From the riverbank, he pointed at the Reynolds plant upstream, the long plumes of smoke from the seven or eight stacks blowing down on the northwest wind across Cornwall Island. "Six thousand tons of fluoride a day come from those stacks—that's what they tell us." Two of his children—he had seven in the camp—were already ill from what is assumed to be fluoride poisoning, one of them with bone problems—he pointed at a young boy on the camp swing—and the other with skin troubles. "Perhaps we may have to go away from here," he said, "but we will not go until all of this is settled. If the leaders go, the state will walk all over the Longhouse People." Asked what would happen if he walked out of this camp, he said, "Four of us [Chiefs Swamp, Porter, Thompson, and Erin Oakes]—we hear they will kill us if they get the chance, so that this won't happen again. They think we are troublemakers, always involved in these things, but we are only doing our duty as Mohawk chiefs."

Jake Swamp spoke about how the hunting and gathering and fishing in this once plentiful hardwood forest region had been ruined by massive pollution by chemicals, waste products, sewage, and acid rain, the fall-out of sulphuric acid that was damaging the forest and destroying thousands of square miles of fish habitat in the Northeast. According to Longhouse prophecies, he said, "something will happen to the rivers and the lakes; near the time of the great purification, the river will become dirty, and the fish will rise up to the surface on their bellies and die. It is like this today along that river; you go downriver, you'll see many fish that are dead and dying.

"In the days of the Thunderers—they are the Grandfathers, the Winds, who bring us water and who clean the earth—there

were evil serpents or monsters that the Creator put under the
ground, and these Thunder Beings accepted the duty of keeping
them there, because they were so harmful that even to see one
might be fatal. We have been thinking that maybe this uranium,
these chemicals like dioxins, all these dangerous things out of the
earth that have ruined our country, they represent those monsters
that are now starting to reappear."

"This is a highly polluted area," Tom Porter had said the
night before, "and we have many children, so our main concern
must be their safety and health. Our attachment to this place where
our great-great-grandfathers lie buried is very strong, but our children's future and well-being is at stake. Even though it is poisoned,
it is difficult for us to exchange this land for somewhere else.
We're not permitted by our beliefs to deal with the earth as a
material thing, because the earth is our mother.

"After 1492, immigrants came here who were in a very bad
way. They asked if they could live here, and our ancestors welcomed them and fed them, brought them back to health, and we
said, This earth is very large and there is plenty, and you are
welcome to be here and share with us. There are still elders among
us today who remember this sharing attitude of our people, a very
humanistic and moral attitude, and it is still solid and firm among
traditional people: we still want to share. We have many white
friends, many black friends, and we are all human beings.

"As far as land claims go, the Longhouse people have never
sold any of this land, it was taken dishonestly by theft and tricks
and bribery. I don't want to cause the people of the U.S. and
Canada to become paranoid," Porter said mildly. " 'That was a
hundred years ago! These are modern times! We bought this land,
and paid for it!' We recognize that cities and towns and farms have
been established in our territories by these illegal means, and that
we cannot undo this.

"I used to wonder why white people got so paranoid about
our land claims; then a white person explained that they expect
to be treated as other whites would treat them, asked to leave the
land and go back to England, France, and Sweden. Well, Indians
don't think that way; there is no need to talk about clouded titles.
The land wasn't given to us as a commodity but entrusted to us;
we are its custodians, you might say, so that our children will have
a place to put their little feet upon this earth. The Creator still

sees the native people as custodians of this land; we think so, too. It is our *duty* to take care of it. If the people of the U.S. and Canada wish to ease their consciences with the Indians, they can't do it with monetary awards for the vast territories taken illegally; they must have the honesty to admit a mistake. Then white people and red people could get together and discuss what would be best to do, how we can *share* things.

"Until the white people, the state, are ready to share with us, we are left faced with the realities of New York State policies. We can't hope for any real justice from the state—not the *people* of New York State, but their leaders—and they leave us no choice but to go to the international courts. We don't really want to go to the United Nations, the World Court, but we are forced to do so in order to survive. They pretty near came in and massacred us the other day: they admit the police were ready to go; they have told us that. And they would have gotten most of our leaders, too. I can't stress it strongly enough: it's a matter of life and death that the truth come out about that day."

• • •

In the last week of July 1980, a group of thirty-five or forty "Concerned Citizens," many of them Vietnam veterans armed with automatic weapons, established a "beachhead" on Racquette Point, a mile from the traditional encampment; this group was led by the brother of an Akwesasne policeman, head of the Hogansburg American Legion, and a man—according to one non-traditional—"in no way Indian in his thinking at all." These Concerned Citizens were located in a trailer park owned by the Tribal Council that overlooks the St. Lawrence, and the traditionals say that shots were fired at boats crossing the river to Akwesasne.

On August 6, a "demilitarization" was attempted. The vigilantes agreed to leave the Point, the state police (mainly for economic reasons: their two-month blockade had cost more than a million dollars) agreed to open up the roads, and no weapons were to be displayed publicly by either side. But in late October, a bomb exploded outside the house of Dr. Solomon Cook, the only one of the three elected chiefs who was seriously trying to bring unity to the Mohawk; a week later, when Chief Tom Porter's house, which lacks electricity and had been vacant for some days, burned to the ground, even the police suspected arson. On November 19, Harris Cole and two other Akwesasne police officers were stripped of their status as Franklin County sheriff's deputies.

In the winter of 1981, after months of wrangling between the factions, Judge Plumadore finally dismissed the controversial indictments against the traditional chiefs that had done so much to perpetuate the tension. The tribal police have been disbanded, and the attention of both sides has turned to the threat of chemical contamination of their land and life. The federal government and New York State are still involved in negotiations with their own creation, the St. Regis Mohawk Tribal Council, to extinguish land rights of the Hodenausaunee, but for the first time in many years, a certain unity has evolved among all factions of the Mohawk people.

· 6 ·

THE HIGH
COUNTRY

Coming up from Pecwan, on the Klamath River, to Low Gap, we could see across the whole wild reach of upper Blue Creek and its forks to the remote High Siskiyous, where we were going. There are no roads into Blue Creek, only rough cat tracks for the loggers, and on this dry summer afternoon, the truck raised a long column of hot dust as it descended the raw eroding zigzag scars down the steep mountainside. Where the trees were stripped off, the stumps, torn earth, and littered deadwood evoked the desolate, blasted hills of war, and the effect was especially depressing where the defoliant called 2,4,5-T had been used by the Simpson Timber Company to "inhibit" broad-leaf growth in favor of the conifers; in these seared areas, there was no life of any kind, no birds or flowers or berries, and the streams were poisoned. "Some people make the mistake of boiling their camp water, to purify it—that just concentrates the poison," John Trull said, glaring out the window. Trull, a big man with a boyish grin, had been a logger and a cat skinner for many years, but as a woodsman and an Indian—though he looks white, he has Cherokee blood and is married to a Yurok woman—he was troubled by the scope of the destruction. His stepson, Richard Myers, sitting beside him, shared his opinion that these poisons being dumped onto the landscape by timber companies and federal agencies were cheap surplus stocks of the notorious Agent Orange that was used by the federal government in Vietnam, and that the use of this 2,4,5-T (its by-product, dioxin, is the most toxic substance, after nerve gas, ever made by man) was excessive and very careless; at one point, ten children were sent home pale and vomiting from the school at Weitchpec as a consequence of wind drift from spraying by the Bureau of Indian Affairs on the Hupa Valley Indian Reservation. Up the river a few miles, at Orleans, a number of dead or deformed babies had been reported.

Where the track descended toward Blue Creek, Dick Myers saw a young black bear in a thicket, but otherwise the summer trees were still. We parked the truck where the cat track ended, in alders by the stream. Five miles downstream from this place, Blue Creek joins the Klamath River, which flows north and west perhaps fifteen miles to the Pacific. Until the great logging boom came to this part of far northern California after World War II, lower Blue Creek was forested by great coast redwoods; the few that remain stand like mourners for the many that are gone. Having logged out the redwoods, Simpson Timber was now seeking access to the old-stand Douglas fir and other valuable timber trees in the inner reaches of Blue Creek and its eastern forks, which lie entirely within the Six Rivers National Forest. For a variety of excellent reasons, the Indians and the environmentalists, the scientists and fishermen, were trying to stop it. Even those local people like John Trull whose livelihood depended on the lumber industry had strong mixed feelings about the imminent destruction of Blue Creek, which is one of the last clear streams and wildernesses in the country.

In recent years, Blue Creek has become a symbol for the fight to save the Siskiyous, which rise seven thousand feet and more above the Klamath. One group of isolated peaks and rocks, traditionally approached through the ascent of the forks of Blue Creek, is a sacred "High Country" for the Indians—the Yurok; the Karuk, farther upriver to the east; the Tolowa, of the northern coast and southern Oregon; and occasionally the Hupa from the Trinity River, which flows into the Klamath at Weitchpec. "Yurok," or "downriver people," seems to be a Karuk ("up to the east" or "upriver people") term for these small, scattered bands of the lower Klamath, from Bluff Creek to Requa, at the river's mouth, and a short distance north and south along the sea. Though all tribes of the region are now quite similar in customs and beliefs, they are very different in origin; the indigenous Karuk are of Hokan linguistic stock, the more recent Hupa and Tolowa are Athapaskans from the Canadian Northwest, and the Yurok are Algonkin, a small western offshoot of those woodland tribes that once occupied almost all of eastern North America.*

In addition to its traditional role in Indian life, Blue Creek is a superb spawning stream for both steelhead and salmon—one of the finest in the Siskiyous, which are the most productive watershed in California—and the people knew that logging would hasten the end of the dying salmon fishery so crucial to both whites and Indians in the depressed economy of this region. As Dick

*For general background, see A. L. Kroeber, *Handbook of the Indians of California* (Washington D.C.: Bureau of American Ethnology Bulletin 78, 1925). "The Gasquet–Orleans Road, Chimney Rock Section, Draft Environmental Statement," Six Rivers National Forest, November 1977, and succeeding documents, include much ecological as well as anthropological information.

Myers says, "Poor logging practices make these creeks run too fast in winter and spring so that they dry up much too soon during the summer. It spoils the rivers, and it spoils the fishing." Botanically, these mountains are one of the most varied regions on the continent, and a reservoir of rare animals and relict plants such as the Brewer's spruce, whose closest relation is found in northeast Asia. For all these reasons, very suddenly, this little-known wilderness has become one of the most controversial in the country.

The traditional way into the High Country is one of a network of old Indian paths known to the Indians of the lower Klamath as *thkla-mah*, meaning ladder or steps (the stepping-stones for ascent into the sky world); the term is transcribed by sentimental bureaucrats as the "Golden Stairs." This path begins just above the confluence of Blue Creek with its Crescent City Fork and climbs the ridge between those streams in a northerly direction to a point off to the east of a huge dark boulder. Perhaps one hundred feet in height, the boulder is poised on the bare saddle of a rocky ridge as if it had descended from the sky. This is *Ha-ay-klok*, Rock Set upon a Rock, known as Medicine Rock in the nineteenth century and now called Doctor Rock. It was and is an important site for medicine training, of which healing is only one part, practiced mostly by women; the men who went to the High Country to "make medicine" were on a vision quest, in pursuit of spiritual power. In recent decades, with the demoralization and acculturation of the tribes that the logging boom served to accelerate, Doctor Rock and other sacred sites have been little visited except by hunters. Dick Myers, who had never visited the High Country, was delighted to be going by the Steps, in case the fight to save Blue Creek was lost. "Nine tenths of the people have never been to Doctor Rock," he said, "and the rest of 'em went up most of the way by truck."

Dick Myers is one of the young Yurok of the Klamath region who are seeking a way back toward traditional Indian life. At Pecwan Creek he was engaged in the unearthing and reconstruction of the Yurok sweat house, last used in 1939, that was silted in, then buried, in the big floods of 1955 and 1964. He was also trying to reconstruct a house for the Jump Dance, a traditional ceremony used by Karuk and Hupa as well as his own Yurok people to "renew the world." A humorous, handsome, easygoing man who does not try to hide his people's ignorance, neglect, and loss of their own traditions, he had finally resorted to turn to a white authority, the great anthropologist Alfred Kroeber, for certain details of the ceremonies. When Kroeber worked along the Klamath just after the turn of the century, Myers' Aunt Queen James, aged ninety-three, was already in her twenties. The last elders, increasingly cut off from one another in the small and remote settlements of the Klamath Mountains, felt that the old ways were lost forever, and when I suggested that bringing these old people together for a few days might exhilarate them and refresh their common memory, thereby preserving at least a part of the old knowledge, Dick politely agreed, but in a way that indicated he would not do much about it. This was not so much apathy or low morale as resignation; Indians, even in these desperate times, are reluctant to share family "songs" or knowledge. For example, Aunt Queen had forbidden Dick to lend the family's ceremonial headdresses (made from the scarlet crests of pileated woodpeckers) to an old Indian down on the coast who was trying to reconstruct the Jump Dance; she declared that this man had failed to learn the traditional Jump Dance medicine from his father. "That old man is only interested in making money," Dick laughed, shaking his head. "Last time we danced, he never even gave us a piece of watermelon and a box of Cokes—'Here, boys, have a good time while you're cleaning up!'"

We shouldered our packs and forged across the torrent, hip-deep and still swift and cold here in early July, to the wooded bench or "flat" on the far side, where we headed upstream. On the east bank, Slide Creek comes swiftly down from Blue Creek Mountain. The huge dead trees that choke its mouth are not the consequence of wasteful logging practice but of the frequent slides that give this creek its name. Natural landslides are common in this region, where the most recent uplifting of two million years ago did not turn the old rivers from their courses but only deepened them, so that the steep mountainsides may fall away even without excessive rain or snow. The soil itself, shot through with intrusions of the beautiful weak slaty jade called serpentine, is poor and shallow, and those slopes that are marginally stable when bound up by forest roots collapse quickly in the first rainfall and erosion that follows road-building and the removal of the trees. This is the main reason environmentalists insist that the Siskiyous should not be logged at all. This situation is worsened by the winter and spring floods that undercut the slopes, causing whole tracts to fall away into the torrent. The Christmas flood of 1964 scoured all rivers in the region and changed the whole appearance of Blue Creek, washing out the forest banks and leaving broad gravel bars that emerge in summer.

We forded the river once again and ascended the eastern bank to Bear Pen Flat, where the mouth of Nickowitz Creek comes into view. John Trull said that in the lower Klamath tongue, what the white man writes as "Nickowitz" is actually *nik-wich*, the grizzly bear, a creature now officially extinct in California. There is an account of an eight-hundred-pound grizzly killed down toward the coast in the 1890's, and on my first visit to the Klamath region, in 1975, I was told that five grizzlies still survived in the Blue Creek drainage. The authority cited was an ecologist at Humboldt State University at Arcata, who wished the news kept quiet, it was said, lest hunters flock into Blue Creek to destroy them. I did not take the report seriously; the source was suspect, and anyway, the grizzly is an open-country species. I was therefore surprised to hear Trull say that about 1952, under Low Gap on the south slope of Blue Creek Mountain Ridge, he saw a huge dark-brown grizzled animal move out of some high grass and cross a mountain meadow or "prairie." "It was so big, y'know, and that damn hump on it— for a minute there, I thought I was lookin' at a buffalo!" John is a logger and a lifelong hunter—one of that old breed, now nearly extinct, who are true woodsmen as well. He had seen hundreds of black bears in the wild and was not likely to mistake one for a grizzly, and the least plausible word in his description, "buffalo," is just the one that made his story hard to discount. Some years ago, I made my way to the main garbage dump in Yellowstone National Park, where I had been told that grizzlies came in numbers every evening (the Yellowstone grizzlies, unlike the black bears, are still wild and stay far from the main roads). When, at dusk, the great bears appeared, rolling through the high brush of an open plain as the nervous black bears loped away in all directions, a young park ranger who accompanied me cried out, "Look! Look! Buffaloes!" before he realized his mistake.

According to Forest Service personnel, the Siskiyous, with no ranches and few visitors, is the only wild region left in California to which restoration of the grizzly has been considered. Blue Creek is still a haunt of the fierce wolverine, one of California's rarest mammals, and also of its scarce mustelid cousins, the marten and the arboreal fisher. An uncommon creature of these streams called the sewellel, or mountain beaver, is considered a "pest" by foresters, who would like to eliminate it. (They are also anxious to eliminate the corn lily on the grounds that it may cause fetuses to be aborted if it is eaten by cows on the nineteenth day of pregnancy. That there are no cows here is a technicality.) The shy cougar comes and goes, and the rare spotted owl frequents the stands of old-growth timber near the creeks.

It was just this primordial forest of immense fir and cedar, concentrated on the shady and well-watered deposits of good soil nearest the streams, that was most coveted by Simpson Timber Company and the sawmills of the coast, which were fighting hard against all efforts to have it protected by the National Wilderness Act, passed by Congress in 1964. As in the Olympic National Forest in Washington, where Simpson and the Forest Service had a special understanding, the industry counted on assistance from this cumbersome and conservative bureaucracy, which tended to oppose the protection of national forest land in favor of commercial possibilities, even where—as in the Siskiyous—other values far outweigh the worth of what will almost certainly be a single "crop" of timber; once that crop has been harvested, this fragile region may not recover for a thousand years.

Both sides of lower Nic-Wich lay on a Simpson holding that penetrated the national forest from the west, and the access road that came down through the national forest from Lonesome Ridge was the only lumber road in the Blue Creek drainage east of the Crescent City Fork. In this lower stretch, at least, Nic-Wich was ruined. The ugly detritus of deadwood and shale pitched all the way down from the clear-cuts high above gave a vivid idea of what Blue Creek would look like if the Forest Service management plan were carried out. Much of the land slope in these dark V-shaped canyons lies at a sixty-to-seventy-degree angle—as steep as the steepest staircase, as anyone will learn who cares to try it, either up or down—and a Forest Service study acknowledges that eighty-three percent of the land area in the Blue Creek Management Unit and the contiguous Eightmile Unit to the north is "moderately unstable or worse." In one region of the Siskiyous, another study shows, the soil loss from new clear-cuts may reach twenty-two tons per acre every year, most of which descends to spoil the streams. (Both of these studies are considered optimistic by outside observers.) Since productivity may be reduced eighty percent with the loss of just one inch of the thin topsoil, and since in the Coast Range thousands of years may be required for a new topsoil to form, the prospects for reforestation here are dismal. Yet despite accumulating warnings (many from its own personnel or from experts hired under Forest Service contract) that the High Siskiyous are too steep, fragile, and unstable to support intensive logging—that owing to the loss of soil, it would not in fact be possible to observe the agency's own legal obligation to manage its forests with a perpetual and sustained yield, and that the inevitable "mismanagement" would therefore be illegal—the Forest Service has held stubbornly to plans to sell 929 million board feet of timber out of Blue Creek alone. The access roads planned for Blue Creek and Eightmile totaled 265 miles, far more than enough to undercut all of these steep mountainsides and bring down a whole rare world into the creeks.

Everywhere else in the Northwest the result of logging (and eroding logging roads) has been the extensive siltation of the waters, the muddying of the clear gravel beds used by the salmon species and the beautiful anadromous rainbow trout that are called "steelhead." The fish must cover their fertilized eggs with stream gravel to protect them, and the gravel must be clean and porous so that cold water providing crucial oxygen can circulate at the constant temperature necessary for embryo development. Logging drastically increases erosion and sedimentation that may smother the gravel beds, and in addition, the clearing of the land, by increasing sunlight, raises the temperature of the water to a degree that may prove fatal to the young. In many places, logjams resulting from erosion slides or wasteful cutting can prevent access to a spawning stream for years.

The sudden and drastic decline in the Klamath fisheries is precisely coincidental with the advent of heavy logging in the region. Already, all commercial fishing has been stopped in the Klamath delta, between the coastal highway bridge and the mouth of the river, which is the traditional gill-netting grounds of the Yurok Indians at Requa. (The Yurok, like the Puyallup-Nisqually and many other coastal peoples from northern California to British Columbia, have been blamed increasingly for fisheries depletion caused by dams, logging, and industrial pollution; where no Indians are handy, sea lions and cormorants will do. When I was in south Alaska's Kenai Peninsula in 1957, the depletion of the salmon fisheries by overfishing was being blamed on the greed of the Kodiak bears.) And so a renewable resource that provides many jobs, not only in commercial fishing but in the tourist-attracting sports fishery as well, may be wiped out by a self-devouring industry that will devastate the mountainsides before moving on.

Since it is generally agreed that artificial reforestation of this region, with a sustained yield, is unrealistic, and since the Klamath sports and commercial fisheries, though much depleted, are worth millions of dollars annually, one wonders at the willingness of the Forest Service to abet the destruction of a natural resource of such long-term benefit to many in order to further the short-term profits of a few. And this is true not only of Blue Creek but throughout the whole Siskiyou wilderness, which is presently threatened with irretrievable destruction despite the warnings of geologists, foresters, biologists, and anthropologists alike that the potential loss, not only to the Indians but to the whole nation, far exceeds the value of its wood.

In recent years, the excuse that has been trotted out for the proposed "multiple-use management" of the Siskiyous is the alleged loss of jobs in the timber and sawmill industries in Humboldt and Del Norte counties caused by government expropriation of coastal forests for the Redwood National Park. But the decline of the vast private timber reserves started more than twenty years ago in Humboldt County, long before the Redwood National Park came into being. As early as 1952, when the lumber boom had just begun, Humboldt County farm adviser W. D. Pine predicted that unless the lumber companies brought their wasteful practices under control, the county would suffer the same boom and bust that had occurred in other timber regions, forcing the companies to intensify their operations here in northern California.

Despite strenuous public propaganda to the contrary (one thinks of all those phony ads in which happy deer and chipmunks gambol merrily among the noble stumps of managed forests), there was no serious attempt at sustained yield. Overcutting, waste, and the wholesale export of unmilled logs to other countries, in particular Japan, accompanied the scare campaigns that threatened America with a lumber shortage, as the companies proceeded with the rapid despoliation of this great conifer forest that is widely regarded as the finest in the world. Increasingly, as private holdings dwindled, and the sawmills replaced the precious redwoods with former "weed trees" such as the Douglas fir and hemlocks, pines, and cedars, the industry sought leases on the national forest lands that lay just inland from the private holdings. That part of lower Blue Creek that lay west of the national forest was already logged, and so was its once beautiful West Fork; the west bank of the Crescent City Fork was under lease and going fast. But its eastern slope was still intact, and so were upper Blue Creek and the whole East Fork, which together constitute the heart of the Blue Creek drainage.

Old paths along lower Blue Creek were overgrown or washed out by the floods. In the woodland heat, we probed and back-tracked for a time before giving up and returning toward the river. "I ain't never been lost," John Trull remarked, "but I sure as hell been confused for about five days." On small sand traces of the gravel bars and on the soft earth of the flats above, the scats and prints of deer and bear and porcupine were common, and everywhere was the sweet scent of wild azalea; in this primeval place, the introduced blackberries so bountiful these days along the Klamath were nowhere to be seen. Rufous hummingbirds came to fire-colored columbine along the stream edge; bright water poured among the rocks, and the white wing patches of mergansers flashed between high silent walls of the great evergreens, upriver. Where steep bluffs or slides prevented progress on the rocks, we forded and forded again, feeling for footholds in deep swirling pools in the swift torrent. Dick sang and whooped in mock alarm. "Just so's you don't get excited, that's the main thing!" he called out, and gave me a big grin.

"I'm pretty young," Dick Myers said (he was in his thirties), "but I can remember when even the lower part of Blue Crick was still blue, a pretty, pretty blue." And above Bear Pen Flat, where the scars made by the loggers faded from view, Blue Creek was still beautiful, still blue. It is a swift cold stream—a small river, really—perhaps thirty feet across and four feet deep in its strong channels even at this dry time of the year, with a bright sparkle in the breeze that in fair weather comes up the Klamath from the sea each afternoon.

John Trull, skipping from rock to rock with his old fly rod, was fishing for our supper, and Dick Myers winked at me, then grinned in the direction of his stepfather. "Come on, Grand-father!" he yelled, to cheer him on. As we moved north, John worked the eddies for the eighteen-inch rainbows that he recalled from other days, but the stream was full of early summer hatches, and the trout were sated, and in the fresh afternoon wind, it was hard to see the fly in the dancing water.

Now the sun was gone behind the steep green walls to west-ward, and the air was cool. By the time we reached the point of rivers where the Crescent City Fork came foaming down under steep bluffs to join Blue Creek in a broad pool, we had forded Blue Creek six or eight times and were soaked and tired. Twilight had come, and we made camp quickly in a grove of hemlock and white cedars—the Port Orford cedar, one of the loveliest of the big timber trees in the old forests. A mature cedar may be worth six thousand dollars, John Trull said, but the species was threat-ened by a root fungus that is spread through the forest by logging machinery that is not hosed clean. The breeze had died, and while John and I cut sword fern and evergreen boughs to sleep on, mixing in fresh pungent braches of pepperwood (California bay or laurel, alias Oregon myrtle) to keep off the mosquitoes, Dick took the rod down to the pool, returning shortly with some small, fat trout for supper.

Trull is quick and agile on the river rocks, remarkably so for a man in his mid-fifties, and it was he who had set the pace as we moved upriver. He was tired now and grumbled a bit about our camp; he preferred the sand of the river bars, where a man might make himself a nest. "Goddamn scorpions in these old logs," he said. "I can handle the rattlers and bears, but I don't like them scorpions." Once he was bitten in an outhouse. "Straightened me right up and out," he said. And, of course, the handgun that he carried—Dick had one, too—was no defense against a scorpion. Firearms are very noticeable in the Klamath region, even more so than in other parts of the Northwest, and John's house at Pecwan Creek was full of them. He took time now to clean his Browning automatic, which had been submerged here and there while ford-ing the river. "Don't know why I brought it," he remarked, in answer to my unspoken question. "After so many years, I just don't feel right without it."

Soon we lay down, and the fire died, and through the black needles high over our heads shone the cold stars of the wilderness.

I stared straight up for a long time in great contentment. I had wanted to come to Blue Creek for three years—I was here at last.

The earliest mention of Blue Creek that I know occurs in the late nineteenth-century journal of James Pearsall (which also contains a vivid eyewitness account of the massacre of Chief Big Foot's band at Wounded Knee).* As a pioneer timber cruiser in the Klamath region, Pearsall became friendly with and knowledgeable about the river Indians a long decade before Alfred Kroeber first appeared, and it is apparent that he did not know of Kroeber's "Yurok." ("Maybe that means somebody's rock," one old Indian told me scornfully; the real name of his people was Pu-le-kl'a. Referring to Kroeber's chief informants, he said, "They made up a lot of stories for the white man.") On one occasion, Pearsall suggested to his guide that they "camp at Blue Creek, but Wau'teen insisted that we return to the village because it was impossible for an Indian to sleep at Blue Creek and live." In former times, the Indians told Pearsall, there had been a large village in Ur-nerth, or Blue Creek, but O-mah-hah had poisoned the water. "Indians all die, get plenty sick in head, make 'em jump in river, turn round and round . . . Indian sleep no more Blue Creek, all die." O-mah or U'ma'a is the "Indian devil" (U'ma'a also means sorcerer and/or his bundle of harmful "arrows"), often summoned as an agent of sorcery, and Blue Creek was apparently its home. On separate occasions, two elderly Indians had described to me the *rakni-u'ma'a*, or "creek devil," thought to be a kind of wild man or "primitive Indian" who used to be in touch with the coastal Indians but took refuge in the inner mountains with the coming of the white man to this region in the nineteenth century. The "creek devil" seems to be analogous to what the Salish nations farther north refer to as Seat-ko or Sasquatch. (Between northern California and Alaska, in fact, there are as many names for it as there are tribes.) To the Karuk, the wild man was the *marukara'r*, or "upslope person," said to be "hairy, large, strong, stupid, crude," who was thought to live in rocky dells deep in the forest. Since 1958, when a celebrated series of immense humanoid tracks was allegedly discovered near Bluff Creek by a crew building timber-access roads (later washed out by the flood of 1964), the Sasquatch

*This unpublished manuscript is in the library of the Six Rivers National Forest in Eureka.

has been widely known as "Bigfoot." Bluff Creek, which empties into the Klamath from the north between the villages of Orleans and Weitchpec, lies on the farther side of Lonesome Ridge from the East Fork of Blue Creek. It was the scene, in 1967, of the only filming of this creature that is considered authentic by most students of this unsettling phenomenon. According to Trull, tradition says that Indian fugitives from white man's justice were sharing caves in the Bluff Creek region with these "wild people," who came there originally from Blue Creek; when the Indians entered the caves, the wild men turned their backs to them and never spoke.

Whether or not there ever was a village at Blue Creek, the region was used in other days for fishing and hunting and the gathering of acorns and wild berries. The Indians would scatter through the woods, collecting basket grass and herbs and wild tobacco, and deer meat, fish, and fruit to be dried for winter. "That's what life was all about in those days," Dick Myers said, "before the Indians got so hung up on shiny things." Though the people avoided Ur-nerth in dark weather, there were a few white homesteaders, often with Indian wives, who established camps on the high forest meadows known as "prairies." James Stevens from Johnsons Landing (known to his friends as Jimmy Skunk, or sometimes "Skunk") came originally from a place still known as Stevens Prairie, under South Red Mountain, and he has spent a lot of time here in the Blue Creek drainage—the last Indian alive, perhaps, who knows it well. In fifty years, said Jimmy Skunk, he never saw a sign of Sasquatch; he told me flatly, "There ain't no such a thing."

As the traditional approach into the High Country, the Steps are considered to be sacred ground, and at daybreak next morning, Dick Myers purified himself in the cold river. The air was dank and gray in the ocean fog that fills the Klamath basin every night, and because we were making a pilgrimage to Doctor Rock, we burned tobacco in ceremonial purification to alert the mountain spirits of our coming and ask for their assistance on the journey. Then we set off into the forest, tracing the lines of moss-covered rocks that were lifted aside by travelers of other days, pushing through the salal and huckleberry that had overgrown the trail where the fall of a huge tree let in light. Among hoary firs, dead still and heavy in their decades of thickened bark, the huge rhododendrons in pink-lavender blossom looked light and fragile.

Trull and Myers inspected small, tough yews that were said to be centuries old: "That's what we used mostly for our bows," Myers said. At a dark brook banked with oxalis and ferns, I paused for a few mouthfuls of sheep sorrel, tart and fresh, and took on a cargo of water; the day would be very hot and the mountain dry, and over the years, I had learned the hard way that if I drank a lot more than I wanted before starting out, there was no need to drink again all day, whereas if I drank along the trail, the need for water increased with the heat, until in the end one could never drink enough.

At a fork in the path, the old Blue Creek Trail headed off toward the east: here rotting Forest Service markers (dating back at least to 1943, when this trail was last brushed out, says Jimmy Skunk) had been clawed down by bears. We followed the north fork, uphill, through forest too huge and dark for brush and wild-flowers; for the most part, the old trail was still plain. Here and there were the flat rocks used as ceremonial resting places by people climbing up the Steps. Higher, there were hollow "pitch trees," in the trunks of which fires were built in time of snow; and the shadows of old camps could be discerned in the oak hollows, where people came to collect acorns for winter. Acorns and salmon were the basis of Indian diet, although other foods were also plentiful. (The driving energy of the great fish as they fought the river without taking food inspired the fasting aspirants who sought power in the High Country.) The white cedar and madrone and tanoak on these lower slopes were the largest I had ever seen, and even my friends were astonished by a heavy tree that rose from its bed of spiny fruits—a gigantic golden chinquapin, which these days is usually seen as a shrubby bush.

Bear scat was everywhere along the path, and John Trull, in the lead as usual, found the big scrape and dropping of a cougar. The cougar persists in the High Siskiyous, though it is not so common as it was. In the 1930's a Yurok friend traveled on horse-back with her family from Cedar Camp Spring, near Summit Valley, across the ridges to Doctor Rock; she told me that cougar screams at night had given the party a lot of trouble with the horses and that she herself had seen a cougar cross the path.

Increasingly as we ascended, the sky appeared among the treetops, and the trail thickened with brush, so dense in places that we just pushed through, feeling for emptiness with our boots.

And so we were astonished, perhaps two hours above the forks, to hear a human voice not far uphill. Whoever this might be had stopped to listen; we stopped, too, as the voice said, "Either that is men or that is bears." Then an old Indian parted the huckleberry bushes; behind him stood a young white man in the green uniform of the Forest Service. Both sides stared, astounded by this meeting on a trail that had scarcely been traveled by anyone in thirty years. But after a moment we nodded, offered our names, grinned, and sat down; among Indians, it was not a situation where one merely nodded and went on.

Guided by the Indian, the Forest Service man was flagging the old trail with plastic streamers, in preparation for the crews that would come in the late summer, when water is low and re-growth poor, to brush the trail; following directions given to them by James Stevens, they had made their way down from Peak 8 and Doctor Rock. To the Karuk man, Cliff Ferris, John Trull said, "Don't you remember me?" And Ferris, a weathered Indian in a black hat and canvas vest, squinted, grinned, jumped to his feet, and crossed the forest path to shake Trull's hand. They had known each other twenty-six years before, when both were loggers, and both had lived for the wild, hard-drinking Saturday nights on Second Street, down in Eureka, and especially the bar called the Golden Horn.

"One time I seen five separate fights goin' on in there at the same time," Cliff Ferris said, and John Trull laughed, shaking his head. "Well, I give up drinking a few years ago," he sighed, a little sadly, and the Karuk nodded. "I give it up, too," he said, "when I found out I couldn't drink it all." To comfort him, John Trull said, "Well, you give it a good try, and I did, too." Both men nodded and let the subject go. Soon we said good-by and went on uphill.

Though seriously injured once when a big log rolled on him, Trull still worked on logging roads with his own cat, and he still had the habit of driving one hundred miles down to Eureka after the week's work, though he went now for the seafood dinner served at his favorite restaurant each Friday night. He is a tall, rawboned man with big arms and heavy fists; it would not have paid to mix it up with him during one of those loggers' brawls in the Golden Horn. "Ol' Cliff," he sighed, remembering. "I wonder if he recalls that time when we was fallin' trees there, side by side, down back of Pecwan. One day there, my brother and me, we both got knocked out by a big limb; it got both of us, knocked us out cold."

It was still early, and for the next several hours the ascent of the long ridge between Blue Creek and its Crescent City Fork was cool and open, as we climbed up out of the fog in the creek bottom. In the soft light of the big trees, the forest floor was clear and airy, with scattered sword fern clumps and salal, and small evergreen plants such as prince's pine and the hollylike Oregon grape. At a step on the ridge where ground was level was the place where Cliff Ferris and the Forest Service youth had spent the night; the Karuk's bed among the needles was set about with a neat arch of stones, "to keep off rattlers," John Trull said, and winked. Dick Myers suggested that Cliff might have used the stones to weigh down a tarpaulin, though it seemed to me that the stones' arch would have been displaced when the tarpaulin was removed. The night had been warm, without much wind, and the forester had told us that mosquitoes had been so bad where they had slept that he had climbed sixty feet into a tree just to escape them. John Trull shrugged. "You hang deer meat thirty feet up, the yeller jackets and flies don't get it, so maybe that Piss-Fir Willie knew something after all," he said. The white fir, known locally as "piss-fir" because of its acrid stink when cut, gave its name long ago to the rangers of the Forest Service, who are treated everywhere and on all sides with mild derision. The loggers resent the bland young college men who dare to tell them how to go about their rugged business; the lumber companies resent the tracts of commercial timber that are "tied up" in the national forests; and the environmentalists and their supporters feel that the Forest Service tries too hard to appease big timber and big mining, destroying the nation's heritage in the process. In the Forest Service management plan for the Blue Creek Unit, the aims of the agency and the ambitions of the lumber companies were very difficult to tell apart.

As early as the 1930's, some of the old trails across the High Country, made originally by Indians, and later used by trappers and gold prospectors, evolved into a series of rough tracks and fire roads that emerged at the mouth of Bluff Creek, on the Klamath. With the advent of intensive logging after World War II came a plan to consolidate this network with an all-weather road, but the Christmas flood of 1964 washed out most of the Bluff Creek section, and in 1965, the proposed road was rerouted. Using a timber-access road already in existence (the so-called Eyesee Road, north from Orleans), it would climb quickly onto the high ridges, then follow the ridge systems north to a point beyond Flint Valley, from where it would follow the old track west along the ridge between the Blue Creek drainage and Eightmile Creek. Passing Chimney Rock on its way to a point north of Peak 8, this track would meet the southbound section from Smith River, which departs Highway 199 about seven miles west of the village of Gasquet—hence the name Gasquet–Orleans Road, or G.O. Road.

In the late 1960's, Robert Irwin of the Forest Service's Gasquet Ranger District had reported to his superiors that the proposed route—and the east–west Chimney Rock section in particular—invaded the sacred High Country of the Indians, and he recommended that this area receive protection. The Irwin report was substantially ignored. In the Multiple-Use Plan issued in 1969, in the customary bureaucratic babble ("This site will be a management unit of the Travel Influence Zone"), the Forest Service conceded that certain ceremonial rocks should be protected from encroachment by the G.O. Road and that a "V.I.S. interpretive display" (whatever *that* is) would be posted at a suitable "overlook." Subsequently it was proposed by the supervisor of Six Rivers National Forest that "core zones" of forty-five acres around each sacred site would be quite adequate; how this magical figure was arrived at was not explained. The Forest Service also offered to erect nice chain-link fences, presumably to protect the sites from "multiple use." But interpretive displays, V.I.S. or otherwise, were scarcely needed by people who had used the place for centuries, and since silence and solitude and a clear unbroken view in all directions were essential to receiving the spiritual power of the High Country, the Indians' idea of encroachment differed widely from that of the Forest Service, which intended to run its road under the south side of Chimney Rock and on across the north side of Peak 8; this route was only three miles north of Ha-ay-klok, which was to become the "Doctor Rock Recreation Area, Zone 7–11A Recreation Area, Primitive Experience."

When I asked Dick Myers if the spiritual leaders of the tribes had continued the traditional use of Doctor Rock, he shrugged his shoulders. He had heard that a few people still went up there, among them a Karuk medicine man named Charlie Thom. A group of younger Karuk, guided by Thom, were doing their best to mend the tattered remnants of the ancient way and had made medicine in recent years at Chimney Rock; Dick was impressed by this because the Karuk had suffered much more than the Yurok in the white man wars, their surviving elders were now very few, and almost all Karuk ceremonial equipment and regalia has disappeared through theft and loss and fires.

But as for the Yurok "spiritual leaders," he looked doubtful. "A lot of people going round these days calling themselves 'spiritual leaders' that wouldn't know the first thing to do at Doctor Rock. Nobody gives a damn what they call themselves, it's only when they get into *believing* it and make themselves spokesmen for us with the Forest Service that people say, 'Hey, wait a minute, who is *that* guy? He has no authority.' Because Indians know just who you really are. And the Forest Service uses people like that, that's where they get their excuse for doing what they were going to do anyway; they pretend they're acting in good faith, listening to them old Indians, but of course they're not."

One of the "old Indians" he referred to would tell me later, "The Indians had power—no more now. They used to train for it. Now they sleep all night instead—they never make it. Nobody ever done nothin' for Chimney Rock, Doctor Rock—nobody said a word. Now everybody kickin' about it, but what do they know about it? They never seen a Indian doctor. I know the songs, lots of Indian songs for a doctor, but I ain't a doctor. Them Karuks that say they been usin' Chimney Rock to make medicine, they must be liars; anyway, they got their own rocks, over east in the Marble Mountains."

On the basis of such testimony, proponents of the G.O. Road claimed that the Indians no longer used this sacred area, and it is true that its use is much diminished. In the century of disintegration that followed the wars with the white man in the 1860's, most of the people had lost the way into the High Country, and apart from a few hunters in the autumn, there were only a handful of Indians who still went there on a power quest, or to make medicine. Much of the medicine that was made (particularly at Ah-Kah, or Bad Place) was dedicated to good luck in gambling, success in murder, and other unspiritual pursuits. One man told me that he had gone up there by the "Golden Stairs" in 1928 with a friend who wished to make medicine to ensure victory in a foot race from San Francisco to Grants Pass, Oregon. However, it has always been true that only a few "high" people, the aspirant Indian doctors and/or priests, were supposed to go there, and that those who did go were not to speak of it, even when the High Country was threatened—hence the criticism of the Karuk Charlie Thom when he testified that he and other Indians still used Chimney Rock for spiritual purposes. Also, the Indians, resigned to being ignored, had failed to speak up until the High Country was invaded, by which time the G.O. Road was substantially complete. In 1975, when I first visited the Klamath region, the highway section through Flint Valley had already been started; by the time I returned, in 1976, the last unpaved stretch was the old east–west track known as the Chimney Rock section, which would not only provide automobile access to the sacred rocks but would lay open the upper Blue Creek drainage to the huge yellow earth-moving machines, and the cable rigs and logging trucks and shrieking saws.

The construction of the Flint Valley section was already well started when it was discovered by two off-season hikers on the day after Thanksgiving, 1974. They alerted the public, and a suit was brought by the Sierra Club on the grounds that no environmental impact statement had appeared. The impact statement came out at last in May 1975, but court appeals delayed the completion of this Flint Valley section until June 1976, when the U.S. district court ruled that the Forest Service might proceed. However, the court took pains to comment that the geological and other surveys conducted for the impact statement had been inadequate, and that on ethnographic grounds (the unconstitutional infringement of Indian religious rights) there was clear basis for another suit. There was also evidence, it said, that the Forest Service had manipulated and suppressed pertinent data. One report (ordered destroyed by a Forest Service officer) clearly supported the Sierra Club's position that the G.O. Road would cause massive landslides and destruction of the watersheds. Another estimated that proposed road-building and logging in the Siskiyous would increase sedimentation in its streams by 1,500 percent.

Though the Sierra Club had no more funds to bring another suit, the Siskiyou Mountains Resources Council was now formed to organize growing public support for the protection of this wilderness, for which the last rampart in a losing battle was the all-important unpaved section of the G.O. Road. In November 1977 there appeared a new environmental impact statement devoted entirely to the problems raised by the Chimney Rock section and weighing the arguments for alternative routes. In this ponderous document of five hundred pages—ostensibly an objective review and summation of conflicting opinions, expert and otherwise—an anthropological survey that the Forest Service had contracted, paid for, and previously approved, and that rejected the proposed route across the High Country, was sharply attacked by regional Forest Service archeologist Donald Miller, who lacked any firsthand ethnographic experience of the region. On the basis of a very suspect paper (which has caused Miller to be publicly criticized by colleagues), the Forest Service determined that the already immense expense of the proliferating and voluminous impact statements should be increased still further by a whole new ethnographic survey from which the only anthropologists with significant field experience of the region's Indians and the High Country were to be excluded. Needless to say, all three of these authorities—Arnold R. Pilling, Thomas Buckley, William Bright—had issued strong statements against the G.O. Road.

By this time, a coalition of environmental organizations (the Siskiyou Mountains Resources Council, the Sierra Club, National Audubon Society, Friends of the Earth, and many others), realizing that the High Siskiyous would be spoiled forever by the completion of the G.O. Road, had made common cause with Indians, scientists, fishermen, and an increasing number of concerned citizens who wondered why their taxes should be squandered on a twenty-five-million-dollar highway between two small and remote villages, crossing a ridge system that is hot and dry in summer (there are no lakes, and the streams lie far down in the steep ravines) and extremely foggy, cold, and wet for the rest of the year. Despite all the Forest Service rhetoric about "multiple use" (known locally as "multiple abuse"), the G.O. Road had no serious purpose besides expediting swift, free access to the Six Rivers National Forest for the lumber corporations, which were being presented with a "glorified logging road" at the taxpayers' expense. Even that old Indian who was offering the Forest Service the kind of testimony it wished to hear had no illusions about the G.O. Road. "All the Forest Service wants that G.O. Road for is haulin' logs out; I know that. They don't think I know that, but I do."

Unless an alternate route was adopted, the Chimney Rock section—the weak central link in this heavy chain across the mountains—would determine the fate not only of the High Country but of Blue Creek. Defenders of the area thought that wilderness designation was the only real protection for the Siskiyous, and they hoped to achieve this in the course of a new series of roadless area public hearings (known as RARE II).*

A Yurok medicine man, Calvin Rube (whom I had visited with Craig Carpenter in 1976), objected to the wilderness designation because it suggested federal ownership of Yurok territory and would require that the true owners take out permits to walk on their own land; the U.S. government treaty of October 6, 1851, with the "Pohlik or lower Klamath Indians," designed to eliminate Indian title to these lands, was never ratified by the U.S. Senate or signed into law by the President of the United States. Rube also objected to the term "wilderness" for a home country that Indians perceive not as "wild" but natural, complete, a perfect place under the dominion of higher powers, a "good place," full of strength and beauty, where Indians may go to be restored. No Indian would quarrel with either of these points (or with the idea of entrusting jurisdiction of the High Country to responsible Indian authorities), but they won't matter much if the towering rocks and clear silences of the High Country are reduced to chain-link fences, car horns, nonbiodegradable litter baskets, and V.I.S. interpretive displays, with forty-five acre "recreation" areas for the Indians.

In Eureka, I had paid a call on Joseph Harn, the new supervisor of Six Rivers National Forest. In the waiting room outside his office the only publications were two neat, unread issues of *Forest Industries* and the *Sierra Club Bulletin*, as if he sought to bring these two into peaceful balance; and in fact Joe Harn turned out to be a hearty, open, friendly man, with a big sunburn and an old-fashioned mustache, who would make a terrific small-town politician. Perhaps this is why he was chosen for this job, which had changed hands several times in the last few years as the plot thickened.

*The right of the federal government to limit exploitation of disputed land while its wilderness survey was in progress was contested in court by a Denver "legal foundation" led by James G. Watt, who later became the Secretary of the Interior.

Rather skillfully, Harn implied that environmentalists were just another "special interest group," like the lumber interests, against which the American people and their national forests must be defended. "If nobody's happy, we must be doing *something* right," he told me with a laugh, and I got the idea that he says this pretty often. It was certainly true that nobody was happy, but what the Forest Service was doing right was very much a matter of dispute. Joe Harn, like all Forest Service people, was courteous and friendly in the face of some hard questioning, having been trained to be politic and "nice" to everyone. But this eagerness to please becomes quite dangerous when, as inevitably happens, the district supervisors and rangers are courted by the local establishment, which does not include environmentalists or Indians. In a sawmill economy, it is led by the big lumbermen, with whom foresters share a "management" mentality that tends to abhor the concept of unmanaged wilderness.

"No one used to care what the Forest Service did," Harn complained. "That's when there was plenty of timber, and forests were just for public recreation. If we said, 'Let us show you what we're doing here,' people would say, 'Don't bother us, we're going fishing.' All they wanted to do was recreate. Now it's different. Some say we try too hard to please Big Lumber, and some say we try too hard to please Environment. But what we're here for is to find just the right balance, to do what's best for everybody." And few people would seriously deny that the Forest Service does the best it can; whether or not that best is good enough is another matter (interested parties on both sides of any national forest issue are apt to think of the Forest Service as wishy-washy). In regard to the G.O. Road, Harn made the point that no one had spoken out against it "originally," which of course was true; but it was also true that in that remote area a great deal of the "improvement" of old roads was done before the public at large knew what was going on, and that even now both ends of the G.O. Road, terminating on the public highways, had been left not only unfinished but unmarked, leaving the public as ignorant as ever about what was going on back in the mountains.

Next day I talked a little while with Joseph Winter, staff archeologist for Six Rivers, whose predecessor, Jerry Wylie, courageously opposed the construction of the G.O. Road before his transfer. Winter acknowledged that the Indian "leaders" who have been most cooperative with the Forest Service might not be the true spokesmen for their people, but said that he wished to work with any who expressed interest, in order that "native Americans would feel included in the process." It was because of Karuk protest, he pointed out, that plans had been canceled for the Red Cap Bridge across the Klamath near Orleans that would have destroyed a traditional site for the White Deerskin Dance. This was certainly commendable, and the more reason to wonder why the Forest Service was persisting in its plan to build a highway through the heart of the sacred High Country.

To complete the picture on the G.O. Road, I rang up Richard Reid, the Western Timber Association's "public relations forester," who does the talking for the big lumber corporations. Reid pointed out that twenty-five percent of "stumpage" fees (fees for trees sold while still standing) received by the Forest Service went for schools and highways of the local counties; in other words, the taxpayers were compensating for the failure of the corporations to reinvest in these beleaguered counties where they made their money. (Louisiana-Pacific had publicly revealed that its local profits were reinvested in the Southeast and in Texas.) "It's in the best interest of everybody to complete the G.O. Road," Reid concluded, pointing out that to leave the road unfinished would be so wasteful. That was certainly true, but there was much more at stake than the waste of money; one might just as well say that it is wasteful for an alcoholic to abandon his unfinished bottle. Since the G.O. Road was a rotten idea in the first place, didn't it make more sense to cut our losses? "I'm afraid I'd have to disagree with you on that," said Reid, whose title had recently been changed to "information forester."

•   •   •

The ridge climbed steeply once again, emerging from cool, early-morning forest into the hot scrub of the upper slopes. Here the trail lost itself in montane chaparral of oak, manzanita, chinquapin; the sharp, stiff, thorny leaves of canyon live oak scratched our bare arms and the open holes in my old jeans. We fought our way uphill through these coarse thickets, stopping every little way to gasp for breath.

The sun was high, the red rocks glared, the air was still. "Got to take it one step at a time," Dick sang out cheerfully. But John, who was still moving in his quick, urgent gait ("Got to move like that—that's the way I go best"), was stopping more and more often, and he showed the strain. He and Dick were halfway through their water, which in summer is scarce in the High Siskiyous— one of the many reasons why few people will ever go there just to "recreate"—and I wondered if we would find any at the summit. Last September, I recalled, there had been water in a rank meadow pool between Doctor Rock and Peak 8, but autumn rains start early in the Siskiyous, and there had been rain before my visit.

Meanwhile, the Steps were growing steeper, the brush fields thicker, the day hotter—the great heat of the day would come in midafternoon. We had pushed uphill eight or nine miles and perhaps four thousand feet, and still there was no sign of our destination. But now small cairns built by pilgrims of other days began to mark the trace, and finally I saw Doctor Rock itself, a dark monument on its bare saddle, toward the west. After eight and a half hours of hard climbing, we had reached the ridge, yet the ridge seemed to be leading us away from Doctor Rock.

"Come on," John said. "I got to see what in the hell we come all the way up *here* for." We were footsore and staggering in the heat, and when we came upon a small warm pool in a rank meadow, blue-flecked with violets and blue-eyed grass, we sank down and rolled out of our packs. The pool was shallow, rather warm, and teeming with dragonflies and torpid salamanders—"water dogs," Trull called them in disgust. (Salamanders are *sok*, or "poison reptiles," to the Indians, and those in alpine ponds are particularly feared, since their stare can detect an evil heart or unclean being.) But I, for one, was glad to see the water; and I drank heavily, after which we lay flat out in the long grass. An hour later we were ready to go on, leaving our gear behind in the small meadow, but our legs felt weak, and we soon found that we had to climb still higher. On a wooded slope, at a cold spring in the rocks, we drank again, then headed west, crossing a beautiful meadow guarded by a great monolithic granite and climbing once more to a bare ridge of red peridotite and wind-worn cedars. Before us lay the gaunt face of Peak 8, but Doctor Rock stood on the far side of a deep wooded gully, a steep descent and another climb away.

We could not believe it; we had imagined ourselves right on top of it, and still we were far off. And I remembered how, the year before, approaching Doctor Rock from the other direction, in broad daylight, we had also had strange trouble drawing near, and how a medicine woman had said that the resistance of the place had come about because we had not been correct in our preparations. Perhaps John and I should have bathed this morning in the cold water of Blue Creek; perhaps we should have paid respect at the ceremonial places and not just flung ourselves down anywhere along the trail.

It was late now, and our strength was gone. We talked about going on, but we could not move. On this high place of incense cedars and knobcone pine, we saw a place where deer had gathered and where a fool grouse had been dusting. To the west, the ridges fell away to the Pacific; to the east, beyond Chimney Rock, lay the horizon of the Marble Mountains. Last year, from just west of Doctor Rock, I had seen the snow cone of Mount Shasta, eighty miles away, and now John spoke about "the line of power" used by the old Indians that ran east and west from Mount Shasta to Red Mountain and included Chimney Rock and Doctor Rock; this "line of power" was part of the sacred solitude and silence. Seeking power, the aspirants would sit in a near-trance, sometimes for days, on ledges or "seats" constructed on the sides of the high rocks; usually the seats faced toward the east, to meet the Creator in the rising sun.

For a long time we sat among the cedars, gazing out over the silence of the High Country. This was the sixth day of July, and still there was a frost of snow on the Marble Mountains. Tomorrow, because we were traveling light and had little food, we would have to return to our camp at Blue Creek, then head downriver to Bear Pen Flat, to Slide Creek and the road on out over the mountains. And so we talked more about going on, but no one moved. I reasoned that I had already been to Doctor Rock, that the purpose of this trip had been to ascend the Steps; the others declared the intent to return another day. And still we sat there, though Doctor Rock was not much more than a hard mile away, and we had another three hours of good light. "This would be a pretty place to make our camp," John said. "Too windy for mosquitoes. But the old people say that you must never sleep up here on these high ridges. There is wind that comes that takes the man away, leaving just the skeleton."

Finally we turned and retraced our steps along the ridge and down through the pines to the beautiful meadow with the mighty granite, then on through the quiet shadowed wood where water flowed ice-cold from the stones and out again into a glade where the glistening beargrass—an extraordinary member of the lily family with tall stalks that bear round full heads of cream-white blossoms—was shimmering with summer light. And there were other lilies, too, and iris and lupine and blue vetch, yellow arnica and buttercups, harebells, mountain penstemon, wild rose—at least fifty species of wildflowers in sight at once, the most various display I have ever seen. The ground rock of the Klamath Mountains, of which the Siskiyous are part, has changed little in the more than a hundred million years of its existence, though these high ridges did not rise until two or three million years ago, an uplift—and a steepening—that is still going on. Because these ancient hills include representative plants of four main botanical regions—the Pacific Northwest, California, the Cascades, and the Sierra Nevada—and because no icecap ever came to obliterate the older forms, the flora includes at least thirteen hundred species of vascular plants, including a few relicts of the Tertiary period, sixteen million years ago. The California Native Plant Society—one of the many groups now fighting to save the Siskiyous—has identified thirty plants as "rare, very rare, or endangered" (the Forest Service refers to these as "a few sensitive species"); and there are a number of flowers and trees that are endemic to this region, including the Brewer's spruce and the Sadler oak. Seventeen of the twenty conebearing trees known to occur here are found in an area of one square mile, near Russian Peak; there are said to be more species of conifers (and lilies) in the Klamath Mountains than in any comparable region of the earth—cause enough, all by itself, to save such country.

Hermit thrushes sang on every side, robins and nuthatches, warblers and chickadees; a jackrabbit came and went away; I saw a skink of brilliant cobalt blue. At camp we made a quick hot fire of manzanita twigs and ate up the last of the food; we were not hungry, and John Trull was already lying down. Earlier a bear had dug a yellow jacket's hive out of the meadow, and we had heard one rummaging back in the bushes. Big bear piles were everywhere, no two alike because of the great range of bear diet, but we did not think we would be bothered. Though black bears are common here, they remain wild in the absence of "refuse areas" and litter baskets and carefully avoid the camps of human beings.

The night was cold, no mosquitoes came, and stars appeared among the silvertip firs and knobcone pines that kept their silent watch around the meadow. Two days before, a Hupa friend had told me about five young Hupa who were up here someplace by Doctor Rock, trying to make medicine; they had come without spiritual training or guidance, and everyone knew that what they were doing was very dangerous. "They never come up here by them Steps, or we'd have seen sign," Dick Myers said. "They had more sense than us, then," John Trull grunted.

Next day there were big thunderheads over the Klamath, not usual at this dry time of the year, and the day after that we were told by Aunt Queen James that she, too, had been aware of the big thunderheads and assumed they were there because "Dick had gone fooling around up at Doctor Rock." For the last sixty years, Aunt Queen has lived alone on the *rancheria* of her father-in-law, Segap, or Coyote, known to the white men of the time as "Coyote Jim." The rancheria lies where Tully Creek comes down on the south bank of the Klamath, facing the sacred mountain of Kay-wet, or Burrill Peak. The old lady was near-deaf and suffered cataracts but was still full of curiosity and humor; she was smiling now but became serious again. "You have to do right up in that place," she warned us. "You can't fool around or eat food or drink water. You can't sleep with your woman for a year before you go. You can't let those white people go up there. The white man, too, can be hurt if he doesn't do right; he can be dead."

"She means you can't go leaving sacred pipes and things up there that would not have been touched by righteous people in the old days," Dick whispered tactfully.

When the first environmental impact statement was in progress, Aunt Queen was interviewed by two Forest Service people in regard to the significance of the High Country. According to Dick's wife, Debbie Myers, who had been present, about two hours of tapes were made, yet Aunt Queen's testimony never appeared on the official record. Speaking against the intrusion of the G.O. Road, Aunt Queen had picked a spoon up off the table, turned it over, sniffed and inspected it, then put it down again before her, asking the Forest Service people, "Why does the white man have to turn things over and upset things, change things, in trying to understand them; why doesn't he accept things as they are and leave the world alone?" Apparently, other testimony of this kind was also disregarded—in the words of a young Yurok lawyer, Abby Abinanti—"because it was inconsistent with what they wanted to find."

Long before dark in the endless summer evening, we were fast asleep, and we slept hard until first light. Even then, after ten hours' rest, it was difficult to bring John back to life. "Come on, Grandfather," Dick said in his gentle voice; it was important to leave before the sun was high in order to bushwhack down through that hard scrub to the cool forest on the ridge. We set off at daybreak, without breakfast, and once underway, we made good time, rounding the mountain and traversing the steep barren slopes that led down into thick undergrowth, pausing just once to gaze at the lovely sunrise worlds below. During the night, the ocean fogs had rolled into the Klamath gorge, pushing thick white tentacles into the canyons of Blue Creek, leaving the ridges all around like green islands in a sea of clouds; this silent world lay far below the rock where we sat perched like three unshaven angels. And seeing the white river flowing in from the white ocean, I understood much better the Yurok concept of the world as a kind of disc bisected by the Klamath, rising and falling minutely on the surrounding sea.

John Trull frowned and cleared his throat. "You're very close to heaven here," he muttered. He glared at us, as if daring us to laugh. Then he spoke about a time, up in the mountains, when he had found himself quite suddenly in a beautiful, strange place where he had never been before and yet which seemed somehow familiar, as if remembered from another life. He had walked along as if entranced, weeping and laughing simultaneously, as if on the point of remembering something that would bring him instantly and forever a profound understanding of the world, of life and death.

Bewildered and uncomfortable, he stopped speaking, and for a little while we sat in silence on the mountainside. But I had been to this place, too, and so had Dick. We were silent, not because we were embarrassed, as John thought, but because we were awed by John's precise description. "That's where I stop," Dick said at last. "Whoo-ee. That's where things get too wild for me." And it occurred to me that what John had described was the world which the aspirant Indians of other days who had come up these Steps into the High Country had wished to enter. In the words of Florence Shaughnessy, an old Indian lady down at Requa, where the Klamath rolls out between huge sandbars, rocks, and cliffs into the sea, "You come upon a place you've never seen before, and it has awesome beauty, everything above you, below you, around you is so pure. That is the beauty we call *merwerksergerh*, and the pure person is also *merwerksergerh*."

John Trull was embarrassed by the suggestion that what he had had was a mystical experience; such experience, he had always thought, was strong evidence of a weak mind. Sighing, he stood up and set his pack, wondering aloud if his old shoes would get him home. He jerked his chin at the red shale and serpentine all around us, then at the stands of oak under Red Mountain; the hardwoods were a soft pale green in the dark pelage of the conifers. "Ain't really worth loggin' the few firs that grow big up this high—firs need good soil." He shrugged his pack into place and started down the mountainside toward the trees. Dick Myers nodded. "But they used up everything else, so they'll cut here anyway. They're even loggin' out the tanoaks now."

To the south lay the scarred slopes of Nickowitz Peak and Barren Butte and Lonesome Ridge, and from far off came the shriek of huge machinery, but in the deep valleys between, and as far as the eye could see off to the east, the only mark in all the landscape was the raw gash made by the deep cut-and-fill construction of the G.O. Road. "I'm sure against the G.O. Road," John Trull sighed, "but I might not be, I guess, if I was workin' on it."

To the west of us, Red Mountain, on the high ridge between the Crescent City and West Forks of Blue Creek, was already a desecrated shrine; we had a full view of the cat-road network that zigzagged back and forth across its eastern face, the blocky hard-edged scars of random clear-cuts that broke the flow of the whole landscape. This was what was planned for the whole drainage. On the far side of Red Mountain, mercifully hidden from our view, the West Fork of Blue Creek had been ruined—"a disaster area," says Tim McKay of the Northcoast Environmental Center, "a catastrophe, the epitome of bad logging practice—Simpson just trashed it." Most of the western prospect from the High Country today is what the Forest Service classifies as "Class C or Discordant

Landscape." In the quiet words of Florence Shaughnessy, "It is just greed that is wrecking this country, just plain greed."

We moved rapidly downhill into Blue Creek, swinging easily along through the old forest and arriving at the river edge well before noon. At camp we made a scavenger's meal of what had been left behind—bran flakes, raw potato, chunks of jarred venison—and kept on going, pausing to swim in a deep hole at the first bend, fording, refording, and fording again, pausing to gather a mouthful of wild strawberries, going on.

· · ·

A few weeks later, coming south from Oregon, I had an impulse to return to Doctor Rock, and I stopped in the village of Gasquet to ask directions for the G.O. Road, which was as well hidden at its northern end as at its southern terminus at Orleans. At the South Fork Road, about seven miles west of Gasquet, there was a large dramatic sign: AUTHORIZED VEHICLES ONLY. EXTREME DANGER DUE TO SLIDING AND FLOODING. Until it arrived at Big Flat, about twelve miles from the highway, there was no indication that this became the G.O. Road, or even a clue that it led south to Orleans. And in fact, this road was in a chronic state of disrepair, owing to the unstable nature of the steep valley sides that were collapsing all around it. In many places, half the pavement had fallen into this South Fork of the beautiful Smith River (which like Blue Creek was one of the best spawning streams in California), and the truck eased precariously along a single narrow lane with sagging edges. Here reconstruction crews were building bridges over the river, to try their luck on the steep, unstable slopes on the far side. A great deal of good money thrown after bad shores this road up until the next flood year comes along, when mountain torrents will wash it out entirely.

In the hot, dry twilight of deep summer—it had been 105 degrees in Grants Pass, Oregon, when I passed through there at five that afternoon—I climbed slowly from Big Flat into the High Country. There were no other vehicles on this forlorn road, and an hour passed before Peak 8 and Doctor Rock came into view; seen from the north, the dark mass of Doctor Rock, where I would go the next day, was emblematic on the southern sky. I parked the truck on an old jeep track off the highway, on a bare point overlooking the Pacific where my small campfire would be no threat to these tinder forests, and made a quick supper before dark, alone with the Pacific sunset, the sea clouds. Just at dark came an unearthly hum, rising eerily over the wash of ocean wind in the stunted spruce beside the truck; a pair of sphinx moths, heavy-bodied, with proboscises like the bills of hummingbirds, whirred on their cyclone wings among pale yerba buena blossoms by the road. Then it was dark, and the sphinx moths fell silent as the earth came to rest. I stamped the fire out to the last spark. Except for the soft wind, there was no sound.

Last September, on my first approach to Doctor Rock, I was instructed by Indian friends from the Hupa reservation to burn ceremonial tobacco north of Flint Valley; on the second trip, with Trull and Myers, we did it at the foot of "the Golden Stairs." Early this morning, before setting out, I did it once again, facing east, then south and west and north, then gazing across Red Mountain to the Pacific. And as I finished, there came an insistent thump upon the earth. Startled, I turned to see an Indian, an older man with a thick walking stick, approaching me along the jeep track from the G.O. Road. The heavy old man, passing by without a glance, only grunted "Morning." I guessed he was making a pilgrimage to Doctor Rock, but I wanted to be sure; knowing I shouldn't, I asked where he was going. He whirled to squint hard at this white man who had no business here at daybreak. "What?" he demanded. "Oh, someplace over there." Not wishing to name a medicine place, he waved his stick toward the south, and kept on going.

I let him go until he was out of sight, then started off myself, entering the forest and walking uphill to the trail head where the path heads south under Peak 8. Last year, in a suggestion box placed at this point by the Forest Service, I had inserted the suggestion that the box be removed; this was Indian sacred ground, I said, and such touristic eyesores had no place here. And I was pleased to see that the box was gone—perhaps some bear looking for food and finding nothing but suggestions had knocked the damned thing away into the woods—and that the Forest Service had not "improved" the path, which was still a dim trace, heavily overgrown.

Though I went slowly through the chinquapin, eating a few huckleberries for my breakfast, I soon overtook the Indian, who was rolling slowly through the bushes like a bear. He whirled on me again and with his stick waved me ahead, but when I said I was in no hurry, he went on without a word. Perhaps my lack of haste had mollified him, for in a little while he paused to show me the big prints of a deer—"There's plenty of doe prints, but this here's a good buck"—and another place where a human being had sat down. "Funny thing is, there's a sign of one man going this way, maybe two, but I can't find no sign coming back." On this dry ground, in this thick scrub, I was impressed that he had picked up any sign at all. It had not rained in several weeks, and, of course, these tracks belonged to Cliff Ferris and the Forest Service man, who had been dropped off on the G.O. Road.

To my surprise, the old man said that he had never been to Doctor Rock before, although he had once worked as a logger in Bluff Creek—was this the path? I nodded. We were now moving out of the forest again, onto the open west slope of Peak 8; last year in this place, at daybreak, I had surprised a sow bear with her cub. Ha-ay-klok, the Doctor Rock, awaited us on its bare ridge, taut and black in the sharp early light, and from below, the huge monolith called Ah-Kah, Bad Place, rose from its dark bed of giant firs. Ha-ay-klok and Ah-Kah are the only huge isolated granites in this landscape, the one high on its crescent on the sky, the other deep down in a ravine; one understands why the Indians perceived them as the Good Place and the Bad. And the man said shyly, "For us, this is like the white man's church, y'know. I been wantin' to come up here for a long time." When I said it was too bad he had run into me, that he must have planned to be here by himself, he nodded. His people used to come up here to hunt, he said, for there had always been a lot of game near Doctor Rock, but once his uncle had come up for something else. "I don't know what he was doin' here," he added quickly.

Slowly we crossed the bare serpentine slope and went down into the saddle between Peak 8 and Doctor Rock. There I turned off the path, telling him that I wished to see if the summer water was still good in that small pool below, where a swampy stream down from a cedar grove made a green meadow. He stopped and turned around to squint at me. "You better go up there by yourself," I said. The old man smiled, and invited me to visit him at Requa. Giving me his name and directions to where he lived, he added, "You can't miss it." He went on up the ridge toward Doctor

Rock, and I went down to the green meadow, all set about with bright, wild tiger lilies and lavender spiraea. A band-tailed pigeon crossed the evergreens, and the jays squalled. The pool was filmed with a light algae, but the spring water down from the cedar grove was cool and good, and the salamanders there seemed full of life; they did not hang around to stare but withdrew into the shadows of the water.

· · ·

Since January 1979, when this chapter appeared in Audubon *(under the title "Stop the G.O. Road"), it has served as anti-G.O. Road literature in the campaign waged by Indians, environmentalists, and others not only in Congress but in the courts, where the sacred "high country" has survived one up-and-down fight after another. In 1980 the California Wilderness Act, sponsored by the late Representative Philip Burton of California, achieved substantial protection for the Siskiyous, and in 1981, the Forest Service recognized the existence of valid Indian religious sites and removed "the Golden Stairs" from its proposed trail system. But the Blue Creek and Eightmile units were excluded from the Wilderness Act, and the Forest Service was still determined to complete the G.O. Road, despite the conclusion of yet another expensive study (commissioned by the Forest Service) that none of the several other routes suggested as alternatives to the uncompleted Chimney Rock section of the G.O. Road would significantly lessen the potential damage to Indian sacred ground, and that the only practicable solution was to abandon the whole idea. To no one's surprise, this $250,000 study was ignored.*

The Forest Service decision to proceed with the G.O. Road and the wholesale logging of Blue Creek was contested by the Sierra Club Legal Defense Fund, but by March 1983, when the case was appealed before the Ninth Circuit Court in San Francisco, the Forest Service and the big timber interests appeared to have triumphed; in fact, the Forest Service had already contracted with an Oregon construction firm to complete the road.

On May 25, 1983, while participating in a reception at the congressional office buildings in Washington, D.C., on behalf of the imprisoned Indian activist Leonard Peltier, I was approached by Representative John Seiberling of Ohio, who had just received news of a court injunction against completion of the Chimney Rock section of the G.O. Road "or any alternate route . . . which would traverse the high country"; it also forbade further logging or logging road construction in the Blue Creek Unit in the absence of adequate measures to protect both water quality and fish populations. This was the first federal court decision ever to protect Indian sacred ground on federal land under the religious freedom provision of the First Amendment; in all other cases, including the Glen Canyon and Tellico Dams, the courts had failed to defend the rights of Indians. While the decision was based mainly on religious grounds, Judge Stanley Weigel of the Ninth Circuit Court noted that Forest Service plans violated the National Environmental Policy Act, the Wilderness Act, the Federal Water Quality Control Act, and Indian water and fishing rights on the Hupa reservation.

The following evening, Tim McKay of the Northcoast Environmental Center, a leader in the G.O. Road fight, telephoned to invite me to a party of celebration. Asked how long the injunction would be valid, McKay said, "The injunction is permanent! And even if the decision is appealed, the case will drag on for years and years—I don't think they'll bother! I think we've won!"

· 7 ·

BLACK HILLS

The old borders of what once had been "the Great Sioux Reservation," established by the Fort Laramie Treaty of 1868, fall strangely close to the shadow boundaries of the great energy empire in the northern Great Plains states, which contain most of the Fort Union coal seam in Montana, Wyoming, and North Dakota, as well as considerable deposits of oil, gas, and uranium; much of this great mineral wealth lies near or beneath the much-diminished reservations assigned to the Lakota (western Dakota or "Sioux"), their former allies the Northern Cheyenne and the Arapaho, and their former enemies the eastern Shoshone, or "Snake Indians," and the Absaroka, or "Crow."*

In the 1960's, in an unprecedented transfer of public wealth into private hands, vast tracts of federally administered land were presented to the energy companies for an average of about three dollars an acre, and the Bureau of Indian Affairs encouraged the tribal councils to share in this bounty. In Montana, the Northern Cheyenne leased mining rights to Peabody Coal and prospecting rights to other companies on more than half of their 440,000-acre reservation; not long thereafter, 125,000 acres were leased out by the Crow. Nearly thirty companies already had leases on Wyoming's Wind River reservation, shared by the Arapaho and eastern Shoshone, and extensive mineral exploration was under way on reservations throughout the Dakotas.

In 1971, the North Central Power Study (endorsed by the Interior Department) decreed that Black Hills aquifers—the only real source of water in this region—could sustain exploitation of their coal, oil, and uranium resources and that the Black Hills should become the nucleus of a multinational energy domain, producing power right in the mine fields and exporting it eastward in a grid of power lines, all the way to Minneapolis and St. Louis. A uranium "gold rush" now began, assisted as it had been a century before by the federal government and later the South Dakota state government as well. Within a few years, more than a million acres were claimed, staked, or leased by about twenty-five large corporations, including the Tennessee Valley Authority and Kerr-

*Some of the energy-industry material in this chapter is adapted from the author's *In the Spirit of Crazy Horse* (New York: The Viking Press, 1983), which included discussion of the Fort Laramie Treaty, the energy development of the Black Hills, the modern treaty claims, court decisions, and related matters.

McGee, which controls a third of the uranium reserves in the United States; Kerr-McGee is the colossus among those colossal companies which, attracted by the overlapping jurisdictions of state, federal, and tribal governments, and a consequent absence of effective regulations, public health monitoring systems, and enforcement, have led the way in the devastation by strip mines and contamination of vast tracts of Indian country in the West.

With the appearance of the North Central Power Study, the Northern Cheyenne of every faction began to question the eventual effect of the coal leases on its lands; fifteen miles north of the reservation, at the great strip mine and power plant called Colstrip, huge green machines were overturning the broad rangelands of the old buffalo country, and even "progressive" Indians perceived that the destruction of their sacred lands could only lead to the destruction of the Cheyenne as a people. New lease applications were resisted, and on March 5, 1973, after an inspection of Peabody Coal Company's effect on the Hopi–Navajo sacred mountain called Black Mesa, the Cheyenne Tribal Council voted unanimously to cancel all existing leases, and sued the Department of the Interior for betrayal of its trust responsibilities in encouraging the leases in the first place. Although these cancellations were fought by the mining companies, the Interior Department was forced to support the unified Cheyenne, who also challenged the construction of further power plants on the grounds of deteriorated air quality caused by the Colstrip operation, and demanded that the Interior Department protect their water by forbidding strip mining within fifty miles of their boundaries. In all these matters, the Crow Nation followed their lead, and so did Montana ranchers, irate citizens, and eventually the state government itself. Realizing that the Yellowstone River might run dry in drought time if the study were carried out, Montana issued a water-permit moratorium in 1977 that brought the headlong rampage of the strip miners under control.

That year, the Department of Interior's final environmental impact statement endorsed the North Central Power Study's grand designs for this "national sacrifice area," despite an acknowledgment that mining and power plant development on such a scale would devastate some 188,000 acres and inflict damage that was probably irreparable on the land, water, air, and life of the Great Plains. A doomsday smog of sulphur, nitrogen, and ash would shroud the big skies of the mountain states even at night, and carry eastward in an acid rain all over the country, while toxic waste and runoff from the huge earth-busting operations would sink into the aquifers and sour the disappearing creeks and prairie sloughs across thousands of square miles. Even the impact statement specified that reclamation, if any, "would be hampered by the severe climate, limited rainfall, short growing season, and . . . nature of surface materials" in the region. Also, Indian people would lose their "special relationship to the land," as the land itself shifted to "mineral extractive use." On the other hand, the Indians would be compensated by exchanging their "isolation" for "a closer relationship with American society" in "the mainstream of American life"—in effect, what American Indian Movement (AIM) leaders were referring to as "cultural genocide."

The companies, insisting on their leases, continued their efforts to divide the reservations through bribery and coercion while exhausting the Indians' limited resources in court. Meanwhile, the industry stuck to its plan to encircle the Black Hills with thirteen coal-fired plants, producing ten thousand megawatts apiece; more than sixty additional plants were under consideration. A nuclear-energy "park" of as many as twenty-five reactors was proposed, with attendant water reprocessing and disposal grounds fed by exploration holes, mines, mills, and the deadly hills of processed ore or mine tailings that erode and leak and blow downwind in eight states of the West.

The waste and ruin of water throughout the western states is a calamity that few public servants have yet found the courage to deal with. The lakes and streams of the Black Hills, and the tilted rock layers that ensure that much of its rainfall restores groundwater to the great aquifers, have provided abundant water for the agriculture and tourism on which until recently the economy of these states has been based. Now the energy industry was seizing this water, which is required in immense amounts in all phases of its operations. The water level in the deep Madison Formation (which underlies much of southern Alberta and Saskatchewan as well as all the northern plains states) is expected to sink at least one thousand feet in mining regions; in fact, the water table in parts of Wyoming and South Dakota has been lowered considerably already.

In 1979, when I first investigated energy development in the

Great Plains, uranium exploration was most heavily concentrated in the Black Hills on the Wyoming–South Dakota border, near the small city in the southern Hills named for General Custer, whose huge expedition confirmed the presence of abundant gold "in them thar hills" a century before. The proposed development of this area was shared by Union Carbide Corporation with the Tennessee Valley Authority, which was seeking fuel for the seventeen nuclear reactors in its long-range plans. The more than six thousand test holes dug by the TVA had promised an eventual return of five hundred million dollars' worth of uranium at the mine mouth, and they also ensured a slow deterioration of all life in the region. Uranium releases dangerous radiation wherever it is exposed to oxygen, as it is throughout every stage of mining and milling—"the most significant source of radiation exposure in the entire nuclear fuel cycle" according to the Department of Energy—and radon, a major uranium by-product easily soluble in water, and odorless, tasteless, and invisible as well, is escaping this very moment from the thousands of exploratory bore holes that these corporations have not bothered to plug up, while the exposed ore leaches down into the aquifers. The mines and mills and tailings piles will add radon to the acid rain from the coal-fired plants north and west of the Black Hills, contaminating land and life perhaps thousands of miles away.

To facilitate the sinking of their mine shafts, the TVA and Union Carbide planned to "dewater" the aquifers, which means pumping the water out of the ground at a rate estimated by the TVA at 675 gallons per minute for each mine. But very similar dewatering operations in New Mexico are wasting water at an estimated rate of 100,000 gallons per minute, and according to the TVA's environmental impact statement for its Edgemont Uranium Mining Project, "Dewatering operations will cause a depression of groundwater levels in the Lakota Formation which will result in some wells to cease flowing." It also predicts "a temporary minor degradation" of air quality "due to fugitive dust and exhaust emissions . . . and releases of radon and short-lived radon progeny from the shafts and ore-piles. . . . There will be a temporary change in land use from rangeland and forest to mineral extraction during the life of the project. . . . it is unlikely that reclaimed communities will closely resemble existing species composition and diversity." Despite admissions to the contrary in the same impact statement, Union Carbide and the TVA have assured the local people that their mines are harmless; anyone acquainted with such mines, not to speak of the knowledge that "ore-piles" (uranium tailings) retain about eighty-five percent of their radio-activity almost indefinitely, will recognize in these public statements the unwarranted optimism that characterized TVA statements on the Tellico Dam.

Eight miles north of Edgemont, at Craven Canyon, Union Carbide has already dug a shaft two thousand feet deep. In the name of the alleged energy crisis, the U.S. Forest Service had exempted Union Carbide from the legally required environmental impact statement, despite the very considerable impact the industry has already had on the Edgemont area; in the same helpful spirit, the state attorney general requested the court to suspend half of the dinky fine that this huge company received in 1979 for digging here without a permit. Ore from the eight proposed mines will be dumped in huge heaps at Robinson Flats, twelve miles from Edgemont, where a sulphuric acid solution injected into the heaps will seep down to a clay base, leaching out the uranium and leaving behind yet another deadly hill of "sand." The clay base supposedly prevents contamination of the water table; even if it works, its efficiency will depend on the care taken with its construction which, to judge from all those unplugged bore-holes in the region, will be minimal at best. Nobody knows if this clay base will really stop the pervasive spread of radioactivity, and since contamination of the groundwater, once started, is very hard to stop, those South Dakotans whose wells run dry may be better off in the long run than their neighbors; already cattle have begun to die in the southern Black Hills, where the companies dig right down into the aquifers.

Edgemont, the site of the first uranium discovery in the Black Hills in 1951, is also the site of the old uranium mill and eroding tailings piles left behind by Susquehanna Western, which sold its property and leases to the TVA in 1974. The 3.9 million tons of tailings have irradiated the ground all around, creating an estimated 7.5 million tons of poisoned substance that the TVA has been directed to clean up: the cost of safe disposal of the tailings has defied all accurate calculation. How can so much poisonous matter be dug up and hauled away—to where?—without further contamination? And so the hills of "sand," as the fine, gray stuff is known locally, sit on or near the Cheyenne River, which is the main source for local wells for miles downstream; in 1962, an estimated two hundred tons of tailings were spilled into the river, washing eastward at least twenty-five miles to the Angostura Reservoir, where— it is hoped—most of them came to rest. But in Edgemont, at least, fear of contamination has so far been offset by the depression caused by the closing of the mill, which has encouraged most of the town's eighteen hundred to adopt a casual attitude about their future.

In 1961, when a local contractor used three loads of tailings fill to shore up a new house, the Denver office of the Environmental Protection Agency had letters on file from the South Dakota Health Department reflecting concern about such use of the tailings, and federal, state, and local officials had proof that the house was dangerous at least as early as 1972, when an EPA monitoring team received high radiation readings from this site and 144 others. But somehow this survey fell "through the cracks," said EPA's Denver office. "We made it available to the Atomic Energy Commission and they chose to do nothing about it." There was no public announcement of the high reading, which another EPA official called "a radiation legacy perpetrated on the community," and no one spoke up five years later when the house was sold to a young Lakota Indian and railroad worker named Neil Brafford. Again in 1978, an EPA study revealed that the Brafford house had one of the highest readings in a highly radioactive town; the Edgemont schoolyard and fifty-four new sites were also found to have high readings. This report was shown to Mayor Pete Ziemet, a former uranium mill superintendent, who saw no reason to alarm people: "We had no local indications of any radon problems." The EPA did not reveal its findings to the public, nor even to the Braffords, who continued to occupy the house until January 11, 1980, three days after a phone call from the South Dakota Department of Water and Natural Resources informed them that Chris Brafford, a child of five, should probably be removed from his basement room. Monitors (which no one bothered to install until late 1979) had confirmed the 1978 findings; radiation levels throughout the house were more than four times the high exposure permitted to uranium miners, who are only exposed for eight hours of the day. In the sickening knowledge that he and his wife Genny and their three small children are condemned to live for the rest of their lives with the dread of cancer, Brafford removed the whole family from the house, which was now worthless, since nobody would buy it. A new apartment was found for the frightened family (secretly paid for, as it turned out later, by the TVA, which sought to "mitigate the circumstances" and perhaps damp down the bad publicity in the process) and meanwhile, the state blandly pretended that Edgemont's predicament was not serious, which the depressed town, with a new boom just over the horizon, was only too anxious to believe. "It's a bunch of hooey," said Eugenia Chord, who with her husband staked a uranium claim in nearby Red Canyon at the time of the first discovery in 1951, and still keeps a piece of uranium tucked "where it's safe" in a dresser drawer.

The fly in all this bureaucratic ointment was Neil Brafford, who tried to share what he had learned with his fellow citizens only to find himself dismissed as a troublemaking "longhair," as traditional Indians are known in South Dakota; he was even resented for having permitted the monitor into his house. Confronted by a hostile town, and realizing that corporations and the state were determined to dodge responsibility for what had happened, he telephoned the staff attorneys of the Black Hills Alliance, a remarkable new environmental group composed of Indians as well as whites. Funded mostly by voluntary contributions and manned by a dedicated volunteer staff of researchers and lawyers, the BHA had joined Indians with environmental groups and an increasing number of white farmers and ranchers in a common cause. While publicizing the deadly effects of mining, it also hauled the huge companies into court wherever they broke or eluded the very lenient environmental laws of South Dakota, in the hope that these delaying actions would suffice until the public could be educated; at the same time, the Alliance supported the Lakota land claim based on the Fort Laramie Treaty of 1868, which, if recognized, would bury the mining leases in the courts almost indefinitely. Not surprisingly, Edgemont's mayor and city council president have accused the BHA of a negative attitude, and Union Carbide dismissed the group as "impatient zealots."

On a first visit, in the spring of 1979, I found the atmosphere at the BHA offices less zealous than exhilarating; I had not seen that interracial dedication, that *celebration* of hard work in a good cause, since working with Cesar Chavez in the late sixties. In the bare hectic offices in Rapid City, at the east edge of the Black

Hills, I learned of the group's origins from Madonna Gilbert, whose enthusiastic participation said a great deal about the character of the Alliance. She was a long-time member of the American Indian Movement and a founder of AIM's sister organization, Women of All Red Nations (WARN); she was also a first cousin of AIM leader Russell Means, who after eight years of harassment had become more vociferously hostile to the whites than any Indian leader in North America.

Help in joining forces with the white community came from Bruce Ellison, a young lawyer from the East, and Mark Tilsen, a young volunteer whose father had served the Indians as an attorney ever since the time of Wounded Knee. Working closely with the Means family, Tilsen and Ellison soon recruited a strong staff of volunteers, both white and Indian; the Black Hills Alliance, joined by WARN (but not AIM, which is still a red flag to most white South Dakotans) as well as a whole range of antinuclear groups, set up office in Rapid City in January 1979.

"The spirit is fantastic around here," Madonna told me. "And it's not just what BHA is accomplishing; I'm thankful that I've found a way to fight the whole damned syndrome of Indian existence." The same enthusiasm was apparent in all of the youthful volunteer staff at the Alliance. Juanita Pullins, a young white woman raised at Sturgis, in the northern Black Hills, believes that her work has brought about "a real education" of her whole family, which once shared the strong race prejudice in this region. "The Black Hills is a spiritual area, and not just for Indians," she said. "There's always been a strong pull back here whenever I've been away. This is my home." Winona Laduke, a charismatic, bright young woman who also works on Indian water and land abuse problems in the Southwest, is one of the most effective speakers and writers for traditional Indians. As an Ojibwa, she was amused by her people's historic wars with the Lakota ("It took us more than a hundred years to run those guys out of the Lakes") but as an Indian whose mother is a white, she knew that the time had come for all sane people to work together: "The Black Hills are an oasis in the Great Plains, a source of water and life to the whole region. They lie at the center of North America, and they are a spiritual center for the Lakota Nation; for as long as the old people can remember, there have been prayers and songs to 'Paha Sapa, our life blood.' Farmers and ranchers as well as Indians, all people who live with the earth instead of exploiting her, can also understand the sacredness of the Hills. For such people, the Black Hills is not just another mine site with a 'potential' for energy production, as it is for the multinational corporations and the U.S. government. Paha Sapa is the great battlefield in the energy wars against the Indians, and the new Indians are white as well as red." ("Red people go up there for our vision quests," one Indian said, "and white ones can go worship at Mount Rushmore.")

"There's a force working to save the Black Hills that's surmounting barriers everyone said were insurmountable, between people—red ones, too—who are pretty damned set in their ways," Ellison told me. "We're doing something that's never been done before—bringing both peoples together in a state where any announcement of an AIM meeting used to send white folks running for their guns. Sure, we're walking a fine line, but it's been working; when the two races start talking to each other, the stereotypes are bound to disappear. They've gotten beyond pointing fingers at each other, and they're looking hard at the real enemy of both."

"The white men stole the Black Hills, sure, but first they raped it," according to John Honerkamp, a local historian who lives at Piedmont, north of Rapid City; it was near Piedmont, in 1874, that George Armstrong Custer emerged from the Black Hills with the glad news of gold "from the grass roots down." "Stripped all the good timber for houses and mine shafts and the like, and what wasn't cut was burnt through carelessness, and they let 'er burn, they were so busy mining. That attitude toward the Black Hills hasn't changed. In my opinion, if we want to collect the revenues from mining, then we are responsible for disposing of nuclear waste, which is going to poison all of South Dakota. What makes me mad is that the rape today is still being done by outsiders who couldn't care less—take the money and run, leaving the people here with all the problems."

· · ·

Marvin Kammerer is a wry, wiry rancher in jeans and boots whose grandfather came out here in 1880, working on a freight train hauling the wire that was already fencing off the range. "Settled that bare ridge where I live now. Something about it appealed to him, I guess, because a lot of the land that's disappearing now under Rapid City was a lot better." Part of Kammerer's ranch— one of the few homesteads where the original family is still living— was taken by eminent domain to build Ellsworth Air Force Base, an enormous storage depot for bombs and missiles, but his youngest children still ride horses to the little school built by his grandfather in 1889. "What my grandfather told my father was, Don't sell the land. I feel the same way the Indians do; I don't own that land, it owns me, because my father and grandfather are buried there."

Kammerer looked up at me; he knew what I was thinking. "The government gave my grandfather that land according to the Homestead Act, and he never questioned it; he'd come from Germany on the run, and he never even knew about the treaties. In those days, the settlers were getting Indians drunk and cheating them out of their land as fast as possible; the only Indians my grandfather knew were the ones who came around to beg for food, so he thought they were all beggars. A lot of people in this state have never gotten over that idea."

Marvin Kammerer was one of the first ranchers to endorse the Black Hills Alliance. Asked what he thought about the Lakota land claim, which is also a strong argument against the mining, he raised his eyebrows, paused a moment, then said flatly, "I've read the Fort Laramie Treaty, and it seems pretty simple to me; their claim is justified. There's no way the Indians are going to get all of that land back, but the state land and the federal land could be returned to them. Out of respect for those people, and for their belief that the Hills are sacred ground, I don't want to be a part of this destruction."

When I asked Kammerer if he saw any way in which uranium mining here would be acceptable, he raised his voice. "There's *no* way it's acceptable! Certainly not for weapons—that's just insane! Hell, we're selling uranium overseas, then importing the waste back, because we don't want other people to make weapons out of it; with a nuclear-waste problem like ours, that's just plain crazy! And as for energy, we just don't need it! We already have an excess! And what are we going to do with all these 'hot' nuclear plants after twenty-five years? Put guards around them? What do we do with all that waste? That's why I'm against *all* nuclear mining; these corporations aren't accepting responsibility for what they are doing, for all that destructive potential that innocent people have to live with.

"Even today, just to hang on to the land, the farmers have to exploit it; they have to abuse it with pesticides and herbicides. And even so, it's more and more difficult because of all the weekend farmers who don't even know that killdeers and meadowlarks are signs of spring. Those people don't really care about the land, and they welcome the mining interests when the price is right. That's what's insane about this country; land isn't a resource, it's a commodity! Those damned realtors are nothing but pimps! Americans have gotten lazy, and along with laziness comes disrespect, not only for land but for food and fuel; that's why we're using so much more than our share. We're so damned *wasteful!* And wasting resources is like stealing from the children to come." Marvin Kammerer shook his head, disgusted; for a moment I thought he might spit on the floor.

"The worst waste of all around here now is water. Farmers are conservative by nature, and like to leave problems alone until they're personally affected, but they'd better start getting concerned about water, safe and plentiful water; I never heard of mining yet that didn't spoil it. We only have about twelve to fifteen inches of rainfall in this state, and most of our groundwater comes from the Black Hills. The pollution of groundwater is very serious, but in the long run, the plain shortage of it is going to be more serious yet. And nobody in this state is taking responsibility for our water; no one I can find will answer my questions about what water supplies and water quality are going to be like in twenty-five years. The state kept mineral rights on all homesteads set up after 1916, with subsurface rights taking precedence over agrarian, and right now the attorney general is serving papers all over South Dakota, demanding proof of water rights from farmers; those who can't prove them could lose them. We ranchers think that's to make sure the mining companies will get the water they need. Homestake has always had a man right in the legislature, Union Carbide keeps its lobbyist right on top of things—the big companies get pretty much what they want. This state has the lowest wages in the country, so these damned companies know that they can count on the politicians. And they count on cheap labor; you can read that right in their publications. They're expecting my kids to become workers in their goddamn mines, because there won't be anything else left for them to do!"

"The argument down there at Edgemont is life versus economics," says Bruce Ellison. "It doesn't matter what political persuasion you are! Suppose I was promised twenty grand a year for twenty years—will that make up for cancer in my child? Look at New Mexico! People were starting to die down there before it was realized that the real problem had nothing to do with people's color. Here in South Dakota, we can't win five years from now, ten years from now—that's already too late. We have to stop these people *this* year, and we're going to do it." He grinned. "We *have* to win. We have no choice, and so we will."

• • •

One April morning in 1980, I accompanied three young Alliance people to Edgemont, which has inherited most of the multiple contaminations of the region. We drove south from Rapid City across bare rangeland not yet warmed by spring, turning west beyond Buffalo Gap into the Black Hills National Forest. Nearing Edgemont, which lies thirteen miles east of the Wyoming border, the road follows the upper Cheyenne River, and Vivian Haskell rapped her knuckle on the car window. "There used to be some big old catfish in that river before they got it all polluted," said Vivian, a lively young Two Kettle Lakota from the Cheyenne River reservation, two hundred miles north and east, where this river flows out to the Missouri. I nodded unhappily, recalling the long wash and swim I had taken the previous year in the Cheyenne near Cherry Creek, from where Chief Big Foot and his people, a fortnight after the murder of Sitting Bull, set out on the ill-fated journey across the Badlands that came to an end in the snow at Wounded Knee.

The town is set among sad cottonwoods and railroad spurs that fringe the dead mill and huge tailings pile on the south side of the river. Apart from a big new access road, the uranium boom is not yet evident in Edgemont, which became a depressed area after its first boom ended; Colleen Ragan, who lived for four years on the Arapaho–Shoshone Wind River reservation in Wyoming, said, "You ought to see the town of Riverton; same boom-and-bust, and Gillette, Wyoming, too—that place is finished." (In 1980 it was discovered that the companies that have leased Wind River land since World War II have regularly cheated the Shoshone and Arapaho and that both Amoco and Gulf, two of the wealthiest corporations in America, had grossly underpaid the Indians on their lease royalties; what Gulf called "errors" in accounting cost the tribes $2.4 million between 1972 and 1978 on the Gulf lease alone.)

Thomas Burgess nodded, pulling at his beard. "Edgemont is a very tense little town," he said. "They want the boom back at any cost, but they don't want to hear what that cost is going to be. One day I was in that café over there"—he pointed at one of the faded buildings on the town's main street—"and the number of fights and arguments in there, I mean one after another, was just amazing; I couldn't believe it! And I got the feeling that if we had said anything at all about the mining, we might have gotten ourselves lynched."

Neil Brafford, whose mother is Lakota, is a tall young man with mustache and sideburns and hair worn long down his back; because he had been laid off from his job with Burlington Northern, he was watching TV in his basement apartment. Brafford had worked in the uranium mill before getting his job with the railroad, and he was still shaking his head over what happened; even when he made a joke, he did not smile. "Those guys in the mill were so brainwashed by the company, they were telling each other they were getting less radiation from uranium than they were from their color TV. The company used to suggest that we wear those little cloth respirators, not over the nose, just over the mouth; I never seen anyone do it, so I never did neither." One of Neil's friends in the mill now has cancer of the thyroid, and too many of his Edgemont neighbors have at least one cancer victim in the family. After the report about his house became public knowledge, "I figured people would come to see us, find out what we'd learned, but they never did. Just two young guys came; no one else wanted to know. And now they say we're just trying to get publicity for ourselves."

"Publicity!" Genny Brafford said, overhearing him as she came in. "This town really makes me laugh. Nobody's got enough courage to pull out, pull up stakes, begin again somewhere else, so they try to blame us, blame the Alliance for stirring up the 'skins. People here don't have the courage to say it to your face, but they're racist as hell."

"Hell, yes," Vivian Haskell said. "I lived in this town for a while. Those eyes follow you into the stores, follow you wherever you go."

"In the mine, too," Neil Brafford said.

"Schools, too," said Neil's younger sister Susie. "Wasn't so bad over in Igloo, the white people were sort of human over there, and when we first moved here in '67, my mom didn't believe what we were telling her about how the teachers spoke to Indians up in that government school. She thought we were just mouthy kids. But when she went up there and listened, why, she jerked us right out. While my dad was still alive, they had to respect the Braffords around here. But after he died, things just got worse and worse. Now the whole town is sore at the troublemaking longhairs: 'You're tearing down the name of this place, just when there's a boom coming!' But nobody wants to help out Neil and Genny."

"When I first heard that report about Chris's bedroom," Genny Brafford said, "I just wanted to punch somebody in the nose." She picked up her three-year-old, Marisa, a beautiful child who had wandered out of her bedroom, still half asleep, at the sound of our voices and climbed into the lap of Thomas Burgess, imagining him to be her father; Marisa had spent most of her young life in the plagued house—the most vulnerable period because of the swift growth of infant cells. "They all say there's nothing wrong, but I don't see nobody stepping up to buy our home."

Because Chris Brafford was still asleep, his mother did not accompany us on an expedition down the hill to 516 Seventh Avenue. The small, red-roofed dwelling, shaded by cottonwoods, has a long yard that slopes downhill from the tailings fill that permitted the house to be built on level ground; the tailings were used by the contractor without permission, Susquehanna-Western says, declining all responsibility, although its own trucks were apparently used to accomplish the job. Because the family vacated so suddenly last January, "Merry Christmas" is still frosted on the window, and from the floor of Chris's room in the basement of the dank, still house someone picked up a polaroid snapshot of the little boy taken last Halloween. "Where you're standing," Neil Brafford was saying, "the monitor got the highest reading of all." Handed the photograph of Chris, swollen-headed in an orange-bearded fright mask, he winced, then managed a wry, unhappy smile. "You see?" he said. "That's what started to happen to him down here." Everyone laughed, very anxious to go outdoors; Vivian whispered that there was a bad power in this place. "I guess maybe the Great Spirit don't want that stuff coming up out of the ground," she murmured angrily. "I signed up with the Alliance because I feel these companies are doing something against *me*—me and my two kids."

Outside again, Neil Brafford gazed at his big yard and garden; in the distress of a few months before, he had not bothered to retrieve his hose and shovel. "This house was the first thing I ever bought in my whole life," he said, "and I had to give it up. We were here only two and a half years, and that was exactly two and a half years too long. Last year I grew two-foot string beans, and cucumbers all swollen up the size of melons, and the baby, he's just eight months old, and he's wearing two-year-old's clothes; nobody could believe it. But maybe we'd better not let that out; they'll be telling us next that nuclear is *good* for us!" For the first time since the Alliance people had known him, Neil Brafford permitted himself to laugh.

Crossing the railroad yards, we had a look at the tailings pile and the abandoned mill that the TVA was ordered to "decommission"—remarkably enough, the first such cleanup ever ordered in this country—but despite the obvious need for haste, nothing has been done, in part because no one really knows how to accomplish it. The area is now surrounded by new chain-link fence brandishing signs reading CAUTION: RADIOACTIVE MATERIALS and NO TRESPASSING. "Used to be just that little cattle fence you see inside there," Neil Brafford said. Even the new fence was not childproof, and we trespassed easily past the chain on the new gate, walking down to Cottonwood Creek and crossing its strange red water on a plank in order to climb the tailings pile on the far side. For many years, the Braffords said, the pile was simply a huge dune of "sand" where all the Edgemont schoolchildren came to play; a much larger pile was visible, not far downriver.

"These sand piles are only a couple hundred yards from the river bank," Neil said, "and the flood waters get to 'em every spring. Carries that stuff right downriver to the reservoir, maybe beyond."

"When we were growing up here," Susie said, "we'd come

on over after school and roll around in the piles, roll right down into that creek there—splosh!—and swim in the little tailings pond, and nobody never come out from the mill and run us off. One day one girl went all the way under, got some in her eyes and ran home crying. We used to bury kids up to their necks in this damned stuff—just let 'em *sit* there!" Susie Brafford laughed, a little startled, but the laugh was bitter. "I remember once I had a bad cut on my leg when I was swimming here." She shrugged, glancing at her brother. Both looked somber. "We have a history of cancer in our family, too."

Neil and Susie will take their families out of Edgemont as soon as they are able to afford it; their mother, who is very upset about the shadow on her grandchildren, will remain behind, since in her case, there is not so much to be gained by leaving. "When I quit this Burlington division, I lose my seniority, and I don't know yet what I'm going to do or where I'm going. All I know is, it won't be anywhere near uranium mining." Neil Brafford sighed. "Edgemont was the town where I wanted to live, but not no more."

• • •

Indian peoples who lived in the Black Hills before the arrival of the Lakota carved beautiful signs into the rock of Craven Canyon. Hoping to see these ancient petroglyphs before they disappeared amidst the mining, we drove northwest on the dirt roads into the hills, where the high rangeland parted by deep canyons of dark pines sloped away westward, down into Wyoming. On both sides of the track, exploratory drilling holes made by Union Carbide rose in barren hillocks like huge prairie-dog mounds; a local geologist has informed the Alliance that more than twelve thousand of these holes have been dug in the southern hills in the last few years. Most of them are still emitting radon, since the state had no capping law until 1975 and no enforcement of that law until three years later. In 1980, there were only two inspectors in the state, both of them answerable to a state government that takes its orders from the industry, and Kerr-McGee, BHA has discovered, dug its exploratory holes north of the Black Hills on a permit obtained through the testimony of a state inspector who lied about conducting the necessary inspection.

Although its lease area lies on public land, Union Carbide had fenced off the broad mud road that its machines have made on the floor of Craven Canyon; to see the petroglyphs, we had to descend from the rimrock above, clambering down steep canyon sides of pine and juniper. Though the canyon was still tight and wintry, spring lilies—small white ones and soft pale blues—were abundant on the lower slopes ("South Dakota flower!" Vivian said proudly) and I picked up a fresh tail feather of a ruffed grouse that glistened with the light rain of the morning. Near the foot of the slope was a group of boulders so harmoniously composed that they might have been set there for ceremonial purposes, and from the canyon floor rose a strange round dome of rock and pine. Surely the two arrangements of wild rock had attracted the makers of the petroglyphs, and perhaps they had also attracted Union Carbide's men who, with the whole canyon at their disposal, had chosen a point just between these places to bulldoze and blast and bore into the earth. In August 1979, Union Carbide's license from the U.S. Forest Service to dig up Craven Canyon without preparing an environmental impact statement was successfully contested by the BHA; until this technicality is straightened out, the company has withdrawn all its machinery, leaving behind raw scars and rubble piles, tin shacks, and fencing, and a state-federal dispute about who should pay the costs of cleaning up. Behind the fencing, on the rock face of the strange dome, we found the petroglyphs— the ancient thunderbird, which is also known in Asia, and a strange, graceful form with finlike wings that looks very like a whale from the distant sea.

· · ·

The antinuclear movement, which has weakened the market for uranium, and legal pressure brought by the Black Hills Alliance and other environmental groups have persuaded Gulf, Kerr-McGee, and certain other corporations to give up their exploration permits in South Dakota until such time as the federal government might restore the nuclear industry to financial health. Union Carbide and the TVA, however, are continuing uranium exploration in the Black Hills, in the apparent expectation of a healthy uranium market in years to come.

    During the 1970's, the Indians had organized to resist the unrestrained despoliation of their lands, but their resolve was weakened by their poverty, and in 1980, the Northern Cheyenne, who had canceled all energy leases seven years before, opened their reservation once again for energy development. With the advent of the Reagan administration, and its brutal cuts in federal assistance to the poor, reservations all over the country became vulnerable to the kind of exploitation that no other areas would permit. The proposed sites for spent nuclear fuel repositories, for example, were mostly on or near Indian territory— one was on Yakima treaty land, thirteen miles west of the Hanford Nuclear reservation, in Washington; and others in Nevada, Utah, and South Dakota (near Edgemont, in the southern Black Hills) were a direct threat to Ute, Navajo, and Lakota populations. Meanwhile, a chemical dump site had been established on ceded lands adjoining the Umatilla reservation, in Oregon, and the huge toxic waste disposal firm in Houston, Browning-Ferris Industries, was investigating dump sites on Chemehuevi lands on the desert border of California and Arizona and also on lands of the Duckwater Shoshone in central Nevada, the Northern Cheyenne in southeast Montana, and even the small Cherokee reservation in the mountains of North Carolina. In 1983, the useless Tellico Lake, which had drowned the sacred valley of the Cherokee, was proposed as a chemical dump site by the TVA.

· 8 ·

AT THE
WESTERN GATE

The most prominent point on the California coast is a rocky headland thrust from the base of the Santa Ynez Mountains into the rough Pacific that has been known since Spanish days as Point Concepcion. For many centuries before that, it was Humqaq, or Tolakwe, the "Western Gate" of indigenous peoples of south-central California, where all new life entered the world and from where the dead departed to the land of the dead on the far side of the sea, an Indian named Maria Solares told the anthropologist John Harrington, who studied this culture between 1912 and 1928. "Three days after a person has been buried the soul comes up out of the grave in the evening. . . . The soul goes first to Point Concepcion, which is a wild and stormy place. . . . In ancient times no one ever went near Humqaq; they only went near there to make sacrifices at a great *shawil* shrine. There is a place at Humqaq below the cliff that can only be reached by rope, and there is a pool of water there like a basin, into which fresh water continually drips. And there in the stone can be seen the footprints of women and children. There the spirit of the dead bathes and paints itself. Then it sees a light to the westward and goes toward it through the air, and thus reaches the land of Shimilaqsha."[*]

Because the Western Gate was threatened by the proposed construction of a huge liquid natural gas (LNG) terminal that would obliterate the silence, solitude, and sacred state of this remote promontory, Point Concepcion became a symbol for Indians all across America, who were waiting to see if the American Indian Religious Freedom Act, signed on August 11, 1978, by President Carter, had any more meaning than the hundreds of other agreements with the Indians that the federal government ignored.[†] In the course of the confrontation, it came to light that the scarily volatile and dangerous LNG (natural gas cooled to

[*]From a manuscript in the Smithsonian Institution. See also Peter Nabokov, "Chumash: The Rediscovery of an Indian Nation," in *Santa Barbara Magazine*, Fall 1980, and Alfred Kroeber's *Handbook* (1925, cited in Chapter 6). Numerous papers are available on the culture, cosmology, and rock art of the Chumash people.

[†]"That henceforth it shall be the policy of the United States to protect and preserve for American Indians their inherent right of freedom to believe, express, and exercise . . . traditional religions . . . including but not limited to access to sites, use and possession of sacred objects, and the freedom to worship through ceremonials and traditional rites."

– 260 degrees Fahrenheit and compressed to one six-hundredth of its normal volume) was to be brought here from Indonesia and unloaded directly on this rugged coast, even though the explosion of an LNG tanker, by conservative estimate, would create a fireball twenty miles long and five miles wide. The four storage tanks, each thirteen stories high, were to be constructed in the immediate area of four earthquake faults that are defined as "active," including the recently discovered Arroyo Central Fault, which lies directly underneath the proposed site. In a staff report issued in September 1978, the Federal Energy Regulatory Commission (FERC) declared that "Point Concepcion must be eliminated as an LNG site because active faults exist on and adjacent to the proposed site." Since the location was also of archeological and religious importance, and since "severe" wind and sea conditions would make the unloading from the cumbersome supertankers very dangerous, the report concluded that "the case against Point Concepcion is unassailable."

Despite these excellent arguments and others (including the prevalent opinion that no such "facility" was really needed) the huge power consortium led by Pacific Gas and Electric (see Chapter 9) called Western LNG Associates, with the nervous "conditional" approval of the state Public Utilities Commission (PUC) and Governor Jerry Brown, persisted in its intention to build its $600-million terminal on this site, which it had leased from California Edison. Should its application be turned down, Western LNG declared, it would take its business out of the state entirely, thereby threatening California with the same shortage scares that oil and timber corporations have employed in recent years to bully the public into acceptance of their swollen profits. Apparently the Indonesian dictatorship, in dire need of income from the U.S. business interests whose investments it protects, was in a hurry, and the Point Concepcion terminal could be completed—and show a profit—faster than the other sites, but in view of the great risks involved, such considerations did not seem to justify the consortium's insistence on this site. Western LNG denied that the American Indian Religious Freedom Act applied to Point Concepcion, and turned to the federal government for a decision; the energy consortium knew that for political reasons having to do with Indonesia, the White House would support the project. The Department of Energy and the Air Force (which at one point warned that space shuttle and missile operations at Vandenberg Air Force Base made the proximity of the terminal too dangerous, then reversed itself just three weeks later) also supported it, and the DOE would probably make the final determination in the matter. Should the department use its powerful authorizing legislation to overrule its own commission (FERC) on the grounds of national emergency and decide in favor of the big power companies, then once again the federal laws to protect the Indians and the environment would be flouted by the government itself.

Tolakwe is the site of a prehistoric settlement, 40,000 to perhaps 100,000 years old: a scraping tool, discovered twenty-five feet below the surface in an early excavation for the terminal, and dating from 13,500 years ago, is similar to much earlier tools found at inland sites. At least one archeologist has suggested that people may have occupied this coast as early as 100,000 B.C. (a skull tentatively dated at 48,000 B.C.—the oldest known at present from North America—was found a few years ago at Del Mar, north of San Diego), and it is generally agreed that there have been at least five villages on this site in the last seven thousand years. Yet in the spring of 1978, Western LNG—without bothering to obtain either PUC approval or a county permit, and without preparing an environmental impact statement, consulting the Indians as to sacred sites (although worried Indians were attending the PUC hearings), or paying any noticeable attention to the state Native American Heritage Act, which protects ancient sites from "severe and irreparable damage"—dug two enormous trenches within thirty yards of a known site and just downhill from the graves of seven Chumash chiefs. This secretive and arbitrary move, and especially "the backhoeing of our ancestors' graves," incensed the remnant Chumash of the coast, who are the "Keepers of the Western Gate," and who, like all Indians, bitterly resent any transgression of ancestral burial grounds.

Strong feelings about the Western Gate have survived the harsh subjugations by the Spanish missions as well as the more casual repressions that came after, as this beautiful and fertile coast that had supported one of the great Indian civilizations of North America passed without recompense into white hands. "There is no group in the state that once held the importance of the Chumash concerning which we know so little," wrote the anthropologist Alfred Kroeber in 1918, unaware that John Harrington was already compiling massive testimony from the last "old ones." The Indian bands that made Juan Cabrillo welcome on this coast (now lumped together as "the Chumash") once formed an advanced and sophisticated society scattered across five thousand square miles of mountains, coastal plain, and large offshore islands of what is now the Santa Barbara Channel; they had seagoing canoes, an efficient economy, and a precise cosmology revolving around the observation of the winter solstice in the so-called "Condor Cave," far back in the hot chaparral-choked mountains of the Coast Range, where a ray of sunlight, striking a point on the stone floor, would isolate that moment when the sun was farthest southward and had to be summoned by ritual and prayer back toward the north; much of this cosmology was painted on cave walls, in what has been called "the finest example of prehistoric cave art in the United States." This was the culture that astonished Cabrillo in 1542, although not until a century later would the Spanish return to stay, and not until the late eighteenth century was the Franciscan mission system established that enslaved, chastised, and all but destroyed a civilized people whose main principles of law were justice, kindness, tolerance, and understanding. In the 1830's, the mission system ended, by which time the broken and disheartened Indians were willing to cooperate in any way with the white men coming from the east, so long as some sort of land and livelihood could be assured them. By the terms of the Fort Tejon Treaty of 1851, they were relieved of almost all their native earth, excepting a tract of perhaps a million acres. The U.S. government now declares that this treaty was never signed by President Fillmore nor ratified by the Senate; since the treaty has mysteriously disappeared, the Indians have no legal claim on that tract of land. As "Chumash," they are now confined to ninety-nine acres of the Santa Ynez reservation near Santa Barbara.

Contemptuously referred to by the nineteenth-century settlers as "Diggers," and accepting the poor opinion in which they were held, the Indians tried their best to become invisible in the white society, and the white men scarcely knew they were still there until the middle of this century. "When we were children there was a lot of prejudice against Indians," says Madeleine Hall, whose great-great-grandfather helped build the original Franciscan mission, and whose son, Kote Lotah, is a spiritual leader, "and people used to pass themselves off as something else, like Mexicans. It was like an insult to be called Indians, and whites would insult us. . . . I'm proud of what I am but we used to be kind of afraid before. . . ." Nevertheless, a few stubborn traditionals had continued to keep what was most precious in their culture from contamination, and when the Point Concepcion episode began, the whites were astonished by their vehemence. "If that place were destroyed tomorrow," Kote Lotah told reporters, "I feel so strongly about it, I would want to die today so that I could pass through the Western Gate." Another Indian declared, "We do not invite violence; we will not pick up a gun. But if it's a confrontation that they want, they will get it. Every Indian in this country knows what's goin' on here; if one drop of Indian blood is spilled, that's it. There'll be more Indians here than they can shake a stick at."*

In early May of 1978, twenty-five Indians invaded the proposed terminal site at Point Concepcion, from which they have been barred in recent years by the utility companies; they announced their intention to lie down in the path of the earth-moving machinery rather than permit further disruption of the sacred ground. When they were not immediately arrested, as they had expected, they set up a camp, and Western LNG, fearing public sympathy for the Indians, left them alone; in July, a PUC ruling that granted the consortium a conditional approval to proceed with the Point Concepcion site, pending the completion of seismic reports and other requirements, also granted the Indians access to the area for spiritual purposes. Meanwhile, a boycott of the LNG operation by local archeologists, who sympathized with the outrage of the Indians over the damage done to the sacred sites "behind our backs" (and whose presence was required before digging could proceed), held up the trenching, and therefore the completion of the seismic report, without which the terminal could not be approved by the PUC. For the next six months, things were more or less at a standstill, with time on the Indians' side. The "spiritual encampment" (all liquor, drugs, and firearms forbidden) at Shisholop Village, named for the ancient Shisholop, or Landing Place, had grown to about one hundred people, and was in clear violation of trespass and zoning laws, but the power com-

*Articles by Herb Fox and others in the Santa Barbara *News and Review*, beginning in 1978, give a detailed history of the Point Concepcion struggle and provide some of the quotations in this chapter.

panies, announcing a belated wish to establish a "relationship" with the Indians, did not force their eviction until late February of 1979, after a young Indian who had been found drinking was shot through the foot. The bad publicity surrounding this senseless shooting by visiting AIM "security men" had broken the Indians' own rules about firearms and weakened public sympathy for the cause.

A leader in the Point Concepcion struggle was Archie Fire Lame Deer, a Lakota medicine man who is married to a Chumash and serves the band as a spiritual adviser. Lame Deer, whom I first met in 1978, had been kind enough to include me in a sweat-lodge purification in the hills behind the town, and meanwhile he and others at the Santa Barbara Indian Center informed me about the crisis. Although the Indians are astonished by the white man's folly in planning such a "facility" in such a place, they have limited their protest to the transgression of sacred ground. According to Lame Deer, one of the many Indians from other parts of North America who support the fight to preserve the Western Gate, Point Concepcion is the most sacred site in all of California, and though he is anxious to avoid the sort of violent confrontation that occurred in 1973 with the occupation of Wounded Knee, he has joined Kote Lotah and others in a vow to give his life, if necessary, in its defense. "Indians come from South Dakota, Montana, Oregon, and throughout the nation to be present in support of our Chumash brothers and sisters, and in support of our Mother Earth," Lame Deer says. "We formed a confederation to offer protection of our holy lands. If we can't count on the state government to protect our religious rights, then we are willing to protect Mother Earth ourselves from further desecration, and the people who came for the conference will return."

Passing through Santa Barbara in the spring of 1979, I visited the Indian Center to find out how the cause was going. Lee Dixon, a young Luiseño from southern California, felt that the eviction from Shisholop Village had actually improved Indian morale, which had been damaged by the factionalism introduced by the AIM "warriors": these people had ignored and even disobeyed the wishes of the traditional Chumash elders, who now demanded that they leave the area.

When the Indians dismantled Shisholop Village in obedience to a court order, they had left behind the central cook shed and two sweat lodges as well as certain religous objects that Lame Deer was anxious to retrieve. I offered to take him out there in my truck, and early next morning I picked him up at his house in downtown Santa Barbara. During the journey north on the coast highway, he told me more about the struggle, and how he himself had come to be here.

. . .

Archie Fire, at forty-three, is a very big man with a bearish walk who wears his long hair in a braid. He has a melodious, resonant, sad voice, and something sad is seen around the eyes; but otherwise, his big-featured Lakota face is without expression until it opens in a sudden smile. During the journey north on the coast highway, he told me some legends and stories of the Minnecojou, the most traditional band of the Lakota, or Teton Sioux, who once lived in the region of the Rapid River just east of the Black Hills, and whose lands have mostly disappeared beneath the pavement and environs of Rapid City, South Dakota. (His great-grandfather was that Minnecojou chief who joined forces with Sitting Bull's Hunkpapa and the Oglala of Crazy Horse in the battle at Greasy Grass Creek, as Little Big Horn is known to the Plains Indians.) Archie Fire was raised in South Dakota on the Rosebud reservation, and his father was the late John Fire Lame Deer, a well-known medicine man who came here to Point Concepcion four years ago and renewed the Western Gate with prayer and blessing. Lame Deer said that his Lakota friends were also sons of medicine people; even though their religion had been prohibited and hidden for many years, all these boys had wanted to be medicine men, not chiefs. But today, he said, every one of them was dead from alcohol or alcohol-caused accidents or diseases, and he himself had a long career of alcohol and prison before finding the will to return to Indian way.

Although Lame Deer was arrested in 1973 for sending medical supplies to Wounded Knee, he has not aligned himself with AIM or become involved in political confrontations. "I just don't want to be where Indians are fighting one another," Lame Deer says. Nevertheless, he feels that AIM has accomplished a good deal in giving Indian people a "new sense of themselves," and that it was now abandoning the armed militancy that had made it so vulnerable to FBI infiltration and self-destructive violence. When we had first talked, in 1978, AIM's leaders were mostly in jail or restricted by parole conditions or indictments, and in Lame Deer's opinion, they had failed to train able young people to take their places. Referring to the AIM warriors who had imposed themselves on the camp at Point Concepcion, Lame Deer said that AIM cannot control these "intertribals," who are not responsible to any traditional Indian community and who wander around "living off the struggle"; he does not think AIM should be blamed for every angry, alienated Indian (or would-be Indian) who stirs up trouble in its name.

Where the coast highway heads inland north of Gaviota Beach, we turned off on the private road that follows the sea cliffs under the Santa Ynez mountains, crossing the Hollister Ranch toward the broad headland at Point Concepcion. Since the February eviction, Indians had been limited to visits during daylight hours; no more than six people on a list of twenty-four names were permitted through the checkpoints in one day. Lame Deer identified me as "Jim Quis Quis," an Indian from San Diego, with whom the guards were unfamiliar. "You look kind of like him," he said to me laconically, when we went through.

The narrow road crossed a sunny plateau between mountains and sea cliffs. Cool ocean air tossed the fresh yellows of wild mustard, one of the many plants still eaten here by Indians; in the liquid light, the harsh notes of the redwings were softened by the sweet song of the western meadowlark. This winter there had been ample rain, and the grass was rich and thick and green, with heavy seedheads, flowing away in waves under the wind; Archie Fire contemplated the grass, remarking finally that it reminded him of spring at home in the Dakotas.

Offshore, the ocean was clear blue, with shining patches of brown kelp and bright whitecaps beyond; Point Concepcion is the meeting place of two strong offshore currents, and its rough seas have been well known to navigators since the Indian canoes traded up and down the coast. To the southwest lay the high mass of Santa Cruz Island, in the Santa Barbara Channel, where the later stage of the Chumash trading culture may have had its start. Lame Deer explained how in the old days, the young warriors being initiated into the tribe would be dropped at sea and made to swim ashore through the cold realm of the great white shark, a sacred creature to the coastal Indians.

Followed by the blue vehicles of the guards, who drove up

onto an eminence to keep an eye on us, we inspected from above the great trenches dug by Western LNG the year before. The company claimed that the trenches had been dug in order to trace the earthquake fault line discovered in a gorge only a few hundred yards from the proposed site, but the Indians suspected that excavations so enormous were not necessary for this purpose, that they were actually intended to serve as foundations for the terminal, which will bury the ancient village sites under heavy concrete.

Lee Dixon's uncle, Therman McCormick, a Luiseño elder from the mountains north of San Diego, has pointed out that the coastal Indians were bands of a single Indian nation whose lands extended from San Diego to well north of Santa Barbara. (The "Chumash Tribe" is a Bureau of Indian Affairs designation of recent years: "We didn't think of ourselves as Chumash," says Conchita Perez. "Everybody was just Indian. The BIA has to determine who's who and what's what, so they decided we were Chumash.") Point Concepcion was sacred ground for all these bands; Indians as far away as Utah and Arizona knew about "That Place," he has said. "We get everything from there. It means more to us than anywhere else, because it's in our prayer." It was a meeting place and shrine for all bands of the tribe, with ritual bathing that continued into the twentieth century, and spring solstice ceremonies at Shisholop, or Landing Place, which gave its name to the "village" established in 1978. There are references to Point Concepcion and Shisholop in the texts of Harrington, the main ethnographer of the Chumash, and references to the spring solstice ceremonies in the Spanish records. Chumash elder Victor Lopez, a tart old man who had no time to meet me but was happy to talk over the phone, said that the Spaniards had respected the Indian religion, despite their exploitation of the Indian slaves for both rancherias and missions, and referred to this place as Tierra de las Animas, the Land of Souls. Mr. Lopez, who first visited "That Place" when he was nine years old, was told by his uncle that he was being taken to see a temple. When he got there, he remembers, he had to "pee-pee," after which he asked his uncle where "the temple" was; he was very embarrassed when his uncle pointed at the ground and said, "Right here."

Victor Lopez, although raised a Catholic, had learned a lot from an old Indian who turned up outside his mountain tent when he was working for the U.S. Forest Service in the Los Padres National Forest of the Coast Range (the last redoubt of the California condor, at one time the Indians' most sacred bird). This man, Joachim de Justo, who died in 1939 at the estimated age of 139, passed on to him the ancient traditions of their people, saying that 25,000 years ago, four continents had been known to the wandering Indians, and that this Red Continent was later invaded by the White Continent of Europe; to these "Immigrant Americans," Victor Lopez informed me, "the only good Injun was a dead one, y'know. Must have 331 treaties with us all across the country, and not a one of 'em was any good—all broke!" It was Lopez, as I later learned, who had accosted John Harrington in the course of one of his local excavations, saying, "You already took the land away from the people, and now you're digging for the bones, and pretty soon you'll dig for the souls. . . . Of course, the immigrants have that as a way of study. They want to learn the ways of the dead, the other culture, yet their forefathers didn't want to learn it. They killed the Indians and *then* tried to find out."

In recent decades, California Edison has denied the Indians access to the Western Gate, but since 1974, when John Fire Lame Deer renewed Tolakwe with his blessing, "from the mountain ridges to the sea"—his son indicated the extent of it with a wave of his big hand—sweat lodges have been maintained here, and also a pit high up in the mountains that is used by young Indians in the vision quest. Lame Deer had come out today to renew Tolakwe once again, and he led the way on foot down past the remains of Shisholop Village, where a solitary wickiup, or "tepee," and the mess hall are the only structures that still stand.

The encampment was situated on a grassy canyon flat above a wooded creek that winds down from the mountains; from a sweat lodge beside the creek he retrieved deer antlers and a tarpaulin. Pushing through a rank undergrowth of sticky thistle that has grown up since the Indians departed, we followed tracks of a raccoon up the quiet stream to a second sweat lodge in a copse of oak and willow. Medicine pouches belonging to Kote Lotah and to Ernie Peters, an AIM spiritual leader to whom Lame Deer had given certain teachings, still hung from a small staff outside the entrance. This place was sheltered from the hard sea wind, and the heat was quiet; everything was still. In hauling back the heavy tarpaulins that insulated the low round hut and its pit of fire-heated stones, we disturbed the soft nest of a deer mouse and the shelter of a skink with a bright blue tail: like the rank thistles, the wild creatures had come back very quickly.

· · ·

Lame Deer was carrying the pipe that I had seen the year before at the sweat ceremony in the hills behind Santa Barbara, a red pipestone bowl that is fitted to a long straight stem of white ash decorated with faded beadwork; a feathered tamper, sweetgrass, and tobacco are carried with the pipe pieces in a beautiful soft buckskin bag. "There is no such thing as a 'peace pipe' or a 'war bonnet,' " he murmured. "There is only the sacred pipe, the sacred headdress." Once the lodge was stripped, he sprinkled some tobacco, explaining that the wind and sun would purify this place of all bad feelings.

Lame Deer believes that Point Concepcion is a "power place." Here his father had called to him from the other world, and here Therman McCormick had heard voices of the Ancestors. As Kote Lotah has said, "With our prayers and with our presence, we bring back the spirits of long ago. We've brought this land back to life." In the words of Kote Lotah's mother, "You wouldn't believe that peace and contentment you feel when you go out there. It's a tremendous feeling you get inside to know you're right there where your ancestors have been and where the spirits go through . . . to the other world. I walked out there to where they dug the trenches and I felt just like bawling to see what they did. I had this weird feeling that bad things were happening there on account of the digging. . . . That is our sacred ground and if they put that liquified gas stuff there, something bad is going to happen, you can feel it."

Lame Deer took pains to repeat his ceremony of respect at Shisholop Village, where we stood facing high feather poles ceremonially decorated with beads and feathers, hawk and owl heads, tobacco packets, and black, white, yellow, and red streamers, which are the colors of the four directions. The warm grass breathed, and meadowlark songs came down the wind on the scents of sweet anise, sagebrush, and the sea. "Oh, I feel good today!" Archie exclaimed, with that sudden grin that breaks his stony Lakota face like a splash in a still pond.

From Shisholop, old dirt tracks climb onto the ridges of the Santa Ynez Mountains. On the far side of the mountains was Lompoc Prison, where Lame Deer had set up a sweat lodge for Indian prisoners, including the AIM leader, Leonard Peltier; the Lompoc "sweat" is one of several he has started in both state and federal prisons. Indian prisoners, he says, are especially eager to find their way back to the Old Ways religion that, in the words of Therman McCormick, "makes an Indian feel like he's living again." In this ceremony of renewal, the naked participants are cleansed by the scalding steam he calls "Grandfather's breath," the heat energy that returns all who breathe it to unity with the Grandfather Sun and Mother Earth.

The sweat ceremony is the oldest ritual among all North American Indian people, Lame Deer said, and the most fundamental one to an understanding of their religions, but very few Indians today know the proper construction of a sweat lodge, far less the significant ceremonial songs. "Our rituals cannot be done properly in English, which is the way that they are done by most of the so-called medicine men. And a lot of these other guys, they're just fooling around; they don't even know that a song they sing might cause the death of a man; sometimes they go in there and sing the AIM song! So I'm trying to reestablish the sweat lodge as the foundation, right in the family; it isn't necessary to have a medicine man so long as there is sincerity and purification. Families break up because they do not pray together the Indian way, in the circular shape— they go into those square buildings with straight lines that are not natural to us. Our grandfathers had very strong hearts, from the heat of the sweats, then plunging into the icy water, and they lived well over a hundred years; today the average Indian dies at forty-four."

Lame Deer regrets that the American Indian Movement mainly neglected the sweat lodge ceremony in favor of the more colorful and dramatic sun dance, which is usually performed improperly, he says, and therefore lacks real spiritual foundation. "You're supposed to do the Sun Dance when the cherries are turning red; most of 'em do it when the cherries have already fallen. You have to pay attention to the time of year, and the *feelings* of that year, and to the wind and weather, and the position of the morning stars—Venus, Mercury, Pluto, Jupiter, sometimes Mars. The positions change every three months, so that all get a chance to be the morning star, and the evening star."

As a traditional, Lame Deer knows that the great disruption that was visited upon the Indian culture for three centuries can never be undone. "We cannot go backwards," he has said. "Everything will run over us, people will run over us, our own people will run over us. . . . We have to leave some of the old ways behind." Like most Indians, however, he is appalled and depressed by the white man's implacable assault on the natural world of clean air and clean water that sustains his life; he believes in the development of solar energy, the "gift from the Grandfather Sun," that even now was warming the cold air off the ocean all around us.

•   •   •

Winding up into the canyons of the foothills, the steep, rough tracks had led us far back into the mountains, though we were still in full sight of the sea. Where there was water, the canyons were shaded by the live oak forest, and near a small brook, wild honey bees went spinning in swift golden circles through the sun and shade of a huge tree. Lame Deer showed me the small sweat lodge of white willow saplings used by Lee Dixon and other young Indians who came here under his guidance to perform their vision quest. From this place we climbed on foot out of the trees of the arroyo, making our way up a steep hillside of wild flowers to a grassy saddle between mountains that overlooked all of Tolakwe, far below. Lame Deer moved swiftly for a big man, and when we reached the saddle, we were breathing hard; we took a moment to observe the silent circles of a red-tailed hawk and the blue triangle of ocean between hills. Then he led me to the vision pit, a one-man hole dug into the hillside, with an earth seat and a small sun shelter of saplings bound with reeds.

"Before choosing this place," Lame Deer said, "I rode a horse all around these mountains. How the wind comes is important, because the wind brings spiritual forces from all over the country, bad as well as good, and it can disturb you if it is too strong." Opening his tobacco bundle, he purified the vision pit with smoke from a braided hank of sweetgrass, after which he assembled the stone pipe. We smoked the pipe together, facing successively in the four directions, giving thanks in our own ways to the Creator, to the Great Unseen, to *Mitakuye Iyasin!*—All Our Relations!—which means not merely our own families, but relationships with all things on this splendid earth. Lame Deer stood for a long time against the California sky, chanting in the Siouan tongue, his big voice rolling down the mountain to the seaside grasslands that reminded him so much of the Great Plains.

A few years ago, not long after his father's death, when Lame Deer climbed onto this mountain on a vision quest, clouds immediately swept up the valley, filling it to just the level of the pit; on this white cloud bed, like a snow field, there was a strange reflection of the moon. A deer came straight up to the pit and gazed at him and went away, and then his father appeared: this was his vision. Encouraging him to go on with his work, John Fire told him to leave the pit immediately and return down the hill, although he had only been there a few hours. On the way (he pointed out the place when we descended), he had slipped into a hole and fallen backwards in his heavy buffalo robe, so hard that he had found himself half-stuck into the ground. Here this huge Indian from the Great Plains had sat laughing in the moonlight, gazing out over Tolakwe and the sea.

· · ·

The Indians won the battle for Point Concepcion. The spiritual camp and the publicity that helped delay approval of the site for two and a half years allowed time for the Public Utility Commission, Governor Brown, and even Pacific Gas and Electric (a Western LNG partner, and the largest public utility in America) to come to their senses and withdraw support for the ill-conceived terminal. This change of heart, in 1981, had little to do with the loss of a valuable archeological site, far less deference to an Indian religion; what turned the battle was the gas price deregulation of 1980 which quickly led to profitable domestic production of natural gas. With the end of the "emergency," shipments from halfway around the world were no longer needed, and Western

LNG gave up its contractual rights to Indonesia's reserves. In April 1983, however, I was told by Archie Fire that the energy and utility corporations had new plans for an oil storage depot in the area, and were seeking out Indians and whites who were willing to testify that the Western Gate had lost all religious significance for the Indian people of southern California.

· 9 ·

EAST OF
MOUNT SHASTA

On Easter Sunday, 1979, I drove north from Point Concepcion to Santa Maria and the Salinas Valley. Everywhere in the green hills, wild ceanothus was in deep blue blosson, with red poppy, yellow broom, and blue amaryllis in the pastures. South of King City, slow, mantis-like machines were sucking the last oil out of the weakened earth of California; the highway traversed a road across the valley that is still known as Wild Horse Road.

In the Gavilan Mountains on the east side of the valley, I picked up Craig Carpenter, who was wanted for kidnapping in northern California and was lying low. Against their mother's will, he had taken two Indian children to a sacred mountain for religious purposes; when the children returned, the mother withdrew all charges and refused to sign any complaint, but the authorities had no wish to forgive this seditious individual who grows most of his own food, owns almost nothing, and refuses to participate in "the American Way of Life."

Although he dislikes the rhetoric and violence associated with AIM, Craig was convinced that the FBI was out to "neutralize" him as an Indian troublemaker, since his name had been mentioned by an FBI informer in the murder trial of AIM organizers Paul Skyhorse and Richard Mohawk two years before. During the Indians of All Tribes occupation of Alcatraz, in 1970, challenging AIM leader Richard Oakes at a rally in Golden Gate Park, Carpenter had attacked Oakes's call to Indians to take up arms—"Go ahead, pick up some guns and see what happens! They'll meet your peashooters with tanks!" Apparently this had been interpreted by some literal-minded informer in the audience as a call for violent insurrection; Craig could think of no other reason that his name could have been associated with the AIM rhetoric that he most deplores.

We crossed the warm hills to San Juan Bautista and on over the Pacheco Pass to the San Joaquin Valley, where we headed north, stopping off for a visit with the mother of the "kidnapped" children along the way. This day was the start of a long circular journey through the West, to the Pit River forests east of Mount Shasta, then north and east across the cold, windy wastes of the Northern Paiute on the Oregon and Idaho borders of Nevada, south into Western Shoshone and far Gosi Ute country of the Great Basin, then east again to the Utes of the High Uintahs of northern Utah; from there we would follow the Rockies south through Colorado to the sage deserts of New Mexico and Arizona—Navajo and Apache, Pueblo and Hopi—continuing west to the Colorado River and the remnant Indian bands of southern California. Carpenter wished to revisit and encourage certain elderly traditionals whom he had not seen since 1969, during the "Traditional Indian Unity Caravan" led by Six Nations spiritual leaders, including Mad Bear Anderson of the Tuscarora, Chief Beeman Logan of the Seneca, and young Chief Tom Porter of Craig's own Mohawk Nation, in an effort to strengthen communication between "the last ones still standing on the land" that had begun at a conference in Henryetta, Oklahoma, the year before. (Indian spokesmen traveled all over the country for the next three years, and many joined in "The Trail of Broken Treaties" march on Washington, D.C., in October, 1972.)

Craig was pleased to hear of my good meeting with Lame Deer at Point Concepcion. "In the sixties," he recalled, "when we had finally established touch with traditional medicine people from coast to coast, the only empty place left on our map was the Sioux Nation. Most of the so-called medicine men were Christian-influenced and showed no interest in what we were trying to do, so that place wasn't filled until I met Archie's father in Los Angeles. Old John was a cantankerous man, but he was a lot of fun, and he was the real thing. He wasn't a miracle worker of the first rank—he recognized that the greatest Sioux medicine man was Victor Youngbear, who came to us later—but John Fire was the first one to stand up with us, and we were grateful to him."

Even in April, the San Joaquin and Sacramento Valleys, with their flat, regimented fields and pesticide-ridden soils, looked bare and desolate, but in late afternoon, north and east of Redding, on steep hillsides parted by swift, sun-filled streams, the redbud and manzanita, dogwood and plum were all in bloom, and in the rich twilight of full spring, a bluebird crossed a meadow of blue lupine and heavy oaks. The road climbed gradually into evergreen forest in the eastern foothills under Mount Shasta, and just at dusk, in soft spring rain, we came down out of the mountains to the forest settlement at Big Bend, on the Pit River.

At Willard Rhoades's house, it was raining hard, and Mildred Rhoades served us a warm supper of stick tea and deer stew. Both Willard and Mildred are wide-eyed, open people who like to laugh,

and both were delighted to see Craig, who had not passed this way in the last ten years. Mildred said fondly, "I thought about you yesterday, and here you are today," and Craig just nodded as if to say, Among Indians, that is how it should be. Willard Rhoades's father was a white who married among the Pit River and was disowned for it by his parents, who shared the violent anti-Indian emotions of all the early settlers in this region. "My dad was more Indian than my mother, Indian way," he said, shrugging his shoulders. Craig likes to say that "Indian way" is a matter of attitude, not a matter of blood, and Willard Rhoades is the spiritual leader of the eleven autonomous bands of the Pit River Nation, having inherited the teachings of his uncle, Albert Thomas, a Pit River-Wintu medicine man who was also the teacher of Calvin Rube.*
Mildred Rhoades, a Wintu who has joined wholeheartedly in the struggle of her husband's people, had spoken with bitter eloquence of the treatment received by Indian war veterans: "That uniform didn't mean a thing to the Veterans Administration, not as long as it had an Injun in it." But now she laughed with real delight as her husband told us his fine Coyote stories, although she must have heard them many times.

"Old Coyote," Willard sighed, looking at me. "He's always ruining things by trying to make things better—dams and food preservatives and stuff—and he just makes everything worse. Before that Shasta Dam was built, we had big salmon over here; our boy Squally caught one nearly as big as he was, couldn't hardly pack it home. Now that's all gone." Willard sighed. "Them dams took our water—they dried up the rivers and just ruined our fishing. There's plenty changes in this land since I was a boy."

The best known of the small Indian bands along Pit River is probably the Achomawi, and this name is sometimes used for the whole nation; the Achomawi are celebrated in the writings of Jaime de Angulo. ("He stretched the truth and shrunk it, both," says Willard Rhoades, "but it makes good readin'.") Otherwise, the painful story of this people, hidden away in remote forested mountains, is almost unknown to white Americans, although very well known to other Indians as one of the last identifiable Indian communities in America that still occupies its aboriginal land and knows

*See Chapter 6, "The High Country."

its boundaries and has never signed a treaty ceding title to its territories.*

Originally, said Willard Rhoades, the territory of Is-s, the People—they were known to the Maidu as "Snow Maidu" or "Snow People"—extended eastward from Mount Shasta to Blue Jay Mountain to Mount Lassen to Horse Lake to Goose Lake to Medicine Lake and back to Shasta—about one hundred square miles, or 3.5 million acres. Most of this land is administered by the U.S. Forest Service and could be transferred to the rightful owners with a minimum of legal complication; furthermore, the Pit River claim to aboriginal title is not seriously contested in the courts. Yet the USFS continues to lease this land to private corporations, and does so without the smallest compensation of the rightful owners, who may be the most poverty-stricken group in the United States.

The man who knows most about his people's struggle is Raymond Lego (pronounced *Lay*-gu) at Montgomery Creek, a few miles away over the mountain. In a fresh morning after heavy rain, with the evergreen needles shimmering silver in the forest, we followed a timber road south from Big Bend past a hillside clearing marked with a sign reading LEGITIMATE PIT RIVER INDIAN LAND. Not far below, a muddy track leads up the hill to Lego's house, where a crew of dogs swarmed out to harangue the strangers. Raymond Lego came out, too, and looked me over; recognizing Craig, he relaxed a little and invited us into the house. Lego is a small, wiry man in his early sixties, with silver-black hair, worn short, that seems to stick up out of sheer exasperation; as spokesman for the five "legitimate" bands which are still "standing on the land"—holding out, that is, for their aboriginal title to the land instead of accepting the government settlement that will take these rights away forever—he is extremely busy, and he said so. Though restless, he had a lot to tell us, speaking rapidly and bitterly with an articulate, sharp tongue. In the end, his manner softened,

*Very little has been written on the Pit River people of today. For general background see "Achomawi," in A. L. Kroeber, *Handbook*; Vine Deloria, Jr., *God Is Red* (New York, 1973); George Ballis, *The Dispossessed* (a published film script; Piedmont, Calif., 1970); John Hurst, "Indians Defeated But Won't Yield in Land Struggle," Los Angeles *Times*, September 28, 1980; and various pamphlets issued by the Legitimate Pit River Tribe, Box 52, Montgomery Creek, California.

and eventually we moved from the small sitting room into the kitchen, where Marie Lego offered us a good noon meal as we continued our conversation around the table. "It's really ironic!" Raymond Lego snapped, with a very un-Indian outburst of real pain. "A few raggle-taggle Indians trying to defend the validity of the U.S. Constitution!"

According to "the discovery doctrine," which was accepted by the United States, the Pit River people still have full claim to their land.

> Upon the "discovery" of the Americas, the debate about whether the indigenous peoples were to be recognized as having the rights of humans was resolved in favor of indigenous rights. . . . The doctrine of discovery under international law of that period protected native title to inhabited lands and gave to the "discovering" nation only the exclusive right of acquiring the land from the indigenous owners by consent or after a just war.
>
> From the earliest times, formal treaties were entered into between European governments and native nations. . . . The decisions of the United States Supreme Court, until about 1845, normally applied the existing international law in determining appropriate issues of Indian relations.
>
> Respect for the application of international law in relations with indigenous governments waned rapidly in the latter half of the nineteenth century, yet there was no other body of law to replace it. . . . As a result, Indian nations, communities, or "tribes" are usually not accorded the legal rights and protections accorded to persons and to other legal entities under municipal law. . . . In the United States and perhaps elsewhere there is at least theoretical, limited protection against purely arbitrary action by the government. But, in general, the national government remains quite free to legislate and to act as it wishes in regard to indigenous peoples, their governments and their property.*

In 1848, the United States acquired California from Mexico by the Treaty of Guadalupe Hidalgo, which specified that Indians held title to their lands through "immemorial use and occupancy."

*Statement submitted by Indian Law Resource Center to United Nations Commission on Human Rights, March 2, 1983.

In 1850, a congressional enabling act, recognizing this title, authorized the establishment of treaties with the California tribes, including the peoples known today as the Yurok and the Chumash, but *not* including the small Pit River bands, which were ignored; by the provisions of these eighteen treaties, the Indians exchanged some ninety million acres of good land for about nine million of the worst land that could be found for them. Even so, the citizens of the new state denounced these arrangements as a waste of land, and California's representatives in Washington fought hard against Senate ratification of the treaties, which were subsequently "lost" among the U.S. government archives. A congressional act of 1853 assigned all Indian lands in California to the public domain, and a Land Commission formed to hear any protests or alternative claims was convened that same year in San Diego, the place most distant from those California Indians whose lands were wanted. Though no one told them so, the Pit River bands were authorized to send a delegation for eight hundred miles on foot across unknown country to an unimaginable place to make marks on a "talking leaf" in unknown language in order to claim title to ancestral lands that they did not know were threatened and had never conceived of "owning" in the first place. By failing to appear at San Diego, decreed the government, California's Indians had forfeited their claims to their ancient territories, about seventy percent of which were seized that year without compensation, just as if those "lost" treaties had been ratified; the Snow People, who had never signed a treaty, were lumped in arbitrarily with all the rest.

The fraudulent dealings of 1853 opened the modern history of the Pit Rivers, which had once lived easily on this land, hunting and gathering and fishing. Already Indians were being killed by the rabid whites who were streaming into California in the Gold Rush. "What are the lives of one hundred or one thousand of these savages compared to the life of a single American citizen? We say shoot them down wherever you find them," said an editorial in the *Shasta Courier* in April 1853. Many of the new citizens were taking this advice, and when the Indians fought back with bows and arrows, the U.S. Army was sent in to clean them out. The Army campaigns, which dragged on for over a decade, were led by George Crook, later celebrated as the greatest Indian fighter in U.S. history for his campaigns against the Apache and Lakota;

the first Indian he ever killed was a Pit River, and he carried a Pit River arrowhead in his hip to his dying day. The blue coats were abetted by vigilante elements from the settlements, and in September 1859, the "Pit River Rangers" set fire to a peaceful Indian village just at dawn and slaughtered every person who emerged; in their exuberance, they chopped the heads off women and tossed live Indian children into the flames. That fall, another local bunch, "the Buckskin Men," kidnapped children to be sold off into slavery, and hundreds of people were rounded up and marched to the Round Valley reservation, near the coast, a detention place where thousands of California Indians would perish of white men's diseases. A few Pit Rivers had remained hidden, and others escaped from the camps and made their way home, and in 1867, they fought Crook again from hideouts in the lava badlands near the south fork of the river—what the newspapers called "The Battle of the Infernal Caverns."

In 1860, at Soldier Mountain, a great many of the Achomawi band were slaughtered. "There was a big area over there where the soldiers massacred *all* the Indians—'terminated' 'em, you might say," Raymond Lego said, with a sour smile. "Would have maybe finished 'em off entirely, only finally the settlers called a halt. There was a commercial side, y'see—they wanted the same kind of free labor that settlers were gettin' everywhere else in California." In 1871, the government repudiated the whole concept of treaties, most of which it had already broken; since the Indians who had not been exterminated were now mostly under control, the remnants could be administered by the Department of the Interior as a "natural resource." The next year, however, the Modoc Indians north of Pit River rose in revolt; with the hanging of their leader, Captain Jack, in 1874, the Modoc were shipped off to Oklahoma, and some Pit Rivers were banished with them for good measure. Others were sent over to Eureka on the coast, where for want of a better plan, they were taken out to sea and drowned. In the thirty years that followed the Gold Rush, starvation, disease, and genocide had reduced the once-prosperous Indian population of California (estimated at about 125,000) to less than 20,000 people.

The mighty forests and steep rivers on the east side of Mount Shasta had already attracted the attention of timber and power companies, and the Pacific Gas and Electric Company (PG&E) was exploring the possibility of dams on the Pit River as early as 1901.

By 1906, when the remnant Indians were released from the disease-ridden detention camps—some walked the long, hot, dry two thousand miles from Oklahoma, returning like Pit River salmon to their ancestral streams—the settlers controlled all the land not assigned to the national forests. They had no intention of sharing it with Indians, who were forced to pay for their few small rancherias, and old people today can still remember when whites felt free to shoot down any Indian who got in the way. Settlement increased heavily about 1912, and the settlers were early shareholders in PG&E, which in 1921 obtained a federal license to build the first of seven dams on the Pit River; inevitably, the settlers were bitterly hostile to Indian land claims and the Indians themselves, and even today, justice for Indians is very uncommon in Shasta County. Meanwhile, the U.S. Forest Service, with its power to condemn, was leasing vast tracts of Indian land to the big corporations. The deer and bear were driven away, and the fishing was ruined by the dams, which provided electricity for almost everyone except the rightful inhabitants; the remaining Indians—they now numbered about six hundred—subsisted on their land in utter poverty.

"The white man never cared for land, or deer, or bear," a Wintu woman has said. "When we Indians kill meat, we eat it all up. When we dig roots, we make little holes. We shake down acorns and pine nuts. We don't chop down the trees, we only use deadwood. But the white people plow up the ground, pull down the trees, kill everything. The tree says, Don't. I am sore. Don't hurt me. But they chop it down and cut it up. They blast rocks and scatter them on the ground. How can the spirit of the earth like them?"*

An enabling act of 1928 gave the Pit River the legal right as "American citizens" to sue the government. These suits have been brought irregularly since 1955 (when anthropologist Alfred Kroeber testified to Pit River title rights) and in July 1959, the Indian Claims Commission concluded that 3.4 million acres had been seized unlawfully from the Pit River Nation after 1853. But rather than relinquish a fair part of the public land, both federal and state governments have sought instead to buy off those Indians who would cooperate. In 1936, the Pit River Indians had voted against

*Quoted in *Touch the Earth*, ed. T. C. McLuhan.

the Indian Reorganization Act, which had set up the system of tribal councils under the BIA, but when the smoke cleared, the BIA announced that the Pit River people had endorsed it: in 1963, after a decade of negotiation with BIA-approved Tribal Council lawyers, the government decreed that any value the lands might have was due to the industry of the white man, and that therefore any recompense should be based on the value of the land over a century ago, which would be paid over without interest. It made an offer which worked out to 47.5 cents an acre, and although other California tribes (lumped into two groups, the "Mission Indians"—including the Chumash—and "the Indians of California") were persuaded by the BIA that this was best for them and were desperate enough to accept the offer, the Pit Rivers refused to go along. Led by Lego and the late Chief Ray Johnson, these people decided to reject the offer, despite great pressure from the BIA, which they still believed to be their ally: the bureau did its utmost to persuade the embattled Pit Rivers to accept a compromise settlement, and when this didn't work, they cited their legal guardianship and authority to speak for the Indians, then remanded the Pit River land claims back to the lowest tribunal, represented by the federal Indian Court of Claims.

To rally Indian opposition, Lego ran all over California—"I slept in the canals," he said—but his efforts came too late. "The bill was run through by them sophisticated BIA Indians; what could a few poor raggle-taggles do? We missed out on the first hearings back in Washington, and they wouldn't let us have no transcripts so we could find out who testified to what. We didn't know the legal process, and we still depended on the BIA to keep us up to date on what was happening." He shook his head. "It took us a long time to learn. Them BIA people been the main factor in destroyin' us." Meanwhile, the Indians were being threatened with the "backlash" legislation that would surely ensue from pursuit of their rightful claims, and their own attorneys joined in this subversive chorus, telling them that the government's indecent offer was "a lot better than nothing." When the time came for the tribe to vote, the BIA, anticipating resistance, discouraged a fair turnout by scheduling the voting for Alturas, which lies more than a hundred miles to the northeast, across the Cascade Mountains. Though many Indians pleaded poverty and hardship, no absentee ballots were allowed until those who managed to get themselves to Alturas voted heavily against acceptance of the money, at which point the BIA reversed itself and opened up the voting to absentee ballots from as far away as Oregon. "The bureau finally come up with a twenty-four-vote majority of sellouts and mercenaries," Raymond Lego said, "and that was it—they nailed it down right there."

A hearing before the Indian Claims Commission had been scheduled for Eureka, on the coast, although the Pit Rivers had asked that it be held in the large town of Redding, which was only a quarter of the distance. This request was refused, and a pathetic caravan of Indians in dilapidated cars made its way across the mountains. There they were confronted by retired Senator Arthur Watkins, Republican of Utah, who, in 1946, had introduced the first bill in the modern wave of so-called "termination legislation," according to which the American Indians "would be freed from the yoke of federal supervision" and delivered to the mercies of those fellow citizens who, in Lego's bitter phrase, had "terminated" them earlier at Soldier Mountain. Watkins was now the head of the Indian Claims Commission, and he made the most of his opportunity to patronize the tired Indians, to stall them, confuse them, and deride them, saying at one point, as Craig recalled, "You ought to be thankful we didn't ship you to Siberia." Apparently Watkins was unaware of those earlier Pit River Indians who were shipped out of Eureka only to be thrown overboard and drowned; they would have been thankful to go to Siberia or anyplace else to escape the Commissioner's spiritual forebears.

Because their own attorney—the one approved by the BIA—was recommending compromise, the Pit River had scraped enough money together to pay the flamboyant San Francisco lawyer Melvin Belli fifteen hundred dollars to represent them on their only day in court. But Belli's advocacy was subverted by the BIA, which said that it had not approved him; since Belli was not "the attorney of record," he could not represent these Indians. The bureau also pointed out that the compromise ballot for the Alturas vote on accepting the government payoff had specified that after this vote, the bureau would make its recommendation, from which there would be no appeal. "They laid a trap for us," Raymond Lego said. "Later the Supreme Court threw out our case, and I don't blame 'em." In 1969, the Indian Claims Commission made an award of twenty-nine million dollars; despite their poverty this settlement was refused by the Pit Rivers and all checks were returned.

In 1965, the "Battle of Big Bend" had drawn the Pit River Nation into the activist movements of the sixties. It started modestly enough when the Indians protested the high speed of the logging trucks on the dirt road through the Shasta National Forest that the people had to use in order to reach Big Bend from the state highway. The huge trucks were not only dangerous but raised big clouds of dust, and the Indians proposed that, since the land involved was theirs, and since they had no share in the timber leases issued by the Forest Service, they should collect a toll by way of compensation. When the Forest Service laughed at this request, the Indians took it to court, and rather than test their title to the land, the Forest Service laid a blacktop surface on the road. The lawyer who won this victory for the Indians was forced to move from the community following the subsequent boycott of his services by fellow whites, and Willard Rhoades, who led in the fight, has been harassed by the Forest Service ever since.

In the spring of 1970, inspired by the Indians of All Tribes occupation of Alcatraz, the Pomo Indians occupied Rattlesnake Island, in Clear Lake, where Boise-Idaho Corporation planned to erect a vacation condominium on their sacred burial grounds. (Clear Lake, on which the Pomo depend for most of their food—mollusks, fish, and tule bulbs—has since become dangerously polluted by industrial mercury.) Indians took over Fort Lawton in Seattle and numerous other locations all around the country in symbolic protest of the theft of Indian land. The Pit River and Wintu, having nothing to lose, challenged the white man's law by spearing salmon in Clear Creek, near Anderson, and in June of that year, after an abortive attempt to stage an occupation at Mount Lassen, they occupied an empty recreation camp set up on their land at Big Bend by Pacific Gas and Electric, which claimed 52,000 acres of their ancestral territory. "We are the rightful and legal owners of the land," declared a young Indian named Mickey Gemmill. "Therefore we reclaim all the resourceful land that has traditionally been ours, with the exception of that 'owned' by private individuals." On the second day of the occupation, thirty-six Indians were arrested, at which point they sued PG&E for prosecuting people for trespassing without having established that they owned the land. This was the showdown on their land claim that finally attracted some publicity to Pit River, and Indians came in from all over the country to give support, including Richard Oakes from Alcatraz, the singer Buffy Sainte-Marie, and Grace Thorpe, daughter of Jim Thorpe, the great Olympic athlete.

"In 1970, we hired that famous champion of the Indians who defended them people in the takeover at Alcatraz, and after a while, he was sayin' the same thing as all the rest: we owned the land, all right, but there was nothing he could do to help us with the law because of all the decisions that had already been handed down against us. By now we were so desperate that we was thinking about a takeover of our own, and this guy said he could act for us if we went ahead and occupied our ancestral land. I wanted us to occupy Forest Service land, so there would be a clear-cut legal issue, but some of these younger ones, these pot smokers and big talkers, they wanted to do it up at Mount Lassen, which would involve the public at the national park and get them more publicity. So we said, Okay, but no alcohol and no dope and no firearms, and Richard Oakes brought up some of his people from Alcatraz, and we went in at night. But somebody had alerted the Park Service, and they had that main road closed off, state cops and even the National Guard, with big lights and machine guns. So I marched up there under them guns, and the park supervisor told me he had a right to close the road, he gave me the usual bureaucratic stuff. And I said, 'If you people were in the right, you wouldn't need all these guns.' When we left, we decided to occupy our own Forest Service land over at Big Bend. We were tailed all the way by police cars, and when he got there, the sheriff told us he was going to arrest us for trespassing. We had no experience of this—damn, it was spooky! So the big part of our people ran off and went home; the only ones that stuck with us was Oakes and his Alcatraz people." ("Those ones who ran were mostly the weak ones who later sold us out," Marie Lego says, "and a lot of them were set up by the BIA in an office over in Burney, where they call themselves the Pit River Tribal Council.")

"So then they came for us, eighty-two of 'em, with Black Marias, M-16 guns, riot helmets—the works! There was thirty-seven of us arrested, and they divided us into three groups down at Redding jail. The trial was in Burney, and the judge sustained every objection by the D.A.; he limited the case to illegal trespass and refused to hear our arguments, so we were deprived of the forum we needed to show who owned the land. The first two groups got convicted, but then the case was removed to Sacramento, where the third group got a fair trial; we were acquitted in June 1971. It was white people there who helped us and got us bailed out: there wasn't one black or Indian organization that helped out or spoke up—I was amazed!

"During the trespass trials, we set up a camp at the Four Corners there, near Burney, where the Forest Service has left a line of beautiful trees along the road, the way they always do, to hide from the public the mess that's being made behind. And that's our land, and we don't get one single cent of what the Forest Service is taking in on that leased timber; PG&E, Southern Pacific, the Los Angeles *Times,* the Hearst Corporation, the Bank of America, and a lot of others, they're *all* making big money off our land and the Indians don't get nothing. So we figured that we had the right to start cutting down some of these trees and sawing them up for logs to build our cabins, and pretty soon, along came a police patrol and screeched to a halt. They couldn't believe it, a bunch of Indians cutting down the Forest Service trees! So I guess there was a lot of frantic conferences that went back all the way to Washington, took 'em four days to make up their minds how to handle it, and finally our local congressman here, Harold 'Bizz' Johnson—he's a great friend of Aaron Forrest, who is the only rich Pit River Indian, so 'Bizz' knows how to handle Indians—Harold 'Bizz' Johnson approved of strong action in handling this."

The Indians had offered to leave if the Forest Service could show title to the land; since it could not, it resorted to main force. Raymond Lego did not bother to describe the gory details of the Four Corners fight on October 27, 1970, but a young Indian named Coyote who fought that day and went to jail with Raymond and the others told us that about 150 Indians, none of them armed, were attacked by a huge gang of police, U.S. marshals, Forest Service personnel, and assorted vigilantes—he estimates about four hundred men. When they came at the Indians with rifle butts and clubs, Mace guns, and vicious dogs, the Pit Rivers picked up sticks and two-by-fours in a desperate effort to defend themselves, and the day was bloody. He remembers best the slow, painful ride next day from Susanville jail to jail in Sacramento, four handcuffed Indians squashed into the back of a police car without handles on the doors.

An attempt to reopen the land claim was rejected by the U.S.

Supreme Court in 1971, and the following year, when the Claims Commission checks came in ($656 per person), the unity of the disheartened Indians fell apart. Many felt that their only hope now was the BIA; others were told by their attorney (who had also dropped the civil damage suits filed against several large corporations for illegal occupation of Indian land) that acceptance of the checks did not invalidate the Pit River attempt to stop payment on the Court of Claims award. The Tribal Council, including Mickey Gemmill, now supported acceptance of the 47.5-cents-an-acre offer, and only about one hundred traditionals, led by Lego and Rhoades, continued to refuse the money. This group occupied a tract of PG&E land near Lego's house at Montgomery Creek, while another group occupied a Kimberley-Clark holding near Big Bend; since the occupations cost them nothing, and since they do not wish their land claims tested in court, the corporations have chosen to ignore the Indians, whose morale has steadily deteriorated.

Today the lines are clearly drawn between the Legitimate Pit River Tribe, representing the five bands (out of eleven) which are still "standing on the land," and the "official" Tribal Council, which represents the BIA. "That's the crookedest outfit in the world," Lego said with cold contempt, referring to the Bureau's willingness to betray the Indians. But of course he knows, as all Indians know, that whatever its weaknesses, the BIA is their main access to the federal government, and their only access to the Department of the Interior, which, in carefully selected cases, had made a certain effort to live up to its trust responsibilities; the elimination of the BIA would only make easier the elimination of the Indian nations by termination, which would always be a threat until a responsible national policy (that would survive the changes of administration) provided enduring protection to the Indians. For certain tribes, the tribal councils had worked well (here at Pit River, the Tribal Council had originally supported the traditional land claim and even the refusal of the settlement checks); and for others, in which traditional tribal government had died out, they were usually preferable to the "white government" of Indian agents and missionaries that had ruled the reservations prior to the Indian Reorganization Act of 1934.

"Christianity really wiped us out here, the way it was used by the missionaries, but the Bureau is always the key instrument whenever the government wants to swindle us," said Raymond Lego. "Today the real Pit River Indians don't get no help at all

from government, no help at all, because we won't organize ourselves under the BIA, the way they want. We're outlaws! The only
reason we're still here is because we stay here, we won't compromise, and we won't move; and as long as we stay here, this is still
our country, still Indian country!" (Or as Willard Rhoades puts it,
"We know who we are because we have never left the land.")
Raymond Lego glared at us with a fierce expression, but when he
spoke again, his voice was sad. "Somebody's got to hang on, that's
all. Them Wintu got terminated, they sold their Clear Creek reservation, but they got to live on or near Indian land to qualify for
their government aid, so they use our Pit River rancherias." He
shook his head. "That attorney told us that accepting them checks
had nothing to do with our land claims, so a lot of the people
went ahead and done it—that was the end of our unity, and that's
what's wrecked us. People ask me, 'How come you don't want to
be a citizen?' The kind of citizen I'd be is third or fourth class,
maybe let in the back door once in a while, and maybe not."

Last year, the indomitable Lego had led an occupation of a
nine-hundred-acre tract that lies not far uphill from his house; the
tract is leased by PG&E, which does not occupy the land or put
it to use in any way. PG&E filed suit for eviction, claiming three
thousand dollars in damages, and the Legitimate Pit River Nation
hired a young Yurok Indian lawyer, Abby Abinanti, and a Karuk,
Amos Tripp, who had had experience in Indian rights cases in the
Eureka area. They lost the case, but at the threat of an appeal,
PG&E offered a compromise, reducing the damages to 250 dollars.
Knowing that any compromise was an indirect acknowledgment
of the company's right to occupy Indian land, Lego's
group refused. "We're going to use our right to appeal, and we
intend to take this as high as we can go, and if that don't work,
maybe we'll take the case to international law, the United Nations,
or maybe the World Court. From now on, we'll represent ourselves
in court, and try to take care of our own defense, and see what
happens."

PG&E has yet to force the eviction of the Pit River Indians:
apparently the corporation wants no echo of the bad publicity that
surrounded the beating of unarmed Indians at the Four Corners,
or the transgression of Indian sacred ground at Point Concepcion.
In any case, since this tract is lying idle, the Pit River occupation
costs it nothing.

"The second night of the occupation, February 5, was the

same night that the sheriff came. There was no moon, it was real dark, and what sounded like a whole army of coyotes sounded off from up there on that mountain, and the next thing we knew, they was being answered by another bunch from over in the next valley. I never heard anything like it, and we never heard them since." Raymond raised his eyes. "It was kind of a spiritual thing, I think."

"If we don't turn back now and remember who we are, the Pit River people are gone. Today we're civilized; we can lie like hell, y'know, and make money doin' it, too. We don't put out no food for strangers; we put up the white man's 'No Trespassing' signs instead. Indians everywhere are fighting with each other and ignoring the real source of their trouble, and meanwhile we're headed for legislative extermination. It's kind of ominous, like thunder rolling in the distance, you try to hope that it's going someplace else."

. . .

The traditional Pit River people continue to be denied any legal forum for their land claim, and this shameful situation remains today one of the most painful in all of Indian country. "Raymond is not with us any longer," Marie Lego told me in an eloquent letter in July 1983. "He passed away on June 13, 1980. The struggle is over for him, the long years of hardship, deprivation, and sacrifice, trying to get the U.S. to correct all the wrongs done to our people and regain some land for our people, is ended. Our people have been terribly weakened by our loss. Two weeks after Raymond's death, Pacific Gas and Electric Company came to the occupation site and removed everything, buildings, personal things, and hauled them off. We again put together what we could to construct a small cabin. The attorney . . . told us we did not have a legal defense, that the U.S. Government could do anything they wanted . . . they were not legally responsible to anyone. We had to disagree, because if this is true, why is there such a document as the Constitution of the U.S.? and why would the U.S. try to offer to settle?

and why would the U.S. have to use all means of crookedness and fraud to dispossess us of our land?

"No corporation holding ancestral land has ever proven in court that land has been legally acquired from the Indian people.

"So this is the way it is today, we have no lawyer, no legal defense of any kind, and no means to hope that we might have, but we'll still try to get some measure of justice for our people, whether it be a hundred years or a thousand."

· 10 ·

GREAT BASIN

From Pit River, our road led north and east, crossing over the Cascades in wet spring snow and descending to the town of Canby, named for that general of the U.S. Army who was shot down in a desperate move by the Modoc chieftain, Captain Jack. Beyond Alturas, the road crossed snow mountains and descended through stiff sunny pines into sage-flat country; this land is traditional hunting territory shared by the Pit River bands with Northern Paiute from the Great Basin. In Cedarville—where in 1969, Craig, Mad Bear, and Beeman Logan, passing through on Indian business, had seen a golden eagle come right down into the village and alight on a porch rail as they passed by—we took a small road to the north through the wide treeless valley of Upper Alkali Lake. In a hard wind, spring killdeers flew across white rangeland in the foothills, which fell away eastward through wind flurries of snow and shifting sun to a strange pale expanse of Soda Lake, over ten miles long. On this slope, silhouetted in a snow whirl, stood a giant bird. "Sandhill crane!" I said, and Craig, who had never seen one, stared at it, delighted; he interpreted this sentinel bird as a good sign for our journey.

At Ford Bidwell, a small Paiute reservation where California's northeast corner touches Oregon and Nevada, we paid a brief call on a spiritual leader named Rose Williams who, like Mildred Rhoades, had "seen" Craig's arrival the previous day and was very happy he had come; his message of encouragement to traditional Indians ten years before, she told me, had given her life new hope and direction. From Fort Bidwell we went north into Oregon, on a dirt road across low hills of juniper and sage. We passed an antelope struck dead into a ditch, and a coyote running; it was a big handsome coyote, flowing easily along between low bushes of black sage in the direction we were going. Farther on, a pair of cranes were nodding together in spring courtship dance close to our road. Off to the west rose a lone snow-capped volcano; the road east crossed a windy country of rock and sagebrush, rough buttes and lost mesas and pale lakes, looming and shifting in a whirl of snow and hail, swift sun and rain. This weather-beaten border country of east Oregon and northwest Nevada has little sign of human habitation; it is the last great redoubt of wild mustang horses in North America.

South of Denio, the land subsides into the Great Basin, crossing open prairie country toward the white snow peaks of the Santa

Rosas, in sunlight now as the sun emerged beneath the clouds. Nearing the mountains, we turned north again toward Oregon, on one of the long, rough, dead-end roads of the desert west at the end of which traditional Indians may still be found.

At twilight, when we drew into the yard of a Paiute holy man, Craig said, "See there? He's not on the government dole, he's a real Indian. He's the leader here, but he still lives in that patchwork wooden house. He's about the only peyote man I know who doesn't cooperate with the Christian churches; he doesn't pray to Jesus, but to Our Father, meaning the Creator." Because this man was not at home, we sat in the truck and talked a while as twilight came. Screech owls, first one, then three or four, began their sad descending fluting as the light began to fade, and a pair of wild ducks in silhouette descended, flared, and climbed again into the cold north sky.

Just at dusk, the medicine man returned from Winnemucca in his pickup truck, carrying a load of groceries and supplies. Although he had not seen Craig in ten years, he did not comment on our presence, and we unloaded the pickup in silence, storing the cartons of canned goods in the derelict iceboxes and autos that fill his yard; on one old car someone had scrawled "100% Junk." The man explained that he stored the food here because there was no room inside. He and his wife were taking care of many neighbors' children; there were thirteen kids now living in his modest house. "They can't take care of 'em," he said mildly, "so we try to help those families out."

A small, handsome man, in a bright yellow shirt and a turquoise necklace, this Paiute leader was wide-eyed and open-faced, soft-spoken; he moved as he talked, quietly, without waste effort. Having no wish to be a "media medicine man" or attract the curious, he was happy to be identified by his Paiute name; Tu-pi, he said, means "Mahogany Shadow," or "Dark Place Where Nothing Can Be Seen." He smiled. "The people will know who that is," he murmured.

Inviting us inside, he said, "I'm very glad to see Craig again, you know." Because his wife was still at work and could not cook for us, he murmured in Paiute to a child, and while we were talking over coffee, this boy came back with a big bag of sandwiches to offer to his father's guests. "We are really of the Pa-na-quit people," Tu-pi was saying, explaining that Pa-na-quit, or "Bannock" (the Anglicized name, now used for closely related Indians in Idaho), meant "People closer to the water"—the Pacific—and that "Pa-ute" was the Pa-na-quit answer to a question from the first white men to cross these deserts. "Where is water?" they would say, and the answer was, "Baiute" or "Paiute," meaning "Water-this-way." The Shoshone were "Horse Paiute," and the Eastern or Wind River Shoshone, now in Wyoming, had adopted the culture of the Plains tribes when they moved east of the Rockies in the early nineteenth century, after the last bison were killed off in the Great Basin. "The Bannocks were like the Wind River Shoshone, they had good horses, and old Henry Crow Dog told me once that the Sioux used to raid the Bannock to steal horses, especially their pintos." He explained that Paiute, Ute, and Bannock people understand one another, and the white men say that these are all "Shoshonean" tongues, but Shoshone, which signifies "Whole Land," as in "We are holding the whole land," is a different dialect; so is the tongue of the Comanche of the southern Plains, who were originally outcast Shoshone, unable to get on with anybody: "Comanche" means "Always against us."

"My father's great-grandfather was called Captain Horse by the white men because he was such a great runner," Tu-pi said. "It was said that he could actually outrun their horses, but of course he had a lot of power. He was the hero of the band. Bullets would strike him, his horse, too, and leave nothing but a blue spot. He was finally betrayed by a white man's scout from his own tribe, who lured him in. They penned up the people like cattle here, took them all off to stockades up in Yakima, including Horse's sister. And on the march, they shot down any lady who had to pee or go to potty; they just had to shit like geese right where they were. That was around 1861–1862. Captain Horse was 119 years old when he died." (An historical marker on the county road outside the reservation assures the traveler that some of these Indians returned here in the mid-1860's and "settled contentedly . . . preferring the generosity and kindness of the military to the Indian agents at Yakima. They aided the local military against the Bannocks and others resisting Caucasian takeover of traditional Indian lands.")

The Paiute, whose words for insanity and war have the same root, were peaceful hunter–gatherers, and their small bands once wandered all of the Great Basin. Being poor and defenseless, and lacking horses, they were hunted and shot down for sport by the fur trappers and frontiersmen who opened up the California trails. From Arizona and southern California north to Oregon and Idaho, such good lands as they could claim in the desert valleys were mainly taken over by the Mormons, who often took these "Digger Indians" as slaves; they were so disregarded that almost nobody spoke up for them in the 1950's, when most of the Paiute bands were "terminated" under the direction of Indian Claims Commissioner Arthur Watkins. Even today, the Paiute bands at Pyramid and Walker Lakes, whose relative strength permitted them to cling to their identity, are severely threatened by white encroachment, while those on the Duck Valley reservation on the Nevada–Idaho border are also fighting for their water rights, and are threatened as well by the proposed construction (on Indian land) of the first nuclear power plant in Nevada. Unlike Tu-pi's band, however, the Duck Valley Paiute have accepted a money settlement for their land claim, and Corbin Harney, a traditional leader, told me in 1983 that he would probably move back south to his own Shoshone people.

In 1863, after the Indians were banished, the white men brought cattle into the region, and they still use the land as if it were theirs, but Tu-pi's people at Fort McDermitt are still insisting on their identity as an Indian nation. "We never made any agreement with state or federal government, and we have never applied for a land-claims settlement, and nobody has accepted money; I am still holding on here, and I think this whole reservation is behind me. What we want is recompense for the timber that was taken, and for the grazing rights, and for our fish. We are the aboriginal people on this land." Tu-pi smiled, but there was a shadow in his eyes. "The original homeland area of our band was about fifty by sixty miles, I guess, all the way south around Orovado. One time we were down that way deer hunting, and we had the deer meat in a wagon bed, and we covered it up with cottonwood logs that we had cut down there, to keep the meat from spoiling. Well, we were stopped by seven ranchers, armed with rifles and pistols; they said we were rustling cattle, and had the meat hid in the wagon. So I told them that the Indians had not been paid yet for the land; if this was their land like they claimed, I wanted to see the title. They said they had bought it from the government, and probably they did have a deed of some kind, but they never had no title. So I said, 'We were on this land a long time before you were, and we never been paid for it yet.' And after that, they let us pass; maybe they didn't want to test it out in court.

"Another time, Harvey Cracker and Joe Sam got arrested up in Oregon for possession of an out-of-season deer—somebody had give it to 'em—and we had to get the BIA to go up there to Vail and testify that they was within their rights because they was on reservation land; we have nineteen thousand acres on the north side of the state border. That was one time the BIA helped out a little, but when it comes to real trouble like we have with the BLM [Bureau of Land Management], they just fall back out of sight and don't do nothing."

Like the BIA, the Bureau of Land Management is an agency of the Department of the Interior, and administers much of the Indian land that the department supposedly holds in trust for the Indian peoples in the western states. By the provisions of the Taylor Grazing Act of the 1930's, the BLM started leasing off this land to the white ranchers, reducing the territory of this Paiute band from 3,000 square miles to about 39,000 acres. Most of what is left is poor and rocky, making it difficult for the Indians to raise the quota of cattle that the BLM has declared necessary for permission to lease what they regard as their own territory. Also, the bureaucrats wish to cut down the number of Indian horses, on the grounds that the horses use up too much cattle pasturage on the thin range; they ignore the fact that the Paiute need the horses in order to get around a very rough country that lacks roads. Finally, a Paiute burial ground about ten miles away has been enclosed in a fenced tract to which the Indians have no ready access. Under the American Indian Religious Freedom Act of 1978, Tu-pi petitioned for removal of this fence, which seemed to be one of the arbitrary transgressions on Indian sacred ground that are so common all around the country—so common, in fact, that Indians suspect the influence of missionaries behind it. The government agencies are inevitably influenced by the numerous Mormons and fundamentalist Christians in the bureaucratic ranks, who see the prayers and ceremonies made to a sacred spring or rock, to the earth spirit, as ungodly, especially when such "pagan" ways stand in the path of economic progress.

Although a descendant of medicine people on both sides,

Tu-pi said that as a youth he drank a lot and "chased up and down the street. I didn't know anything better." But while still in his twenties, he realized that he had gifts as a healer and was destined to learn medicine, and for the past twenty years he has sought out the few elders among the Paiute and Western Shoshone who could tell him something of the old ways. "Our old people had quit talking," he said. "They had been left behind." In recent years, he carried spiritual teachings to those Paiute who still live among the Yakima in Washington. "It's like me teaching you, that's how bad they were! Now ninety percent of them are trying to relearn their language and culture. They're very impatient!" Tu-pi smiled. " 'Hey! When we going to speak our own Indian language?' "

. . .

The previous night had been clear and cold, with a northwest wind down off Blue Mountain, up in Oregon. The screech owls had drifted off before we slept, and when I awoke, just before light, the frozen air was tinkling with spring songs of redwings and the creak of magpies. I went for a walk onto the hills above the houses, where I watched the sun rise; to the north rose a strange small mountain that the Pa-na-quit know as the "Red Spot That Is Sitting There." Over the night, the frost had formed tiny snow flowers on the yellow rabbit brush, and three cow ponies hunkered their round, hairy rumps to the raw weather.

Craig and I sat in the truck, watching the small house come to life; one by one, thirteen children came out to use the outhouse, then ran back in, to get ready for school. Someone had brought a lurid girlie magazine into the outhouse, and though it had found an appropriate use, the sight of this white man's pornography in a place used by young children made me ashamed. When the children had gone and his house was quiet, Tu-pi came out and politely invited us to come in and get warm. Over a good breakfast of eggs, coffee, and deer stew, he told us about the Indians' Longest Walk the year before, across the country from Sacramento to Washington, in protest against the latest wave of anti-Indian legislation, the new threat of termination, and the mass relocation of thousands of Arizona Dineh ("Navajo") people from their homeland at Big Mountain, on Black Mesa. Tu-pi, who had taken part, was proud that a Paiute boy had volunteered to carry the sacred pipe through the blizzard that met the marchers in the Donner Pass across the High Sierra. "He used prayer," he said. "And a boy from here said that the next seventy miles east went by like nothing because he had been praying all the way." At another table, where women of the community were talking in the soft Paiute tongue while they did beadwork, his wife smiled, saying, "We're *strong*! They say Nevada Indians are stupid—well, I'm glad we are!" All the women laughed, then resumed their conversation in their own language.

"Well, those people suffered a lot, you know," Tu-pi resumed, "with cold and heavy snow, and hunger and blisters; in that stretch between Fallon and Ely, they were searching for firewood in snow that came up to their waists. But all the same, they felt so good, and people took care of them all along the way, white people, too, donations, benefits, and everything opened up for them, even in Colorado!* And eagles followed them all the way to Kansas, sometimes two and sometimes four!

"In Kansas there was a lot of argument over leadership instead of correct ceremonies and preparations. Some AIM people even stole the sacred pipe and drove away with it, but then they realized they didn't know what to do next, so they brought it back. Anyway, all that unity they kept talking about was gone, and after Kansas, the ones who stuck with it were mostly AIM people and their followers, and they had trouble all the way, I heard, and when they got there, nothing opened up for them." Tu-pi sighed. "A lot of people said that the Longest Walk was a failure because the President wouldn't see the Indians, and nothing much came out of it, but it accomplished one very important thing: it brought a lot of spiritual leaders together who didn't know that others existed, and from now on, we're going to work together. I pray all the time for these good leaders who try to bring the Indian people back together." (In 1980—the year after our visit—Tu-pi convened a number of spiritual leaders at Fort McDermitt and held, with the guidance of Lakota medicine men Pete Catches and Bill Schweigman, the first sun dance in many years among the Paiute and Western Shoshone.)

---

*Colorado is still notorious among Indians for its attempts to exterminate the native peoples, notably in the Sand Creek massacre of Cheyenne and Arapaho, in 1864, but also in campaigns against the Ute.

In 1981, under the direction of Secretary of the Interior James Watt, the Bureau of Land Management drastically increased its fees for grazing leases, in an apparent effort to clear the way for the white ranchers by driving the Indians off their own land. "They know we have no money," Tu-pi told me when I visited him again in April 1983. "So they're really pouring it on.

"My grandfather was a big eater," Tu-pi said. "One time he was at this barbecue, and a white man, watching him, said, 'I wish I had your appetite!' And my grandfather looked at him for a minute, and then he said, 'You white people took our buffalo, and our women, and our land; you took everything that we had. You want our appetite, too?' "

· · ·

To the east, in desert sun, rose the white Santa Rosas; to the west, behind low hills, a snowy plateau sailed off into blue sky. Ravens blew across the empty landscapes, and rough-legged hawks hovered over the low sage. We headed south for Winnemucca, named for a great Paiute chief who had been delighted by the coming of the first white men, which was predicted in the prophecies: "My white brothers, my long looked-for white brothers have come at last!"* But even though the Indians followed them for days, making peaceful entreaties, the fearful white brothers had driven off every approach.

East of Winnemucca, the deserts, piñon ridges, and sparse valleys of central and eastern Nevada and southern Idaho are the territory of the Newe, or Shoshone. After thousands of years on foot in the Great Basin, certain bands of Newe, The People, had traded or stolen Spanish horses from the Navajo and Ute to the south and east; those buffalo hunters who crossed over the great eastern mountains remained on the Wyoming plains. The Shoshone woman Sacajawea had befriended and guided Lewis and Clark, and the redoubtable Chief Washakie had befriended the Mormon pioneers under Brigham Young. Led by Washakie, these eastern Shoshone or "Snake Indians" (now called Wind River Shoshone) would be allies of the whites in wars against the Lakota and Cheyenne, and those Western Shoshone who remained in the Great Basin also remained friendly with the white men.

*See Sarah Winnemucca Hopkins, *Life Among the Piute* (New York, 1883).

In 1860 gold and silver were discovered in Nevada, and the following year, the United States attempted to force a treaty on Chief Tu-to-aina by surrounding his camp with armed cavalry. Tu-to-aina held fast, saying, "We will both drink the water. The wild game belongs to the Newe. The Sogobia (Mother Earth) will never be sold and cannot be bought." Since the Civil War was already under way, the Lincoln administration, anxious to guarantee safe passage of gold shipments from California, was willing to sign a fair treaty with these Indians, which was duly approved by Chief Te-moak in 1863. The Treaty of Ruby Valley provided for "definite acknowledgment . . . of the boundaries of the entire country that they claim," a twenty-four-million-acre territory in southeastern California, eastern Nevada, and western Utah; for their part, the Western Shoshone granted the right to safe travel across "Te-moak's Territory" as well as reasonable use of treaty land for military posts, rail, telegraph, and stage coach lines, mining, ranching, and mills. In the exercise of this right, the white men, growing stronger every year, seized any land they wished, often shooting down Indians who got in the way, and within a decade the dispossessed people were reduced in many places to starvation: today most of the Newe are confined to small, poor "colonies" at the edges of the bony high-plains towns. Yet the land was never signed or sold away, nor was Indian title seriously challenged, since until recently, few outsiders had much interest in this vast near-desert, and those who did went unimpeded by the rightful owners.* As early as 1910, however, the Indians felt obliged to ask the U.S. government to stop referring to their land as "public domain."

In the 1920's, the Newe were harassed for attempting to hunt, fish, and gather piñon nuts—the basis of their subsistence— on their own land, and in the 1930's, when increasing mining and ranching became a threat to this sparse range and its sparse water, the elders called a meeting in Elko to discuss their treaty rights. Judge Milton Badt, who agreed to defend their interests, was well aware that the Indians wished to assert their land rights; however, he judged this hope impractical and worked from the start toward financial compensation, turning over this task, in 1946, to an attorney in Salt Lake City. This enterprising Mormon, Ernest Wil-

---

*General background information on the Western Shoshone land claims may be found in *Newe Sogobia: The Western Shoshone People and Lands* (Battle Mountain, Nevada, 1982).

kinson, wished to lobby for new legislation that would provide compensation to the Indians for "lost" land. Although very poor, the Shoshone declared that they had not lost their land and wished no money; all they wanted was a confirmation of their treaty title to ancestral territories. Nevertheless, Wilkinson persisted in his plan, supported by Senators Pat McCarran of Nevada and Arthur Watkins of Utah, who would later become Indian Claims Commissioner; Watkins was also the leading sponsor of the "termination" legislation designed to end all federal services and responsibility for Indians once their claims to land had been extinguished. The Indian Claims Commission, established in 1946, was largely the creation of Wilkinson's Salt Lake City firm, which opened offices in Washington for the main purpose of representing Indians before the ICC and its Court of Claims; this court had no authority to restore Indian lands but only to put an end to claims through monetary settlement. In the thirty years of the ICC's existence, claims attorneys' fees amounted to more than eight million dollars while their clients lost tens of millions of acres of land.

With the Court of Claims safely established, and negotiations underway with the Paiute and Ute, Wilkinson turned over his Western Shoshone clients to his partner, Robert Barker, who informed the Indians that financial settlement was their only hope of recompense since the settlers had "taken" their land by "gradual encroachment" in 1872 (the same year that Major John Wesley Powell wrote of the Shoshone that "their hunting grounds have been spoiled, their favorite valleys are occupied by white men, and they are compelled to scatter in small bands to obtain subsistence"). Eventually he persuaded the BIA Tribal Council of the Te-Moak band to support a money claim without making clear that in doing so, the Indians were signing away their land—in effect, acknowledging federal title to land that the United States had never owned. In 1951, Barker filed a claim for compensation for the alleged loss of twenty-four million acres (including about sixteen million acres that had never been encroached upon in any way); since the ICC had the earnest support of almost all congressmen from Indian country, the government made no serious effort to contest it.

Despite misgivings among traditionals, Indian resistance to the claim remained unorganized until the early 1970's, when all of Indian country was in ferment. Across the mountains, the Wyoming lands of the Wind River Shoshone were being ravaged by energy development and a serious threat to their water, while here in Nevada, the Bureau of Land Management, planting grass on marginal range for the cattle of white ranchers, ripped out the piñon groves that had provided pine nuts to Great Basin peoples for ten thousand years without bothering to consult the land's true owners.

"We have to work together as a whole people," the Paiute leader Tu-pi said to the Western Shoshone, some of whom took a while to understand this. Among those who understood was old Chief Frank Temoke at Ruby Valley, descendant of that Chief Te-Moak who had signed the treaty; he said to Tu-pi, "You are a part of me," and asked him to be spokesman for their peoples. If Tu-pi's people "became lost," he said—that is, lost their land—the Western Shoshone would take them in. Another who understood was a traditional leader named Glenn Holley. "We think of Tu-pi and his people as 'Snake Shoshone,'" Holley says. "They are much closer to us than they are to the southern Paiute, and closer to us than the Wind River Shoshone, too. We don't understand those Shoshone people over in Wyoming; in all the Indian fights of the last fifteen years, you never hear those people mentioned, despite what's happening to their land and water. They sure haven't offered to stand behind us in our fight; they have always looked on us as some sort of Comanches, and they stay away from us."

In 1974, an emergency organization known today as the Western Shoshone Sacred Lands Association filed a petition with the ICC that accused attorney Barker of collusion with the U.S. government in the seizure of Indian ancestral land. Before a sympathetic Court of Claims, Barker argued successfully that the Temoak Band Tribal Council had authorized him to seek a money settlement. By now, however, even the Tribal Council was alarmed, and with the support of the Sacred Lands Association, it requested the ICC to suspend its money claim until further notice. When Barker contested his clients' wishes, he was fired (he contested this, too), but not before persuading the Court that it was too late to delay the claim.

In 1977, the Indians' new attorney proposed a compromise, according to which the Indians would agree to abide by Article VI of the Ruby Valley Treaty, which specified that "whenever the

President of the United States shall deem it expedient for them
to abandon the roaming life, which they now lead, and become
herdsmen or agriculturalists, he is hereby authorized to make such
reservations for their use as he may deem necessary within the
country above described; and they also do hereby agree to remove
their camps to such reservations . . . and to reside and remain
therein." The Indians asked for a three-million-acre reservation—
about one eighth of their treaty land—and the Department of the
Interior as well as the Justice Department approved the plan. But
in June 1979, a few weeks after our visit, these sensible negotiations were abruptly broken off "in the best interests of the Indians"; two weeks later the U.S. government revealed that the
"public land" administered by the BLM in the Nevada desert—
almost all of it in "Temoak's Territory"—had been selected for
deployment of the MX missile. The largest construction project
in man's history would bring ten thousand miles of roads and at
least twenty thousand people to a land where scarcity of water
was already serious, and no one needed to point out that this
grotesque "system" would be the foremost target of the enemy
in the event of nuclear war. "Probably the U.S. figures that's
okay," Glenn Holley said. "There's nobody out here but us
Indians."

In the fight against the MX-missile system, the Indians were
joined by antinuclear and environmental groups as well as ranchers
and local citizens in what was to become the Great Basin Alliance,
which eventually persuaded the state governments of Nevada and
Utah to reject the plan: the Air Force acknowledged that the
Western Shoshone treaty claim was a major obstacle. But the
threat to the Indians continued in the so-called Sagebrush Re-
bellion, endorsed by Secretary Watt, which sought to transfer to
the state administrations the so-called public-domain lands in the
West.

In April 1983, I spent an evening with Glenn Holley at Battle
Mountain, east of Winnemucca. A descendant of Chief Tu-to-aina,
Holley is a big friendly man with big tattooed arms and expressive
gestures; he served five years in the U.S. Army, reaching sergeant,
first class, and was twice decorated in the Korean War. For many
years, he worked as a cowhand and ranch foreman here on the
high plains of northeastern Nevada. Then one day the traditional
elders reminded him of his heritage and asked his help in the

Western Shoshone effort to reclaim their ancestral land. In 1974, he founded the Western Shoshone Sacred Lands Association, which directs the land claim; he has also served as chairman of the Te-moke Band Tribal Council and is still a member of the local band council at Battle Mountain, where his house in the small Indian colony serves as headquarters of the WSSLA. "We try to be so-phisticated with our office here," he laughs, pointing to the office equipment and stacks of printed matter on his front porch. Like other Indians now making land claims all around the country, the Western Shoshone will make no attempt to repossess privately owned land within their territory; it is only the "public-domain" land that concerns them.

When Glenn Holley joined his people's fight ten years ago, about three quarters of the Newe, by his estimate, were in favor of accepting money for their claim; today, he thinks, less than one quarter would do so. In most Indian nations, the BIA-dominated tribal councils have endorsed money settlements rather than the return of land, but here the tribal councils now support the tra-ditional claim. "Part of our job has been to educate the people against accepting money for our Mother Earth—what would their grandchildren think of them?—and to unite the traditional people against those 'apples' who are only interested in the money. And we had to re-educate ourselves. We have a sweat lodge for the family now, right out in back of the house, and my son and his uncle are pipe-holders for the Newe, and my son pierced at Tu-pi's sun dance. The northern Paiute and Western Shoshone are really one people, as Tu-pi says." Glenn sighed, shaking his head. "The whole Indian nation is one people, but we haven't yet learned to put this into practice."

In December 1979, the Western Shoshone were awarded twenty-six million dollars—slightly more than one dollar per acre for land now worth two hundred times that much. "We never lost that land, we never left it, and we're not selling it," Glenn Holley declared. "In our religion, it's forbidden to take money for land. What's really happening is that the government, through this Claims Commission, is stealing the land right now in 1979. . . . Most of our people never understood that by filing with the Claims Com-mission we'd be agreeing that we lost our land. They thought we were just clarifying the title question. Barker kept saying the claim was for land we had already lost—that we weren't selling anything."* Holley and his group were dismissed as "a small vocal minority" by Robert Barker, and his firm, Wilkinson, Cragun and Barker, was paid 2.5 million dollars, deducted from the Indian award. The traditionals' attorney argued all the way to the Supreme Court that the Indians had never been given a day in court to present their treaty title to the land; the Supreme Court confirmed this view by refusing to hear the case.

The last hope for the traditional Shoshone lay in a trespass case that heretofore had been obscure. In 1974, Mary and Carrie Dann at Crescent Valley, southeast of Battle Mountain, were charged with trespass by the BLM for grazing their cattle in the "public domain" without a permit: the Dann sisters declared that no permit was needed, since this land belonged to the Western Shoshone Nation. In the U.S. District Court in Reno, their attorney demanded that the government show proof that it had extinguished title to their land in 1872, as claimed earlier in an ICC decision; to no one's surprise, the Commission's finding turned out to be based on the unsupported assertion of Robert Barker, who had simply picked an arbitrary date from which to figure his nineteenth century valuation of the land. However, the land question was evaded, the Dann sisters were convicted, and not until March 1978 did the Ninth Circuit Court of Appeals reverse the conviction, ordering the lower court to retry the case on the basis of the land title. At this point, the original judge acknowledged on the record that he was "sympathetic with the government's strategy"; he would not hear the case until after December 1979, when acceptance of the ICC award by those Indians who wished it might legally extinguish Western Shoshone title and the Danns' claim, as well.

On April 25, 1980, this judge decreed that at the time the trespass charges had been filed, the United States had not yet extinguished title to Western Shoshone lands. The same decision specified, however, that the Indians had lost title to the land at the time of the ICC award a few months earlier, and that henceforth the Danns must not permit their livestock on "the public lands of the United States" without a grazing permit. The first finding of this decision was appealed by the U.S. government and the second by the Dann sisters, on behalf of the Western Shoshone Nation.

*See Jerry Mander, "This Land Is Whose Land?" *Village Voice,* December 17, 1979.

Then, on July 26, 1980, at a public hearing sponsored by the BIA, more than eighty percent of the Indians present voted against acceptance of the claims award. In the words of Raymond Yowell, Chairman of the WSSLA, "What is at issue is the honor of the United States. . . . Throughout the years, our strength as a nation of people has lessened as the strength of the United States has increased. But is the honor of the United States conditional upon the political strength of the nations it enters into treaties with? Now we see the United States, an attorney supposedly representing our treaty rights, and the Bureau of Indian Affairs working together through the Indian Claims Commission to deprive us of our land rights. The land to the traditional Shoshone is sacred, it is the basis for our lives. To take away the land is to take away the lives of the people." A fortnight later, acknowledging that Indian resistance to the land settlement went far beyond what Barker had called "a small but vocal minority," the Senate Select Committee on Indian Affairs ordered postponement of distribution of the award pending the outcome of the Dann case, which "could clearly have a strong bearing on the course of action the Congress, the Department of Interior, and the Western Shoshone people might wish to pursue."

The Interior Department lawyers were uneasy about the outcome of *United States* v. *Mary and Carrie Dann*, and in April 1981, at a meeting on the Duckwater reservation, the Newe were notified that the government wished to negotiate the land claim. After considerable indecision, the WSSLA decided to negotiate with the United States (although some of their fired-up traditionals believed that any negotiation with the government would be a sell-out) and pursue the Dann case at the same time. The significance of this case, which tests the validity of the Ruby Valley Treaty, can scarcely be overestimated, and the federal courts are in no hurry to arrive at a decision which might reverberate all over the West.

·   ·   ·

Twenty-five miles south of the main road across the high deserts of northeast Nevada, in a winter rangeland surrounded by snow peaks, the Danns' small ranch house is set against the foothills, way over east under the Cortez Mountains. The house, in a grove of cottonwoods at the end of a long gravel road across the sage,

was surrounded by farm sheds and dismantled machinery, dead
trucks and autos; it is separated from the silver-green wool of the
sage plain by a stock corral where a small herd, with its new calves,
waited to be turned out on the sparse range. To the west lay the
Shoshone Mountains—"That's how they're known to the BLM
and local people. To us they are A-ken-doia, 'That mountain range,' "
said Carrie Dann, a handsome woman with big strong teeth, a big
strong laugh, and big eyes rounded by thick glasses. It was Carrie
Dann who had yanked open the door and looked me over before
inviting me inside the house, which she shares with her older sister
Mary, their brother Clifford, their niece Sandy, and Carrie's little
boy. We sat down over good coffee at the kitchen table, where
we were joined after a little while by Mary Dann. "You know,
sometimes now, we forget the real name of those places, and the
old people who remember are all gone," said Mary gently; she is
older and more reserved than her brash sister. I said that they
lived in a beautiful place, and Carrie Dann shrugged, saying, "It's
a place."

Sandy Dann, a pretty girl in braids, said hello as she passed
through the room—"She's an outdoor girl," said her Aunt Mary—
but Clifford Dann came and went without a word. "That's my
brother Cliff," Carrie Dann said, as a kind of introduction, but
Clifford Dann, perhaps in shyness, ignored my nod of greeting,
as if pretending that I was not there.

"Our father, he was Dewey Dann, lived in Grass Valley"—
Carrie pointed toward the south—"but the non-Indians over there
would destroy his crops. When he married my mother, he moved
into this area, because our grandmother's aunt lived over here; he
worked on a ranch—that was the one way he could protect himself
from white people—and he got this place under the Homestead
Act in the 1930's."

"Couldn't get in otherwise," Mary Dann said carefully. "Everybody sent him away."

"Well, the non-Indians didn't want him here, and his neighbor
told him he would run him off this place, one way or another.
And they went after him, okay, but he stuck it out; he had that
kind of strength of spirit and mind. And so we were born here
on the 'public domain'—that's what they call Western Shoshone
land!"

Like most traditional Shoshone, this family lived almost entirely off the land. Until two years before her death, the sisters' grandmother lived in a tent that she carried from place to place by pack horse as the seasons changed. "Our grandmother would tell us stories of the past, over meals, you know; she never tried to tell us what was what, she taught us Indian way, by her example. In those days, our aunt was involved in traditional activities, and Mother and Dad used to go to annual meetings at Ruby Valley, so I guess we were always traditional in this family. Anyway, we were in this land fight right from the start, and because she"—here Carrie pointed at her smiling sister—"don't like to talk, she always sent *me* out, and I go and say all kinds of crazy things!" Carrie laughed loudly. "I used to give that Robert Barker fits. I remember a meeting over in Ibapah, when us traditionals and Buster McCurdy's Gosi Ute people were arguing their land claim, and I spoke right up against that money settlement. And Mr. Barker gets mad and he hollers, 'I've known Carrie Dann for fifteen years, and all she's good for is arguing at these meetings!' Anyway, this family openly resisted the fencing of our land, our stock just always found a way through all their fences; we notified the authorities that because this was our land, we would continue to graze our cattle here as we had always done. Then, in 1974, the BLM took us to court for 'trespassing'; they wanted us to pay range lease permits on our own land, and we refused."

The Dann family is one of the few that has not been forced into one of the decrepit Indian "colonies" on the outskirts of this state's hard-bitten towns. "Most of the people *had* to move to town, or starve; they *had* to take up the economic way of life. That economic way is what has ruined us. If you try to live Indian way, the spiritual way, you are so poor and so humble—it is very difficult to stand by it. Tu-pi is one of those who does it; he is a poor man, but he shares everything. I guess that is what white people call socialism: if you have something, you share it."

Mary Dann nodded, gazing out the window toward the south. "If the government was halfway fair with us, we wouldn't be so very poor," she murmured mildly. Though quiet, Mary Dann is a strong woman. Once she burned a book that had been given to the family, refusing to let her younger sister read it. "It told lies about the Indian people," Mary explained, gazing at me with an odd smile of warning. "I'll read your book, and if it's no good, well, I'll just burn it up!"

· · ·

At the Utah border, a road heads south along the west edge of the Great Salt Desert, a waste of white alkali flats and old dead lakes, stretching away between far small archipelagoes of dry mountains. At each turnoff, the road diminishes, tending east into the remote Ibapah Valley where good water comes down from the steep ridges of the Deep Creek Range into an ancient territory of the Gosi Ute. Near the south end of the valley, where the land is green and there is forest on the steep valley walls, a dirt lane turns off past a well-made garden, meandering uphill to a large farmhouse set about with weathered sheds built out of logs. The house has been rebuilt for Molly McCurdy by her brother, who lives in a trailer on the property; it was Buster McCurdy we had come to see.

Craig said he had enemies on this reservation. Not sure of the reception we might get, he told me to park the truck for a quick getaway. While I listened to the bells of the home-coming sheep and the howls of a retarded Indian boy who was wandering here and there behind the farmhouse, Craig got out and talked for a long time in the cool spring twilight with a stocky, guarded man in khaki shirt and coveralls who came out to meet him.

Eventually they came over to the truck, and because it was cold, we sat in the front seat as in a pew, gazing northward up the valley toward high Pilot Peak. "This is Chief Buster McCurdy," Craig said, after a while. "Chief!" Buster McCurdy exclaimed, still a little bewildered by our visit; like most of the people we had gone to, he had not seen Craig since 1969. As if not sure what we might want, he sat motionless and quiet for a while, thick heavy hands square on his knees, a surprised expression on his face; the white stubble and soft dark eyes are the inheritance of Basque shepherds in his ancestry. "Ute" is the real name of his people— their own name, that is, for "the Indians," "the People"—and Ute-ah, or Utah, he explained, "just means 'Them Indians Over There.' Gosi Ute, or Goshute—that's 'Dusty Ute,' " he said, "because we'd be goin' along covered with desert dust on the way to the meeting grounds over in Provo Valley, where we wintered sometimes with Paiute and Shoshone." These days the few hundred Gosi Ute were divided between this band and another across the mountains in Skull Valley. "Wonderful huntin' grounds, used to be, duck grounds, too, and plenty to eat in winter, and we played all kinds of games. Ute and Paiute understand each other pretty good, but we don't understand much Shoshone language, just a few words to get by; the books say we're all the same bunch, but we ain't."

Buster McCurdy was raised here in Ibapah, but he married a Ute woman from the High Uintahs and lived over in the east part of the state for many years as a hardworking and very successful mechanic; in the late fifties and early sixties his auto-repair work had supported the journeys on Indian business made by his wife Etta and other traditional spokesmen. Buster himself won respect as a courageous and outspoken leader, and was jailed more than once for his beliefs. "Among real Indians," Craig had told me, "Buster McCurdy was a hero from coast to coast."

In 1954, the three Ute bands were offered an ICC award of thirty-two million dollars, negotiated on their behalf by Ernest Wilkinson; the Northern Ute traditionals refused the award, and subsequently Wilkinson turned them over to another partner in his firm named John S. Boyden. Representing the Northern Ute Tribal Council, Boyden assisted the BIA in promoting natural gas leases on Ute land, and he also leased away precious Ute water rights to supply large diversion canals to Salt Lake City. Of Boyden, Buster McCurdy said, "That is my worst enemy."

McCurdy chuckled over the fun that he had had when he first knew Craig; he didn't regret a single day, he said, except the ones he had to spend in jail. Smiling for the first time since our arrival, he recalled a meeting held by Beeman Logan at Tonawanda, New York, and how a Lakota woman had come there all the way from South Dakota to plead for help for her son, White Hawk, who was soon to be executed for a controversial murder. Buster had gotten very excited—he raised his voice now, sitting in the cab—telling the assembled Indians that it was all very well to sit around and talk, but that if they didn't *do* anything in a case like this, talk didn't mean much; in fact, they were helping to execute White Hawk by their inaction. "It tickles me still," Buster McCurdy said. "A way-out-in-the-sagebrush guy, talking that way to them educated Indians! I guess I stirred up a hornet's nest!" But the others responded, interceding for White Hawk and saving his life, and later the woman sought out Buster McCurdy and thanked him. Buster told her, "It wasn't just your son I was talking about; we were trying to save all Indians. It was to save me, too." Buster McCurdy turned a little and gazed at me for the first time; his face was sad again. "To save you, too," he said.

Eventually, Buster McCurdy was asked by the last traditionals at Ibapah to come back home and help out his own people, who found themselves under increasing pressure from white ranchers; these ranchers wanted to rechannel Indian water from the mountain streams at this end of the valley onto their ranchland farther north. Although Indian water rights had been affirmed on behalf of Montana tribes as early as 1908, in the Winters Doctrine, this plan had the support of the BIA and its Tribal Council Indians. "As usual," Buster said, "the BIA was workin' one group of Indians against the other." McCurdy and a few friends set up a roadblock to stop a BLM bulldozer that was preparing to dig irrigation ditches for the diverted stream on reservation land; for this act, he was sent to jail.

Ever since he has been treated as a troublemaker; he and his coworker Earl Baker were the first ones questioned, about 1960, when persons unknown blew up two microwave towers up at Wendover, on the Nevada line, "because these two Indians were the only guys around here who were against the government." Buster laughed, shaking his head. In 1962, he evicted some beryllium miners who had negotiated a lease with the Tribal Council. "Them puppet resolutions were being signed by the BIA without approval from the traditional leaders, which was illegal," Buster McCurdy said. A party of U.S. marshals sent out to enforce the permit was disarmed by a group of Indians led by McCurdy and a white U.S. Air Force major named Don Armstrong; Armstrong was offended by what he saw as a transgression of the Constitution, which as an Army officer he had taken an oath to defend, and for his principles was sent to Lompoc prison for three years. McCurdy was sentenced to two years, but was let out a few months later on probation.

In the late 1960's, McCurdy and Baker agreed to join the Tribal Council in an effort to hold the Gosi Ute together. ("Them BIA Indians needed our traditional 'authority,' but traditionals weren't sharing any of the gains.") When they kept passing resolutions that the BIA would not approve, the Bureau solved the problem by rigging a charge of embezzlement of Tribal Council funds. "That's how they got us kicked off," McCurdy said, without surprise and therefore without outrage. The FBI was summoned to harass and discredit them, and eventually they were brought to trial in Salt Lake City. After one look at the evidence, the federal judge called the prosecutor, the BIA people, and the FBI agents into his chambers, where he chastised them angrily for bringing such a trumped-up case into his court and swore that if they ever tried such tricks again, he would jail the lot of them and throw away the key. Apparently the Indians were not supposed to hear this angry and contemptuous denunciation of white men; they only learned about it two years later, when Buster ran into one of the attorneys in the street.

In the course of one of his brushes with the law, McCurdy managed to secure a tape of the obscene abuse and threats to which he and Baker were subjected by a sheriff who had waved them off the road; they submitted this tape to state authorities, and the sheriff was fired. To understand anti-Indian prejudice and retribution in the West is to know how much courage this small act required.

Most of the traditionals here in the Ibapah Valley have died out, and Buster McCurdy has been threatened more than once by armed BIA Indians. "There's nobody on our side; we got nobody to turn to." A girl he had mentioned to Craig ten years before as his potential successor as a leader here had "died from too much liquor." Craig quoted Little Turtle, a war leader of the Miami, who said that the white man's guns had killed many Indians and that his diseases had killed many more, and that liquor had killed more than both of them put together. Buster McCurdy nodded in agreement; they discussed the Northern Utes up in Uintah, one fourth of whom died from alcohol-related diseases or accidents in the years after liquor sales to Indians were legalized in 1952, as part of the termination program. "And those Gosi Utes over in Skull Valley, those poor people are shot; that Tribal Council guy they have has driven them right down the drain. They're going to have their piñon trees, their deer-hunting grounds, all taken away from them because all they can see is dollar signs. Liquor is the main trouble here, too, and it's going to be a dead place pretty soon. I told 'em that, but they won't listen." He sighed. "I kind of give up now. Just flare up once in a while, is all." Buster McCurdy talked a little about the fighter jets passing through from Las Vegas to Mountain Home, Idaho, and how they buzzed this remote Indian valley, scaring the animals; the Indians had protested, of course, but nothing had been done.

"I got a white friend here," Buster McCurdy said, "and he leaves my religion alone. But one day there were three Mormons over there, and they wouldn't let up, they wanted to sign me up right then and there. So finally I got mad and said, 'I *got* my religion. I'm *it*. I carry it with me wherever I go—there's no Sunday in my religion. You leave *your* repent in church, your book in church, and you go out and steal all week and sell liquor to the Indians. Maybe I'd trust you if you took your liquor and your religion back where you come from.' I didn't mix my words, I just told 'em. And so they left, and my friend there wasn't mad at all, he was delighted."

Not long ago, Buster had been in terrible pain, and because his sister doesn't drive, he drove himself all the way to the hospital in Elko. By the time he had located a doctor who would treat him, he could barely drive himself to the emergency room, which was where he belonged; the doctor told him the next day that his ruptured appendix had nearly cost him his life. Concluding the story, he was silent, staring out into the dusk, as if reflecting on his own loneliness, and intuiting this, Craig told him he was still a good man, and that he ought to find himself a woman. Buster McCurdy nodded. "I got no children, y'know, and I never re-married. I looked all over the place—don't look in the right direction, I guess. I met one there was a little on the strong side; maybe she would have beat me up!" He tried to smile. " 'Course anybody who come with me, she would always be afraid of community opposition. They been telling me for years how I was neglecting my family by not having children, y'know, and I try to tell 'em that I'm speaking for *their* children, but they don't understand."

The night before, Buster McCurdy had led us to a hill pasture behind his sister's house where one of the two streams coveted by the ranchers comes down the steep mountainside from the high evergreen in a ribbon of poplar, willow, and red birch. At daybreak he came to sit on his heels at our campfire, and we spent a long, slow, peaceful morning in the sun while Craig cooked us up some of his mush. "I never thought I would see Craig again," Buster had told me when Craig had gone to the stream to wash. "We had some fun, all right, in those days."

Buster McCurdy laughed. "Maybe I'll sign up with the BIA, get greedy, too; maybe I'll go prospecting. I had ideas for a fish hatchery here, or maybe I'll go into cattle-raising; we got good ground and good water." Aware of Craig's eye, he said ironically, "Some days I'm an Indian, and some days not." Tactfully, Craig spoke in abstract terms of the split among Indians that has come about due to the painful choice between Indian way and the white man's culture, and Buster McCurdy changed the subject by addressing a meadowlark that flew over: "Cut out that crazy song now! That's not your song!" He explained to us that in recent years, a number of birds had changed their song or stopped singing entirely, and that rattlesnakes hardly ever rattled any more. "I blame it on that stupid atomic energy," he said, referring to the wind of atomic pollution that had blown out of Nevada and contaminated people in St. Georges, Utah.

Recently, McCurdy had a dream that "didn't feel like any dream; it was a vision. I saw Salt Lake City, all of them nice buildings, smoke was coming out, and some were ruined, and there were no people—there was nobody around. The man with me said it must have been an earthquake, but I didn't think so; it was something else."

Before leaving, we filled our bottles with good mountain water and complimented Buster on how well the farm looked, the animals and gardens, and also his reconstruction of the house. He nodded. "Molly boasts to everyone around about her house, but she never said nothin' to *me* about it yet, not even once!" He laughed a little, standing there in the late morning sun; we had been talking for five hours, and even so, he seemed sorry to see us go. We offered him a lift back down the hillside to the farm, and he shook his head. "Might as well walk," he said. "I'll see you again," Craig said, taking his hand. Buster McCurdy held Craig's hand for a long time, looking him over. "I don't know when," he said at last. And looking back at the still figure on the mountainside as the truck rolled down the slope in the spring ruts, I remembered a moment the afternoon before, when Craig had asked him how many people here at Ibapah were still standing on the land. Chief Buster McCurdy, saying nothing, had raised up a solitary finger.

• • •

The High Uintahs lie in northeast Utah, and the Northern Ute live on flat plateaus south of the mountains, which rise to Kings Peak at 13,500 feet; broad and rolling despite their altitude, they are the only east–west range in the United States except the San Juans of Colorado, where what is left of the Southern Ute now live.

At the house of Bear Dance Chief Alfred Root, nobody was home, and we took the back road past the sun dance grounds east to Tridell, where we found Sun Dance Chief Jensen Jack warming up his tractor. Jensen Jack wears his hair long in a braid; he has gat teeth and his English is not good, but he is an eloquent storyteller. Two days ago, he saw "sparks traveling in his eyes," which was sign that an important visitor was on the way; when he saw Craig emerge from the truck, he said, he understood.

Craig Carpenter had been here in the Uintahs in 1962, when Jensen Jack was jailed in the "Ute Uprising," the newspaper term for a small protest when a group of "True Ute" (as opposed to Tribal Council Ute), in a protest over the threatened loss of precious water rights, had commandeered the BIA office in Fort Duchesne and held it for three days; this was one of the early water-rights fights that in recent years have spread all over Indian country. And that first night, Jensen Jack recalled, they heard huge footsteps outside the "agency" office, and knew that some strange thing was there; they knew it was the Big Man, and that this was a good omen. But later, he said, there were policemen all over the place, and he ran around waking up the Indians. They had a little prayer there in that office, and there was a reporter there with a tape recorder. He said, "How are you going to protect yourselves?" "We're going to stand up on our own two feet, that's all," Jensen Jack told him. But the police rushed them, using tear gas; Jensen Jack himself was shot right in the face and knocked over a table. "Guys was cryin' all around, tears in their eyes. So they grabbed us and throwed us in jail, at Vernal, because the jail at Fort Duchesne was already full of Indians, and I was in there pretty near a month—I was the last one out."

Craig said, "I brought you some Bull Durham in that jail. The Sun Dance was going on that day, and I told you there might be somebody praying for you, to help you out of jail, and that same day you got out." Jensen Jack nodded. "I knew that the Great Spirit would help me out of that," he said, referring again to the big footsteps he had heard outside the "agency."

Jensen and Craig discussed the local lawyer who had stuck his neck out to defend the True Ute in court. "He ain't doin' nothin' now," Jensen Jack said, "Just walkin' around the streets." On impulse, we drove back west to Roosevelt to look up George Stewart, a tall, elderly man who is still full of curiosity and enthusiasm. "I guess I was the only guy who would defend them," said Mr. Stewart, who has Ute blood and speaks the language. "I had advised them to defend their rights, and fight for them, especially their water rights, which are the most valuable asset that they have." Stewart explained that four fifths of Utah's water, including the Green River, originated here in the Uintahs, and that there had been a distinct threat that most of this water would be transferred to the so-called "Wasatch front," to supply the Salt Lake City–Provo complex. "Look at the Duchesne," he said. "All the water west of that sand ridge between here and Vernal drains into the Duchesne, and it used to be dangerous at this time of year, a real ripsnorter; in volume, it was the second-largest river in the state, after the Green. Today it's just a trickle of yellowish-green water—they've killed that river." Today, he said, the Ute were still contesting the Central Utah Project, because according to law they "have priority over all waters sufficient to meet their needs." Even the Ute Tribal Council was adopting many of the resolutions fought for by the True Ute for many years.

Stewart recalled that Buster McCurdy had been around at the time of the "Ute Uprising" and that his wife had been among those thrown in jail: in fact, Etta McCurdy's child by her second marriage had stayed here at the Stewarts' house. "The FBI was here to reinforce the Tribal Council police, and they had a big roundup of True Ute—the most unfair thing I ever saw. A friend of mine, an old medicine man called 'Elephant,' was one of the few who still wore his hair in the long braid, and they threw him into jail just on hearsay; why, he didn't belong in there at all! How woebegone he was! They didn't realize how much damage they were doing to that old man's dignity."

Court hearings on the "Ute Uprising" were eventually removed to Salt Lake City, where John Boyden, as the Tribal Council's attorney, claimed that the True Ute had no legal basis for appeal from a prior conviction by the Ute tribal court, and no right to their own lawyer. As Jensen Jack had said, "Boyden was supposed to be working for the good of the Ute Indians, but he turned against us; he was working for the BIA." Lawyer Stewart had taken the position that since American Indians had been made full citizens in 1924, they were entitled to full access to the white man's courts, this one included; he was upheld by Judge Willis Ritter, in a landmark decision that opened the way for the Indian struggle to win back at least a part of their usurped heritage. Craig was also there that day, and recalls Boyden's consternation with delight: "That big tall thin man was so excited, he was jumping around that courtroom like a grasshopper." Subsequently Boyden had represented the Hopi Tribal Council while his firm represented the Peabody Coal Company, which was strip-mining coal on Hopi and Navajo land, and the True Ute had joined Hopi traditionals in demanding a grand jury investigation of Boyden's alleged conflicts of interest involving energy development and the Mormon Church.

•   •   •

Crossing the Green River, we headed east to Dinosaur, Colorado, then south across bare reddening hills of the Roan Plateau. Near the road, a dust devil held aloft a strange column of tumbleweeds; Craig saw this as a negative sign and became subdued. From the oil town of Rangeley, we took the road south over the Douglas Pass through snow and spruce and quaking aspen; to the eastward, in bright sinking sun, rose the twin peaks of Bear Ear Mountain, a sacred place in the Bear Dance legends recounted by Jensen Jack.

In late afternoon, the road came down into the Colorado River Valley. Above spring riverbanks of red tamarisk and willow and new cottonwood in light-green bud rose the monumental red walls of the Roan Cliffs, and on the east side of Grand Junction rose Grand Mesa, a spectacular pink-purple in the sunset snow— "the largest flat-topped mountain in the world," Craig told me. At twilight, twelve to twenty elk come down out of the mountain trees into horse pasture, not far north of the Gunnison River crossing; at Delta, the huge white masses of the Rocky Mountains loomed in the high darkness.

Originally a number of Ute bands, speaking different languages, hunted the forests on the far side of those mountains, in what is now eastern Colorado and New Mexico, wandering west into Utah and Arizona. About 1820, it is thought, they obtained horses and became fierce raiders who captured their Shoshone relatives in Nevada and sold them as slaves to the Spanish in the Southwest; later they harassed the Mormon settlers. In 1859, when gold was discovered in the vicinity of Denver, a rush of prospectors and settlers moved into Ute territory, shooting down any Indian who got in the way. These were the same citizens who, a few years later, endorsed the vigilante massacre of Black Kettle's peaceful Cheyenne people at Sand Creek, as part of a well-organized plan to clear all Indians out of Colorado. Even then, the Ute resisted the white clamor for their lands, but finally, in 1868, faced with utter destruction, they signed the first of several treaties, all of which moved them ever farther toward the desert; they gave up eastern Colorado and all Ute territory in New Mexico and moved to poorer lands west of the Rockies. "The agreement that an Indian makes to a United States treaty is like the agreement a buffalo makes with his hunters when pierced with arrows," remarked their "talking chief," a half-breed named Ouray. "All he can do is lie down and give in."

By 1879 valuable minerals had been located in this new territory which had been guaranteed to them "forever," and already the whites were agitating to get these redskins the hell out of the way. Said Colorado Governor Frederick Pitkin, "Unless removed by the government, they must be exterminated. . . . The advantages that would accrue from the throwing open of twelve million acres of land to miners and settlers would more than compensate all expenses incurred." In a view of traditional Indians that still survives in the western states today, a Denver *Tribune* editorial declared: "The Utes are actual, practical Communists and the government should be ashamed to foster and encourage them in their idleness and wanton waste of property. . . . The only truly good Indians are dead ones." No more encouragement than that was needed to shoot Indians almost at will; others were sent on long marches into Utah, where many died of grief and deprivation. "I realize the state of my people," Ouray mourned. "We shall fall as the leaves of the trees when winter comes and the land we have roamed for countless generations will be given up to the miner and the plowshare and we shall be buried out of sight." Those who were left were eventually removed to a narrow strip on the border with Utah and New Mexico that was already overrun by white men and their cattle. This place was hated by the fiercely traditional band called Weminuche, which took shelter in Mesa

Verde Canyon and wandered west into the deserts; some of these people, called White Mountain Ute, still live in the vicinity of Blanding, Utah. Today the Weminuche, or Ute Mountain Ute, occupy the arid western section of Colorado's one small Indian reservation, with the so-called Southern Ute band in the east.*

In 1897, an Indian agency was established at Navajo Springs, now called Cortez; when the whites found this place to their liking, the agency was moved to Towaoc, a few miles west of Mesa Verde. But Weminuche hatred of the whites remained so fierce that for a time the Towaoc agency was closed down and the Weminuche left to their own desperate devices; even more than most traditionals, they were penalized by the bureaucrats and missionaries, the state and the federal government, for trying to persist in Indian way. Unlike the affable Southern Ute, the reclusive Ute Mountain people were entirely unsophisticated, and when, in 1954, the two bands were awarded Claims Commission money for the land which had been lost or stolen, and when, only a few years later, oil and gas leases brought further income to this poverty-stricken people, the great majority of the Weminuche could not handle it and, in Buster McCurdy's phrase, "went down the drain." Drunk, idle, hostile, or indifferent to almost everything, even the money, even one another, these lost people remain all but ignored by the crass governments of Colorado and the United States. The suicide rate at Towaoc is twice as high as the high Indian average elsewhere in the country, and twenty-two percent higher than anywhere else on earth.

(Two years before, we had camped on the San Juan River in the southwest corner of this reservation, then headed north out of Cortez into Ute country along the Utah border. An Indian had speeded up his car when we tried to pass him, refusing to let us back into his lane; I nearly ran him off the road to avoid a collision with an oncoming truck. When Craig got his breath back, he had said in a stiff voice, "That guy did that on purpose. There are a lot of angry ones like that; they just don't know how to get out their frustrations.")

Next morning we headed south again, up the Uncompahgre River to Montrose, where the white man's "talking chief" Ouray had been given a white man's house by a grateful government; we

---

*See Nancy Wood, *When Buffalo Free the Mountains* (New York, 1980).

passed through a small settlement named after the same man, in the San Juan Mountains. At Red Mountain Pass, just east of Telluride, at over eleven thousand feet, snow was still heavy, with snowslides on the road, and the old mining town at Silverton was shining white. The road climbed again to Molas Pass, then followed the Animas River down into Durango.

* * *

On May 19, 1983, the Ninth Circuit Court of Appeals, deciding in favor of Mary and Carrie Dann, held that the ICC award (repudiated today by Western Shoshone of all factions) did not legally extinguish Indian title to the land established by the Ruby Valley Treaty. While the formal decision must await additional clarification from the district court, this ruling is certain to affect a number of other cases in the West, including the Northern Paiute claim based on the Treaty of Fort Boise, and it represents an important victory for the Indian people.

· 11 ·

FOUR CORNERS

On a bright Rocky Mountain day we rode down out of Colorado into a strange and beautiful country in the great ellipse between the Colorado River and the Rio Grande, known to the Indian peoples of the Southwest as a sacred center of the earth: Mesa Verde, Shiprock, Chaco Canyon, Canyon de Chelly, Rainbow Bridge are only a few of the many shrines and dwelling places of the Old Ones, and such places were used long before the advent of the Europeans, who fixed this region on their maps in a grid of squares. Here the four states of the Southwest come together, and here the Four Corners Regional Commission wished to build (on Indian land) a sprawling city complex of 28,000 square miles, complete with airports, ski resorts, and tourist ranches, with a few Indian villages thrown in for local color.

In 1951, when Craig Carpenter made his first trip into this "red rock country" that he now regards as his spiritual home, he was, by his own account, a "half-baked detribalized Mohawk from the Great Lakes country trying to find his way back to the real Indians." Traveling alone from Moab, Utah, he descended the Colorado on a rubber raft, and after a river voyage of 120 miles, arrived at Rainbow Bridge in Aztec Canyon, where he walked up to the trading post and startled hell out of the trader, a former horse wrangler named Bill Wilson, known to the Navajo as "Crippled Hand." Before Wilson could figure out where the young Indian had come from, Craig demanded, "I hear there are Navajos starving to death up here—is that true?" It was true, and it still is, despite the fact that the Navajo reservation sits squarely upon the so-called Grants Mineral Belt, one of the richest mining regions in the world.

Craig worked that winter at Dunn's Trading Post on Navajo Mountain, which rises more than ten thousand feet above the Colorado, and after that, for several years, he was a "river man," or guide, out of Green River, Utah; for a time he also lived at Hite, a remote settlement that was the farthest place from a post office in the "lower 48." (In 1963, Hite disappeared beneath the artificial flood that backed up behind the new Glen Canyon Dam.) For the next five years, from 1951 to 1956, Craig was based mostly at Navajo Mountain; in the same period he made contact with the Hopi, for whom he was later to become a trusted "messenger." Having lived with both peoples, Craig shares the Hopi view that the Navajo are like white men, adaptable and domineering. "They're the most aggressive Indians in North America except the 'Mighty Sioux,' and maybe it's for the same reason. The Navajo are Athapaskans who arrived from the far north not more than five centuries ago, in the same way that the Sioux came late to the Great Plains. Neither tribe had a strong culture of its own, and they both improvised, taking what they could from other Indians who arrived before them, and making it their own. Maybe that's what makes them so boastful and so insecure." He shook his head. "That's what the Hopi say about the Navajo—'they're easily led.' They don't have the ancient spirit of brotherhood and cooperation that the older tribes have, although I have Navajo friends who are very generous. They will feed you." He sighed. "And they will also steal from you." He pointed out a pickup truck full of Indians. "See that? The white man's pickup, and his jeans and cowboy hat. Their sheep and horses and their silverwork came from the Spanish, and the so-called Navajo culture—the sand paintings, the weaving, the ceremonial dancing, the designs for their turquoise and silver, and a lot of their religion—was all adapted from the Pueblo culture, especially the Hopi."

But Craig acknowledged that the Navajo had transformed the arts of weaving and silversmithing, and that in remote parts of their reservation, such as our destination at Big Mountain, there were still "real Indians" who understood that this still, timeless land was full of imminence and power, full of the beauty of its own perfection, as in the Navajo phrase *Nih zhonigo*, or "Walk in beauty." Once he had camped with Navajo hunters near the junction of the San Juan and the Colorado, under the leadership of Ashe'teatla—One Salt. A hunter making propitiatory medicine could not get the Colorado to rise and take the offering of turquoise dust, and finally he shook it off his hand—a very dangerous gesture of disrespect to the harmony and balance of the natural world. Deer remained exceptionally scarce until one of the hunters came across a cougar print. "Good—that's my medicine," the hunter said. After that, as Craig recalled, many more deer were "called in" than could be supported by the desert country.

In those years I was a naturalist doing research on the disappearing wildlife of North America, and traveling the back roads of the West. One day in New Mexico, I gave a ride to a young Navajo, very stiff and quiet, perhaps because he didn't speak much English; he was also angry, and not knowing how to handle that,

I was quiet, too. He rode with me as far as some place in southern Nevada, an entirely silent seven hundred miles. That desert crossroads was not his destination, if he had one, it was just where he decided to get out, and he closed the door quietly without thanks and without good-bys. I see him standing in the heat, against the mountains; his expression disturbed me, and disturbs me still. Approaching the small town of Aztec, I related the episode to Craig, who merely nodded; he was staring out across the desert to the west. "Shiprock," he said disgustedly. "Can't even see it."

When Craig and I, on separate roads, first came this way back in the 1950's, the great rock monument called Shiprock might have been visible a hundred miles away, so pristine was the dry bright air in this empty space. The country to the west, between Lukachukai and a point north of Round Rock, in Arizona, was a clear landscape of towering pinnacles and monuments, of window rocks pierced by blue pieces of sky, set about with wind-worn amphitheaters of sun-filled rock and strong sand-smoothed figures like the giant *Yei* of Navajo mythology, rising and turning out of the sage and greasewood, the red hardpan of the desert floor, watching the stranger come, watching him go.

But in 1977, when we came this way from Hopi, crossing Navajo country from Black Mountain and Burnt Corn Wash to Canyon de Chelly, and from Mexican Water Trading Post to Teec Nos Pos, the great rock eminence off to the south was only a shadow in the pall of yellow-gray haze that had descended like an evil spell over the desert. Excepting the Great Wall of China, the smoke plume of the Four Corners plant near Farmington (just one component of "the largest energy-generating power grid in the world," transmitting electricity through an ugly web of lines and towers as far away as Texas and southern California) was the only man-made phenomenon observed by the astronauts in 1966. It has been called the greatest single source of pollution in the country, greater than the entire city of Los Angeles, and its awesome shroud has been darkened in recent years by the fallout from one of its sibling plants, only ten miles away. Four others are also in operation on or near the Colorado and San Juan rivers—the only permanent rivers in the region—which are used to cool them; in this near-desert, the Four Corners plant alone has lost an average twenty million gallons of water to evaporation every day since it opened in 1963. And this water loss from the shallow San Juan may doom the Navajo Indian Irrigation Project, a 110,000-acre agricultural enterprise near Burnham, to the south, which was guaranteed to the Indians as early as the Navajo treaty with the United States in 1868 and remains their best hope of healthy food as well as employment.

Now it was 1979, and here in the sacred Tukunavi, the spring light of late April came darkly through the haze of ash, the unseen mist of lead, mercury, dioxides, sulphuric acid, and other sickening pollutants that all dwellers in one of the most dramatic regions of the earth are doomed to breathe. Most of the human inhabitants are Indians, who watch in silence as their bare, clear world is turned into a wasteland. Five of the six plants now in operation are fired by coal from nearby strip mines, which contribute their own poisons to the air and water, but coal is not the only menace. In 1948, Kerr-McGee, attracted by cheap defenseless labor as well as the lack of health, safety, and pollution regulations, became the first company to mine uranium on Indian lands. Not far south of Shiprock are dead mines into which, for sixteen years, the overseers of Kerr-McGee sent Navajo miners when the air was still choked with uranium dust from the blasting; as late as 1966 (three years before Kerr-McGee abandoned its operation), there was no ventilation system in the mines. Perhaps because they had no concept of "radiation," the Indians were given no protective masks, nor were they ever warned of their great danger: since no drinking water was provided, they often drank from the puddles of "hot" water on the mine floor. Within a few years of the mine-closing, twenty-five Navajo—about one miner in five, including young men in their thirties—had died of anaplastic cancer of the lungs, with a like number dead and many others dying of dust poisoning, or pulmonary fibrosis, and no end to these ravages in sight. Two brothers named Billy and Lee John who worked together for seven years were dead of cancer within five months of each other; a woman named Betty Yazzie lost one husband, then another, to the same disease. Yet Kerr-McGee and the Atomic Energy Commission, which was buying the milled uranium produced, dodged all responsibility for the deaths; they left behind a poisoned and poverty-stricken community, a radioactive mill, and seventy-one acres of spent uranium ore that is estimated to retain up to eighty-five percent of the original radiation. These "tailings," exposed to wind and rain, were dumped about twenty yards from the banks of the San Juan River, the crucial source of water for the region. Such tailings piles, together with unfilled exploratory holes that did not pan out but are spreading surface radiation nonetheless, are unmarked death traps for Indians and others all over the Southwest.

In the dim light and cold wind off the mountains, the beautiful wildflowers of the spring desert seemed to be missing; everywhere we had traveled, the atmosphere in this empty land was filled with foreboding. Not long ago, fourteen thousand tons of spent uranium tailings were washed by flood into Utah's Green River; at Grand Junction, Colorado, this deadly material has been used for landfill. This morning we had come south through Durango, where wind-blown radon dust from a gray pile of uranium tailings 2,300 feet high had recently settled in a deadly ash upon a town where a sharp increase in acute and chronic respiratory ailments has already occurred among the children.

. . .

From Aztec, a narrow road heads east across a bleak, bare country: thin ponies wandering, poor bony cattle, an Indian shepherd on horseback, hunched in the wind. The only birds were torn disgruntled ravens, and a solitary hawk blown down the mesa. The road stretched out for miles and miles across plateaus of stunted sage and greasewood; sheep became scarce, and the few Indians stood clustered at the windswept trading posts and missions, awaiting deliverance or some unknown sign.

Beyond the road to the ancient ruins at Chaco Canyon (in a region now coveted by uranium prospectors for Mitsubishi and Getty Oil), this easternmost part of Navajo territory gave way to a still more bitter land assigned to the Jicarilla Apache. Due to the minerals beneath this land, the Jicarilla are members of the Indian bargaining coalition known as the Council of Energy Resources Tribes (CERT), but the riches have never extended very far beyond the tribal councils that deal with the energy corporations and the U.S. government. Like the Navajo, from whom they separated upon arrival in the Southwest, the Apache (a Zuñi word for "enemy") are Athapaskan-speaking people from the vast spruce muskeg regions in the interior of northwest Canada. But unlike their kinsmen, who have increased tenfold since the late nineteenth century, the Apache have scarcely maintained their numbers, and the Jicarilla band, Craig said, was all but finished, so far as its ancient traditions were concerned. Just east of the crooked dog-leg of bad land that comprises the Apache reservation lay a well-watered region heavily wooded in big piñon trees, presumably the property of white men.

Although not a part of the large Navajo reservation, this area of New Mexico is presumed to be where these Athapaskan nomads became settled; it was here that the Dineh, The People (Canadian Athapaskans are called Deneh), who may or may not have acquired a little agriculture, a little weaving on their southward journey, first encountered the settled, agricultural societies of the pueblo-dwelling tribes of the Southwest. By the time they appear in the Spanish records, in the early seventeenth century, the "Navaho" or "Navajo" (the meaning of this Tewa Pueblo name is still disputed) had learned the dry-farming agriculture of the Pueblos, as well as many of their arts and ceremonials, and soon acquired the livestock of the Spanish. The acquisition of horses and sheep permitted a return to their former nomadic existence; as their herds increased, they began the expansion of their range that has continued intermittently until the present, moving westward into Arizona and as far east and north as what is now Nebraska, where they traded with and raided the Pawnee. (Even today, the Dineteh, or Dineh homeland, according to Indian tradition, is not the abstract squares on paper of the white man's "reservations" but a spiritual region, bounded by the San Juan and Colorado rivers and the Rio Grande.) The Dineh had little contact with the Spanish missions that had been established in the region of Tsah Dzil (Mount Taylor), one of the four sacred mountains that marked the four directions of the Dineteh, and their taste for marauding brought them to the attention of the American authorities when this Spanish territory became "New Mexico" after 1846. To protect its new citizens, the United States established a military post and set forth on punitive expeditions, but not until 1860 did the Indians dare to express their resentment in an all-out attack on Fort Defiance. In doing so, they assured themselves a hostility from the U.S. government which many feel still exists to the present day. In June 1863, Colonel Kit Carson was sent out on a campaign of attrition, laying waste their fields and herds and killing those Indians who did not immediately submit to capture; he was guided by Hopi and Ute, whose people had suffered from the nomads' raids. Carson, who had been respected by the Dineh, lives in their memory today as the barbarian who, in 1864, destroyed the thousands of fine peach trees in the old Indian orchards in Canyon de Chelly. Within the year, most of the Indians were penned up at Fort Defiance, and the next year, half-naked and half-starved, some 8,500 were herded east in freezing weather on the notorious Long Walk across three hundred miles of arid desert to Fort Sumner, at Bosque Redondo on the Pecos River, an ordeal that has never been forgotten by the descendants of those who survived. (General James Carleton, who organized the relocation, observed that it cleared Navajo territory for exploration for minerals, which even in those days were thought to be present in promising amounts.) Not until 1868, in a period of searing drought, were the Dineh permitted to return to their ravaged homestead, and their ordeal was not over; as the Indian wars came to an end, there began the century-long siege of exposure to white civilization and the white economy which for these people, as for most Indians of North America, spread a slow plague of disruption, alcoholism, and abject poverty.

> Although there were several trading posts on the reservation by the early 1870's, it was the building of the railroad across New Mexico and Arizona in the 1880's which brought intoxicants, diseases, and other disrupting forces of white society to The People. The gradual but steady increase in white population in surrounding areas came to mean economic exploitation and a mounting general pressure upon the Navahos. . . . Even those Navahos whose direct contacts with whites are limited or negligible have a heightening sense of a net being drawn ever tighter around them, of being at the mercy of a more powerful and often unfriendly people. As more of their own number became bilingual and conversant with white ways, informed individuals spread bitterness among the tribe by quoting chapter and verse as to the deceit and trickery of the white rulers. . . . Even recent administrations have found their serious practical problems complicated by the bewilderment, cynicism, and resentment bred by three generations of treatment that was often vicious, mostly stupid, and always based on the attitudes toward "backward" peoples current in white society at the time.[*]

[*]Clyde Kluckhohn and Dorothea Leighton, *The Navaho* (New York, 1962).

· · ·

Crossing the Continental Divide, our road descended gradually to Coyote and Gallina and Abiquiu, where in the mid-eighteenth century the Spanish resettled some Apache and Comanche captives in abandoned pueblos; these Genizaro people, as they are known, still use a Spanish architecture and Spanish names. The stream here is one of the headwaters of the Rio Grande, and we followed it down to San Juan Pueblo, near Española. Craig's friends were absent from San Juan, and we drove north again to Taos Pueblo, taking the river road up the Rio Grande, which is narrow here in north-central New Mexico and swift and beautiful in its spring flood, rushing down through foothill ravines that descend from the broad and melancholy plateaus under Wheeler Peak in the Sangre de Cristo Mountains. Taos and Ranchos de Taos are strip-development, tourist-shop towns tacked on to this monumental landscape, but the old brown pueblo grows out of the earth. Parted by a mountain stream, the ancient village is a maze of dirt lanes and corrals, fences and gardens, surrounding stepped pueblo structures of worn abode; to the north rise the steep sides of Mount Wheeler, hiding the sacred Blue Lake. Craig's friend Paul Bernal, traditional spokesman and a leader in the successful fight to recover Blue Lake for his people in the early 1970's, was also away, and that night we went on south to Santa Fe and Albuquerque, where we slept in a lot on the west edge of that town.

At daybreak, in dry, sunny weather, we headed west, crossing good rangeland to the red cliffs and small mountains beyond the Rio Puerco. Once this river was a large one, to judge from the dimensions of its bed, but now it has been reduced to a mere trickle, even at this flood time of the year. And this is true of so many rivers in the West that one must wonder where the end will be, as the growing cities of these desert sunlands, and the mines, suck the earth dry of its last uncontaminated water.

At Mesitas Pueblo, Craig asked a boy if the kiva was in use; did his people dance? To both questions the boy answered, "Naw." At Laguna Pueblo, a white mission church sits on the highest rock in town, and a child called out, "Hello, Bahana!," using the Hopi word for "white man." Being close to the main east–west highway, Laguna profits from the tourists, and until recently sent its men into Anaconda's Jackpile mine, the largest uranium mine on earth.

Not far away, Acoma Pueblo remains isolated on its beautiful high rock some sixteen miles south of the highway, in a land of strange buttes and window rocks and soaring birds. Although it could trade on what must be the most striking location of all the pueblo villages of the Southwest, Acoma has so far resisted the temptation of both electricity and running water, and its people are silent and reserved. Resistance to the intrusion of our truck was so manifest in the dead silence of the stone dwellings in the rock that we turned around and left immediately, on a shared impulse, feeling exhilarated rather than rejected, as if we had glimpsed a rare vanishing creature without scaring it away. "They're still together here," Craig said, eyes shining. "Still standing on their land."

.   .   .

On the way to Big Mountain, we passed through Grants, "the Uranium Capital of the World," a neon boom town under the south slope of Mount Taylor; here an antinuclear demonstration by whites and Indians would take place in the next few days. Despite the statistics at nearby Laguna Pueblo, where tailings from the Anaconda mine, used for fill in construction of Indian schools and other public buildings, have apparently caused serious birth defects in over one hundred Indian babies in the past five years; despite the massive radioactive poisoning from "unknown sources" of deep-well water at nearby Martinez Camp, and elsewhere; despite the known water depletion and pollution at nearby Crownpoint (to dry out the uranium strata for more profitable mining, the precious desert aquifers around Crownpoint are being "dewatered" at the rate of four hundred thousand gallons per minute); despite the fact that every wind from the northwest carries radioactive dust from this mountainous pile of poison right across their town, prosperity has encouraged the citizens of Grants to accept the glib assurances of the mining companies about their prospects for long life. One of these companies is Kerr-McGee, which made this comment on the Shiprock deaths (to the Senate Select Committee on Indian Affairs) in the face of overwhelming evidence to the contrary: "We are not aware of the sources of the allegation that Navajo Indians who worked in those mines have died of lung cancer resulting from radiation exposure. We doubt that any evidence to support this allegation exists anywhere." Fearing massive litigation, Kerr-McGee continues to refuse all responsibility to the destitute families of the Shiprock miners, a point that their employees in this community would do well to keep in mind. This roughshod company (best known for the smelly Karen Silkwood case) has another New Mexico mine on the Navajo reservation at Church Rock, where it operates a training school for Indian miners. Despite an Oklahoma judgment on this corporation's negligence toward the public, Kerr-McGee's school is funded by the Labor Department, and American taxpayers might well inquire why they and not the uranium profiteers are paying two million dollars annually to train an estimated one hundred people for the mines of a private corporation.

(In addition to mines and tailings piles, the Church Rock Navajo are also threatened by what the Nuclear Regulatory Commission has called the worst contamination in the history of the nuclear industry: not long after the antinuclear demonstration at Mount Taylor, on July 16, 1979, the dam at a United Nuclear Corporation tailings mill pond gave way near Church Rock, releasing ninety-five million gallons of radioactive water into the Rio Puerco, that once-great, now-dead tributary of the Rio Grande. Although the pond had been overfilled, and the dam itself was known to be cracked and fissured, this event got almost no publicity, unlike the spectacular episode at Three Mile Island, Pennsylvania, which reminded the world that a nuclear disaster was "inevitable." In northwestern New Mexico, events have been unspectacular, insidious, and slow, and so far, most of its victims have been Indians—conditions which apparently permit the authorities to ignore a nuclear tragedy that has already occurred.)*

*In 1978, a Supreme Court decision (*Oliphant* v. *Suquamish Indian Tribe*) denying reservation governments criminal jurisdiction over non-Indians asserted that these "quasi-sovereign" governments could not exercise power "inconsistent with their status": "Upon incorporation into the territory of the United States, the Indian tribes thereby come under the territorial sovereignty of the United States and their exercise of sovereign power is constrained so as not to conflict with the interests of this over-riding sovereignty." In the absence of any limitation on this "over-riding sovereignty," this ruling renders the Indian nations completely vulnerable to any judicial abrogation of their rights. Thus a federal district court ruling in 1981 (*UNC Resources* v. *Benally*) forbids the Indians from suing

It is estimated that about seventy-five percent of known uranium reserves in the United States are currently controlled by the seven major oil corporations (Kerr-McGee and Gulf control more than half, mostly through leases on Indian lands)—hence the huge power of the uranium lobby to prevail over human welfare and common sense, not to speak of the law of the land. Most or all of the companies exploiting the Grants Mineral Belt are here illegally, since they have rarely or never bothered to prepare the environmental impact statements that are required by the National Environmental Policy Act, far less submit to public hearings and obtain approval from the government agencies involved.

In regard to Indians, the U.S. government has customarily suspended its own laws wherever these got in the way of commercial expedience, and never more so than in collusion with the great energy consortiums that are looting the Southwest (and the Great Plains) under the red-white-and-blue banner of "energy independence" for America. In 1977, for example, in approving an Exxon lease for uranium prospecting on four hundred thousand acres of Navajo land, the Secretary of the Interior waived thirteen regulations of his own department, including the lease area limit of 2,560 acres. According to a 1978 report of the Anthropology and Resource Center in Cambridge, Massachusetts:

> The Navajos who resided in the uranium-exploration region and who would be relocated when uranium extraction began were not asked whether or not they desired to be moved. Nor were they asked whether or not they favored Exxon's extracting uranium ore from under the houses they lived in and from under the vegetation that sustained their sheep. Neither the BIA nor the Secretary of the Interior sought information on Navajo attitudes about their environment; their beliefs about sickness and health, relations among the gods, rituals, kinship groups, and land; the importance of family households and their functions in Indian society; and

United Nuclear in Navajo Court for damages or injuries, declaring that the Navajo tribe's exercise of jurisdiction on its own territory conflicted with "the over-riding sovereignty" of the United States. United Nuclear also triumphed in a related suit in Arizona, where the court found that Navajo jurisdiction "conflicts with the superior federal interest in regulating the production of nuclear power."

a hundred other pertinent questions. The BIA should have gathered and analyzed such information before making any recommendations about the Navajo–Exxon lease. In this case, as in so many others, the federal government did not adequately inform Indians about the consequences of their actions in signing contracts and did not learn what Indians desired.

Indians were not the only ones who were inadequately informed about the despoliation of the desert. "There were no announcements prior to signed contracts, no questions or congressional hearings, no chance for anyone to ask questions or receive answers. . . . The atmosphere and environment fundamental to the quality and future life of a huge part of the Southwest, encompassing thousands of square miles in many states, was literally appropriated by the members of the power consortium. The confusion, wonder, frustration, and anger that resulted when word did get out—after everything was firmly signed and in the works—underscores how grave has become the government failure to protect and even inform the public."[*]

This high-handed attitude has prevailed since 1921 when Standard Oil, finding petroleum on these arid lands that were fit only for Indians, persuaded the obliging Indian Bureau to come up with some "chiefs" to sign the leases; the five who agreed were given a semblance of dignity by being appointed as a "tribal council." In recent years, the Navajo Tribal Council under Haskasilt Begay, or "Peter MacDonald," has continued this tradition, negotiating leases that often ignored the expressed wishes of the Indians it was supposed to represent. For example, the great majority of Dineh at Burnham, near Shiprock, who live in a perpetual fallout of lethal poisons from the Four Corners and San Juan power plants (including the boron that threatens the crops of the Navajo Nation Irrigation Project) have opposed strip mining and gasification plants since 1973, yet the BIA approved the Tribal Council's 1976 lease of forty thousand acres in that region to El Paso Natural Gas.

In May 1978, the Navajo of Crownpoint and Dalton Pass issued a resolution stating: "We have become increasingly alarmed at the present and planned uranium mining activity in our com-

[*]Alvin M. Josephy, Jr., in *Clear Creek*, 13 (1971).

munity and are most fearful of its effects on our health, welfare, property, and culture, as well as the well-being of future generations. . . . We are unalterably opposed to all uranium exploration in our boundaries." Because of its lease of 12,470 acres to Mobil Oil in 1972 without the approval of the local Indians, the BIA was sued by ninety Navajo of the Crownpoint area for violation of its trust responsibility; in the same multiple suit, a number of mining companies were also being sued for failure to file environmental-impact statements. Indian lands are held in trust for the Indian people by the Department of the Interior, which advocates mining development. The reservations are unprotected by the moratorium on strip mining of public lands in effect throughout most of the West, and the authorizing legislation for the Department of Energy would theoretically permit it to seize and hold any mineral lands that it deemed strategic even where the courts had decided in favor of the Indians. As John Redhouse (Dineh) has observed, "We are in the way of progress. . . . The Indian people have always been on the right side of the law. Unfortunately they've been on the wrong side of the issues."

The Navajo find themselves confronted with the real or imagined energy needs of an apparently insatiable white economy. Many of these adaptable people would welcome a fair share of this economy, and most still endorse the Navajo Tribal Council, which has cooperated with the mining corporations; yet the great majority of The People will receive little or no benefit from the huge complex of mines and power plants that is destroying all life in the Dineteh. On paper, at least, the Navajo should be one of the wealthiest people on the earth; in fact (according to the U.S. Civil Rights Commission), they are the poorest ethnic group in the United States, with the great majority living well below poverty level. About one house in five has electricity, and the average per-capita income remains more or less steady at nine hundred dollars a year, largely because of the ludicrous terms in the leases signed by the Tribal Council, with the encouragement and approval of the BIA; here again one must conclude that the BIA and the Department of the Interior have made rich white men that much richer at the expense of a helpless and destitute people they were sworn to protect. (In 1975, for example, the Navajo were paid sixty cents a pound for uranium ore that sold for twice that much on the open market; in 1977, Utah International, on the basis of a contract signed twenty years before, was paying royalties of fifteen to thirty-seven cents a ton for strip-mined coal worth fifteen to twenty dollars.) Council Chairman MacDonald infuriated Senator Barry Goldwater and his associates in energy development by trying to renegotiate these leases; he also infuriated an increasing number of his people, who saw some of the income from the leases poured into the support of MacDonald's regime. The chairman, a golf-playing Republican who traveled by Lear jet and Lincoln Continental, raised the annual salaries of his council members from seven thousand to twenty thousand dollars, or more than twenty times the average per-capita income of their fellow tribesmen, who were kept in line by threats of bad medicine and evil spells that would come their way from one of two male witches who were never very far from MacDonald's side; despite their material sophistication, the Dineh are beset by witchcraft, reflecting a pervasive anxiety and frustration.

In recent years, "Peter MacDollar," as he is known to other Indians, has spoken in high praise of Secretary of the Interior James Watt, and was himself appointed to President Ronald Reagan's Energy Task Force; as chairman of CERT, he also accepted government funding for this Indian energy cartel, from which four tribes soon resigned in the suspicion that MacDollar had sold out to the corporate state.

· · ·

Tsah Dzil, or Mount Taylor, is a sacred mountain not only for the Dineh but for the Pueblo, and the Apache and Hopi had joined in a mass protest against the digging by Gulf Oil of two new deep uranium mine shafts on its western slope; these mines would be worked by "de-watering" wells designed to pump five thousand gallons per minute from the sinking water table in order to expedite the removal of an estimated fifty thousand tons of uranium ore. From this vast excavation, one hundred pounds of uranium might be yielded; all the rest would be dumped on the open desert in yet another tailings pile of lethal waste.*

---

*"The companies are showing a total disregard for the problem of waste disposal," said Dr. Joseph Wagoner, a cancer consultant for the National Institute for Occupational Safety and Health, in an interview in *The New York Times* in May

The road north to the Indian protest camp west of the mountain passed the immense pyramid of uranium tailings, at least one third of a mile long and a hundred feet high, cast off by the multimillion-dollar operation of "United Nuclear and Homestake Partners." High to the eastward, on Tsah Dzil, a wavy line of snow came down the ridges of the dark volcano; on the dirt roads, big trucks loaded with gray waste for the deadly pile left plumes of dust. One road led westward through land leased to Kerr-McGee and Gulf into low rolling piñon hills of Cibola National Forest. There a film crew was interviewing a Dineh activist named Larry Anderson, head of the Dineh Bii Coalition, which was formed in 1974 to resist the policies of the Tribal Council. Anderson, a big man in braids and long moustache, dressed in the red wind band, dark glasses, and green fatigue jacket that sometimes serve as an informal uniform for activists of AIM, had led a group of Indians 150 miles on foot, all the way across the deserts from Big Mountain. The Dineh had established a peaceful camp in the sunny piñon groves under Tsah Dzil, where they planned to erect a ceremonial sweat lodge that afternoon; awaiting Indians from other tribes, they chanted and played softly on hide drums.

From Mount Taylor we headed south along the western side of the Malpais Lava Flow that comes down from Tsah Dzil—the crusted blood of the *Yei* giant from whom the Dineh were delivered by the monster-slaying twin of the old tradition—then west again toward the great rock monument known as El Morro. About 800 A.D., this road was an Indian trail between Acoma and Zuñi, and seven centuries later, the Spanish made good use of it in their searches for the gold city of Cibola; eventually it became the old Fort Wingate Road, much used by the U.S. Army in the years they were rounding up the Navajo for the Long Walk to the detention camps at Bosque Redondo on the Pecos. On the lovely rock face at El Morro are Spanish graffiti made by the early travelers as well as the scrawls of fools who have come since, and there are also ancient petroglyphs, perhaps giving directions to the next spring in this hot, dry pineland country of sparse water. At Zuñi Pueblo, an Indian told us that he would not go to Grants

1979. This bore out a report on nuclear waste management issued in 1978 by the Department of Energy, which discovered entirely unsafe conditions for storage at all twenty-two of the inactive tailings sites in eight of these western states.

to join in the antinuclear protest: "What they going to do about it anyway?" he said, still angry because his girl had kicked him out for being drunk.

At Gallup, on the Arizona border, we spent the evening with three journalists (Dan Budnik, Jerry Kammer, and Molly Ivins) who had followed the Big Mountain crisis from the start; the talk was instructive, but Craig was restless in this place which, among Indians, is widely considered the most racist town in the United States. (A few years ago, in Gallup and Farmington, near the Four Corners, there were at least ten torture-murders of helpless Navajo, whose high alcoholic intake is a main source of income for both communities. In 1973, the most profitable liquor operation in New Mexico was the Navajo Inn on the edge of the Navajo reservation, just north of town; it was owned in part by Gallup's mayor, who served simultaneously as head of an alcoholism project and had recently been made a regent at the University of New Mexico; in 1973 a young AIM organizer named Larry Casuse was shot and killed by the police during desperate efforts to protest this man's exploitation and abuse of the Indian people.)

At Window Rock, across the Arizona line, where we visited next morning with the Navajo artist Carl Gorman, the sacred golden window on the stone-blue desert sky—revered by the Old Ones as a place where man emerged from the darkness of an earlier world into the sun—has been reduced to a decorative background for the new Tribal Council offices of Peter MacDonald.

• • •

From Window Rock, we headed west toward Hopi by way of Ganado and Keams Canyon. Off to the southward could be seen the uninhabited mesa of the doomed village of Awatovi; to the northwest was the long escarpment of First Mesa. On Second Mesa, where we arrived in time for the lively and colorful Basket Dance at Shungopovi, a large Hopi crowd filled the village plazas and flat roofs of the ancient stone houses in the light spring air of this blue windy afternoon.

In the southern distance white mountains rose above the dun haze and heat of the spring desert. Despite the land dispute being encouraged by their tribal councils, Navajo and Hopi are united in their distress over the threat to the sacred San Francisco Peaks, home of the great rain beings, or kachinas, on whom life in this bare, arid place depends. In a recent decision, the U.S. Forest Service had granted a permit to the Arizona Snow Bowl to expand its facilities for skiing in the Coconino National Forest, thereby destroying the already damaged sanctity of the evergreen forests and high peaks. In the words of a Navajo Tribal Council resolution, "The rain and snow will cease to fall; the Navajo people will be unprotected from the forces of destruction; our traditions will die, and Doo-ko-oslid [the San Francisco Peaks] will turn away from us." "Once we lose the San Francisco Peaks, we got no place to go," said Jacob Bahnimtewa, Mina Lansa's nephew, whom we had last seen in Oraibi two years before: Jacob spoke quietly, eyebrows raised, watching the long slow line of old women in red, black, and white ceremonial dress, chanting and sidestepping in the sun and dust of Shungopovi's plaza. (There was talk that day that Jacob would become the next kikmongwi of Old Oraibi, but in 1982 he would be found dead near the Life Plan Rock; those who knew him did not accept the conclusion of the Hopi police that he had died of drunkenness and exposure.)

"The Anglos only see the peaks," Harold Koruh said next day. "There are many other things." In his house in Mishongnovi, surrounded by his family, I sat facing the big loom on which he was weaving a blanket and a belt. "All since time immemorial, that is the home of the kachinas, and we go over there maybe twice a year, get our green spruce and the medicine people gather their herbs. There is still an Eagle Clan shrine over there, and an ice cave that belongs to the Snow Clan. And Long Valley—what we call the Snow Belt, we can see it from over here—that belongs to the Snow Clan people, too. At sunset, that place is important to us when we look out toward the west. Those peaks will always be there, but if they are dirtied with a lot of cinders—no, we don't like that. When we disrespect the San Francisco Peaks, we will have no rains; and the snow will be heavy, or there will be no snow."

Harold Koruh's strong hair stands straight up in a brush; in a weather-lined face, the eyes are sad and gentle. "We can't really depend on the courts in the United States; we might have to go to the United Nations, or the World Court." He pointed east. "Thomas Banyacya [the Hopi traditional spokesman] is over there in Washington to see about that. If the Hopi don't give up, maybe all Indians will get their rights back." (While in Washington, Banyacya submitted to the White House a report documented by the Indian Law Resource Center that the law firm of John Boyden, the Hopi Tribal Council lawyer, was representing the Peabody Coal Company at the same time he was representing the Hopi Tribal Council in connection with the Peabody leases on Black Mesa.)

We returned to our old camp under Shungopovi, very different from the cold March camp of two years before; in a warm wind, the cottonwoods were in green leaf on a blue sky, and two boys with .22 rifles were hunting birds for "paho feathers for our grandfathers." For the first time since we had come to Hopi, Craig emerged from the truck and walked around a little in the sun; he feels he must hide from the many enemies among BIA Indians that he has made over the years, any one of whom might report him to the police, and while we were parked in Shungopovi and in Walpi, he was wrapped up in a blanket in the rear. It seemed to me that he was being paranoid, but at Shungopovi Jacob Bahnimtewa had said, "We ain't seen Craig around here at all. The last I saw him was on a FBI flyer over there in the post office at Keams Canyon; I guess he got himself in trouble, huh?" Asked how long ago he had seen that flyer, Jacob thought it had been less than a year. Perhaps Craig had been right all along: he was regarded as a troublemaker, and the authorities would get him on any pretext that they could. Later that day, when he was seen by a pickup truck full of Indians coming in off the mesa, we decided to move out; we camped on the desert, and next morning, when we paid a visit to David Monongye at Hotevilla, Craig wrapped a blanket all around his head and shoulders before leaving the truck and slipped into the small house like a sick man.

David Monongye's full head of gray hair was tied up in a white wind band; he wore a shirt that was buttoned to the top and a pair of blue sneakers. Though well over ninety and nearly blind, his voice is sure and firm and his step strong. "I don't even know how old I am; I dropped out after the fourth grade. But I was in school when the Split took place over there in Oraibi. The policemen would come and chase us all around, shoot pistols to make us stop. I ran away, but finally I got caught, and my brother, too. So I was sent away to school." He nodded his head, looking straight ahead over his breakfast bowl. "I remember very well what happened over there at Old Oraibi."

David Monongye had just returned the day before from the anti-uranium-mining demonstrations at Mount Taylor—"Digging weapons from our Mother Earth; that is what we are against"—and he felt that the problem at Grants was essentially the same as the problem at the San Francisco Peaks—the greed for money. In his opinion, the U.S. Forest Service that was now so anxious to drastically increase commercial operations in the Peaks was dominated by Mormons, who "force things upon people"—from a traditional Hopi, a very stern rebuke. "The Hopi people escaped a corrupt life in the other world, and they came up here with the permission of the Great Spirit. The Snow Clan was the first people in that area, and the Kachina Clan was next; they have always been there, and we don't want the spirits to be desecrated. The people in the White House—their policy will lead to genocide. That kind of life that the white man leads must not go on forever. The Great Spirit gave us good instructions, and we are the tongue of the Great Spirit. We're still under the Great Spirit, Maasa'u, but the Tribal Council doesn't know that, it makes its own laws—those people will do *anything*!" he exclaimed suddenly, offended anew. "They wanted to put their Community Hall right on top of sacred ground, and a lot of young people who were against us before that, who wanted electricity and all, why they came right back to Hopi way when they saw *that*!" He managed a smile. "So that Tribal Council helped us after all."

In the traditions of both nations, the Hopi are ultimately responsible for protecting the Techqua Ikachi, "Land and Life," while the Dineh serve to protect the Hopi and see that their sacred instructions are carried out. David Monongye emphasized this strong sense of the Hopi's role. "Most Indian people, their land has been taken away from them; if the Hopi can accomplish something, those other people might get back their land."

He shook his head, then spoke again in the firm voice of a much younger man. "We are trying every way to accomplish something for the good of all people, white people, too; we don't try to push anyone aside, we pray for everyone. I was taught by my uncle, a great chief, that the Creator made people like a grass with a single stem and many different colored flowers. That is the way that the Creator made us." It was six in the morning, and the old man sat straight up at his breakfast, unable to see the expressions of his visitors but alert to every nuance in their voices.

Not long after our visit, it was revealed that uranium had been discovered on Black Mesa, and it is generally assumed that the mining corporations and the U.S. government have known about this uranium for years. David Monongye issued a warning:

> Just recently, uranium has been discovered on our sacred lands. In order to gain access to this mineral, the federal government has a plan to forcibly remove all the residents from the land. These people are thousands of traditional Navahos who share this land with the Hopi. We know we must resist the removal of these people because, if they are not here to guard this sacred land, the miners will move in and destroy everything. They will use this uranium, which poisons everything, and cause death and misery for thousands of years. We who believe in the sacred instructions of the Great Spirit must resist and protest, for the sake of all life, both present and future.

Told that we were headed for Big Mountain, David's son-in-law, who is a Navajo, wished us a safe journey. Coming to the window of the truck he said, "Navajos say that when a coyote crosses your path, you are not supposed to go that way. But if you spread corn meal and tell him to go in peace, it will be all right."

· 12 ·

TO BIG MOUNTAIN

Big Mountain, a remote eminence on Black Mesa, is perhaps seventy-five miles from the nearest town at Tuba City; it is one of the corners of this silent land where small bands of Dineh went into hiding at the time of the Long Walk in 1864, and its inhabitants remain today the most traditional and culturally intact of all Dineh communities. Having lived here since the time of the Grandfathers, the Big Mountain people have no doubt about who belongs here, but legal dominion in this region according to the white man's law has been confused since that day more than a century ago when 2.4 million acres of northern Arizona desert were set aside for the exclusive use of the Hopi and such "other Indians" as the Secretary of the Interior might choose to banish there. The Dineh, though few and widely scattered in small sheep camps due to the poor quality of the range, had long since spread westward from their own reservation into this territory; in the next century, while the sedentary Hopi, staying close to their home villages and gardens, barely doubled their numbers, these Athapaskan nomads, following their herds over the empty mesas, became ten times as numerous, and their sheep overgrazed the wiry grass of this hard range.

In the twentieth century, a few "progressive" Hopi families acquired large herds of livestock, and in the 1940's, they began to contest the Navajo presence on the land. After all, it was said, the Navajo had never been legally recognized as those "other Indians" who might use the Hopi reservation, quite apart from the fact that they had a large reservation of their own. The Navajo disputed this on the grounds that their presence in the region had been validated by the U.S. government through the federal services extended to the tribe.*

In the 1940's, the only known coal reserves in Arizona were discovered on Black Mesa, and from that time forward, by coincidence or otherwise, the U.S. government intensified a drastic stock-reduction program among the Navajo, after sixty years of

*General background information on the so-called Hopi–Navajo land dispute and the threatened relocation of traditional Dineh people from Big Mountain may be found in Jerry Kammer, *The Second Long Walk* (Albuquerque, 1980), and various articles by Kammer and Peter Melnick in *The Navajo Times*, 1978–83; see also Navajo affidavits filed with the Department of the Interior, 1974.

encouraging them to raise sheep. Many of these bewildered people lost their livelihood and were forced to leave the Dineteh in order to find work in the towns and cities; within a decade, the majority had abandoned Indian way for the "American Way of Life," and the cow pony was replaced almost everywhere by the pickup truck that became the symbol of this people's conversion to the white economy. Meanwhile, the Hopi Tribal Council had begun legal proceedings to expel the Navajo from Hopi land, and in 1962, all further construction of houses and even maintenance of clinics, school, and roads in the disputed area—almost all of it located on Black Mesa—was forbidden by a federal court order; the same court ruled that the tract of 640,000 acres immediately surrounding the Hopi villages ("Grazing District 6") was the exclusive domain of the Hopi, and that the rest of the 1882 reservation was to be shared equally as a Joint Use Area. Since few Hopi used it except to hunt and look for firewood, the JUA, as it is known, remained a rangeland for the Big Mountain Dineh, who could not imagine any change in their existence and were not much troubled by deterioration of the white men's roads.

In 1972, another stock-reduction program further reduced the number of Navajo homesteads, and in 1974, in response to continued demands from the Hopi Tribal Council lawyer, John S. Boyden, the U.S. Congress, led by Wayne Owens (Democrat from Utah), Stan Steiger (Republican from Arizona), and Boyden's friend Senator Goldwater, passed the Navajo–Hopi Land Settlement Act (Public Law 93-531), according to the terms of which the residents of JUA—almost all of them Navajo—were compelled to sell off most of their herds in yet another stock-reduction program intended to reduce the number of animals to the carrying capacity of the range. Doubtless this ruling made good sense as plain land management, and the payments for stock that were offered by the BIA were fair enough, but to the older Navajo, for whom livestock and the sheep especially were the very manifestations of their security and their well-being, representing not only food, clothing, and livelihood, but their main source of trade, the stock-reduction program was a fearsome threat. Even so, it was much less serious than the authorization of an equal partition of the JUA, which, later defined by a state court (February 1977), condemned some 5,600 Navajo* to eviction from Hopi land (it also affected ap-

*Estimate of the Federal Relocation Commission.

proximately one hundred Hopi who happened to reside in Navajo territory)—the greatest mass relocation of an Indian people since the Long Walk of 1864.

At first the people way out there at Big Mountain had tried to ignore the white man's words and papers; the new law was too foolish to be taken seriously. But a few weeks after our visit to Hopi in March 1977, the five-year relocation plan had been set in motion, and those Navajo who intended to move anyway accepted the relocation benefits and bonuses. For most of the rest, including the Big Mountain people, the promised benefits ($27,000 or a new house, plus a bonus of $5,000, which diminished according to length of delay) were no compensation at all. Despite desperate poverty, few availed themselves of the government offer, though most stopped short of a tendency around Big Mountain to chase Relocation Commission agents and their forms and papers off the land. Threatened anew with eviction from their homelands, and realizing that there was no place for their old ways in the outside world, they promised quietly to resist with guns if that was necessary. "They tell us to get rid of our stock and after that they will get rid of *us*," said the people bitterly, wondering why the Hopi Tribal Council was pressing so hard for their eviction when Big Mountain was forty miles from Hopi and when this same Tribal Council, in 1976, had waived all Hopi claims to the land in question by accepting a government "recompense" of five million dollars that cleared the way for further mining leases on Black Mesa. Why was the government willing to spend so many millions of dollars relocating them? And why had Peabody Coal Company's Vice President for Government Relations, Harrison Loesch (an unabashed agent of the mining companies in his previous job as director of the Bureau of Land Management), and its attorney, John Boyden (who apparently perceived no conflict of interest in his firm's working for Peabody Coal while he represented the Hopi Tribal Council), lobbied so vigorously for the partition in this matter that did not or should not have concerned them? In the light of bitter Dineh experience at Shiprock and Church Rock, Crownpoint and Mount Taylor, the Big Mountain people had begun to suspect that their eviction would expedite the efforts of the mining companies to obtain leases on the emptied territory, which was now known to contain uranium as well as coal.

Anthropologists sent out by the Federal Relocation Commission concluded, a little late, that Dzil Ntsaaii, or Big Mountain, has an important place in the origin myth of its people: "Big Mountain is the most prominent feature in the heart of Black Mesa, and Black Mesa in its entirety is sacred, [as] sacred as the four sacred mountains of the Navaho people." They also concluded that the mountain has been a sacred place for a long time and is still used for gathering medicine herbs and for ceremonials, and that the sense of spiritual continuity manifested by the mountain is crucial to the culture and well-being of its people—so crucial, in fact, that leaving here seems to the elders to be leaving life itself, to being dead people. Big Mountain includes at least fifteen locations of sacred significance; most are springs, used commonly to offer prayers for rain and blessings, but there is also a strange circular stone platform about twenty feet across which supports a cubical stone structure. This structure, which represents a sacred hogan (the traditional Dineh house of logs and mud), has the hogan's opening toward the sunrise in the east, and here offerings are made to two holy beings, one of whom, called Begochidi, has various important attributes, and has been identified as the "One Who Created Man." Dzil Ntsaaii is the traditional home of Begochidi, "whom the sun never leaves, who time and again transforms into sunlight, into wind, who is found absolutely everywhere."

The Big Mountain people feel that they have been here since the Beginning, and that this place and its sacred springs were used by their parents and grandparents, who were buried here after passing on the teachings and rituals that are still associated with these places. "The mountain is ours," says a herder named Kee Shey. "It is the place we go to pray for our livestocks, and our medicine men go there to get herbs, and it is the place our women gather the medicine they use when they bear children. We need the mountain to live." For Indians, Dzil Ntsaaii is as vibrant and alive as Begochidi, and mere "access" to the mountain, as provided for in recent legislation, is of no use and not much interest to a people who conceive of themselves as not separable from this place.

> The mountains, I become part of it. . . .
> The herbs, the evergreen, I become part of it.
> The morning mists, the clouds, the gathering waters,

I become part of it.
The dew drops, the pollen, I become part of it.*

An old lady named Ashikie Bitsie, in a document filed with the Department of the Interior before the passage of the Land Settlement Act in 1974, could say in part: "Ashikie's father told me and my children never to leave or let go of the Big Mountain area . . . handed down from our forefathers. The holy shrine is for our Dineh people: these were some of his last words before he passed on. . . . We ask the right to live and pursuit of happiness like any other human being. I ask the federal government to protect our given rights." It did not do so. In the blunt words of Senator James Abourezk of South Dakota, who fought the passage of P.L. 93-531 in vain, "Lack of knowledge, unawareness, insensitivity, and neglect are the keynotes of the federal government's interaction with traditional Indian religions and culture."

The federal order to leave their land was without meaning to the elderly traditionals on Big Mountain. "We were here many years ago," explained an old shepherd named Biakeddy of the Bitter Water clan. "The spring is ours. Big Mountain is where my prayer is at. This is where I was raised as a child. Why do you talk about us, our land, our springs? We will stay here forever."

Isolated on their remote mesas by dirt roads that are often impassable in winter and spring, with most of their elder leadership unable to read the white man's words, the Big Mountain people took no interest in politics until 1974. That year they turned out to cast their vote against Senator Goldwater, who had not only sponsored the Land Settlement Act but declared his opposition to relocation benefits for these powerless people because they were using property that—by white-man law—did not belong to them; almost certainly, his denial of their identity with Big Mountain seemed more outlandish to the Indians than the threatened loss of relocation benefits, since the whole idea of relocation was incomprehensible. As Tribal Chairman MacDonald said, "We can go to them and say 'It's written here; the Congress says it or the courts say it.' But they have no appreciation for anything that is on paper. Throughout all these years the only law they know is

*Dineh chant, quoted by Joseph Epes Brown in *The Spiritual Legacy of the American Indian*.

the law that has been handed down by the legends and traditions of the culture in which they live. But when you say it is written down, they say 'Don't talk to me about it—tell me where it is in my culture and I'll understand.' It is a very difficult thing to go out to these communities and talk about the law, because they don't understand that. They say 'Don't talk to me about the law; I don't understand it; I probably never will.' "

* * *

In the summer of 1978, after the partition line had been decreed, Pauline Whitesinger and four others from Big Mountain joined the Longest Walk across the country made by Indians of many tribes in protest against the wave of backlash legislation that their latest demands for justice had evoked: the name of the greatest gathering of Indian people in this century was adapted from the Long Walk of the Navajo in 1864, and its leaders included David Monongye, Russell Means, and Mad Bear Anderson. Among other wrongs, the Indians protested the "genocidal" mass dislocation of the Dineh people here on Black Mesa, and the seizure of Indian lands unprotected by treaty without due process of law and compensation (as authorized in the infamous 1955 Supreme Court ruling known as Tee-Hit-Ton). In Washington, D.C., Roberta Blackgoat and Violet Ashikie were promised by Senator Goldwater that he would make a three-day visit to Big Mountain to inspect the situation from the Navajo point of view: Goldwater confessed that he had sided with the Hopi due to his natural tendency to support the underdog. Others felt that he had sided with the Hopi to revenge himself against his old friend and fellow Republican, Peter MacDonald, who had withdrawn his political support because of Goldwater's endorsement of the Steiger bill and who also wished to renegotiate the discriminatory leases on Navajo land. Because the whole reservation felt so strongly, MacDonald seemed sympathetic to the Big Mountain people, but eventually his unwillingness to compromise with those such as Senator Abourezk who were trying to find a fair solution would do the Big Mountain people almost as much harm as the New York City-born Steiger's need to project a right-wing "Arizona" image, or Goldwater's outrage that his Indian sidekick had gotten out of line. For the vanity and ambitions of these politicians, the Big Mountain people had begun to die.

According to reports in *The Navajo Times*, an "official" tribe newspaper in Window Rock, Senator Goldwater arrived at Big Mountain in late August 1977 and assured the desperate Indians that "no one could push them around." The statement displayed an astonishing ignorance of the consequences of the disputed legislation including the stock-reduction program, the fencing of the partition line, and the role of the Federal Relocation Commission, which would move at least fifteen hundred families off their land: "I have a very, very full understanding of the sacredness of this area to you," announced the man who had done so much to take it away from them.

In the matriarchal Dineh society, the strong Ashikie sisters are leaders at Big Mountain, and it was Katherine Smith who fired the first questions at this self-proclaimed friend of "my Navajo." Faced with the bleak eye of Katherine Smith, the senator began to babble, to judge from the response that is quoted in *The Navajo Times*: "I'm glad you asked about the fence," he told her, "because it is something I wanted to explore today. What I wanted to ask today was, Who built the fence, and is the fence, is the problem solved now? . . . Oh, did you build the fence to keep the Hopi out? . . . I understand from the girls [Mrs. Blackgoat and Mrs. Ashikie; both of these tribal elders are in their sixties] who visited my office that the fence prevented access to water or something. I think I'll have to know more about this fence to answer your question." This last desperate utterance was the only one that made any sense at all, and Katherine Smith gave up on him, disgusted. Those who followed fared no better, and under the circumstances, it seems amazing that the Indians were able to remain polite, and serve their food to this wealthy white man who had doomed their way of life in careless ignorance of the facts and human consequences, then tried to deny them all financial aid besides.

After a few painful hours, the senator said that he wished to thank the wonderful Indians who had visited him in Washington (for some reason, he appeared surprised that this "was only the second time in twenty-five years that any Indians have bothered to stop and see me") and retreated to his helicopter. In other years, Goldwater had demonstrated a sincere if sentimental interest in Indian welfare (and also in Indian blankets, rugs, and jewelry according to Craig, who had lived at Navajo Mountain when Goldwater had a trading post up there) and he was visibly annoyed that these ungrateful people were so disrespectful. "I've lived here fifty years," he snapped to a reporter, "and I probably know this land better than most of these Navajo." The farce was completed when Roberta Blackgoat followed him right to the helicopter, imploring him to keep his promise to remain three days and eat Navajo food and sleep on sheepskins. "I even washed out a sheepskin for him," she recalled later, with a grin of malice, "and hung it out to dry."

In a grim way, the Indians were amused by Goldwater's Retreat, but Roberta Blackgoat says that at least fifty-eight elders have died in self-destructive ways since the passage of the Land Settlement Act; one was a suicide by hanging, and the rest succumbed to alcohol and apathy, having lost that identity with the land that is vital to traditional Indian life. This catastrophe had been anticipated by a California Institute of Technology anthropologist named Thayer Scudder, who had studied relocation problems all over the world and who predicted widespread mental and physical illness, depression, and premature death. "It's about the most rotten thing you can do to people, especially low-income people who are relatively illiterate and relatively immobile and tied to the land. It's a cultural disaster . . . the equivalent to . . . the loss of a wife or son." Those Dineh who have been driven off their land quite literally have no place to go except slum housing in the racist towns (Flagstaff, Grants, Farmington, Gallup) around the reservation; many of these families have already disintegrated under severe financial and emotional difficulties, and those who still cling to the land are suffering, too. A recent report by the Navajo Area Office of the Indian Health Service concludes that Navajos who face relocation are "currently utilizing the mental health facilities of one of the IHS at a rate which is eight times greater than that of Navajos who will not be relocated."

> I learned to ride a horse bareback
> > And go as fast as the wind.
> I learned to take a cool bath in Tinaja pools
> > On the Yellow Top Mesa
> > In the hottest summer
> > To cool-off!

I help my grandmom
    To harvest pinto beans,
    Haul melons, watermelons and squash
    In a horse-drawn wagon
    To underground storage cellar
    For winter uses.

But now they say, "This belongs to the
Hopi";
    "You have to move away";
    "Anyway: it's only a land."

HOW DARE THEY CALL IT—ONLY A LAND!

My heart and soul—is part of that land!
    Can't they see
    The anguish and turmoil
    In my soul and heart?

How can I part with something
    That is part of me?*

A rough road north from a point west of the Hopi pueblos follows Dinnebito Wash to the region of Big Mountain, which lies off to the west of the dirt track about fifteen miles beyond the trading post at Dinnebito (Navajo-Our-Water) and perhaps thirty miles south of the Black Mesa mine, in a country of red dust, juniper and sage, sand, rock, dry piney hills, and mountain bluebirds.

The cabin of Ashikie Bitsie's sister, Katherine Smith, lies on an open hillside under the east slope of Big Mountain, facing across Black Mesa toward the rising run. Though the cabin was empty, we were greeted amiably by a large dog—"the first friendly dog I've ever come across in all my wanderings in Navajo country," Craig Carpenter remarked. "There are good people here." Eventually a pickup truck appeared that contained Mrs. Smith's sons Junior and Ricky, together with Ricky's wife and baby. Discussing the forced relocation of the Navajo, and the stated intention of the Big Mountain people to resist, Ricky Smith said quietly,

*Sandy Anderson (Navajo).

"We're pretty serious about it; we'll have to be pushed out or thrown out, or we won't go. We have no problem with the Hopi traditional people—it's the Hopi Tribal Council. There's oil here, I guess, and the white people behind that Tribal Council want it bad."

The Smith brothers led us across the mesa to another cabin, where their mother was tending sheep for her niece, Jane Biakeddy. Katherine Smith, whose own herd of sheep has been reduced from well over two hundred to about thirty, is a big, handsome woman with a pleasant laugh. After looking us over in silence, she said mildly, "I think it is better if you take me to my house; there I will show you something." She accompanied us back to her own small cabin, with its wood stove and kerosene lamp, and changed into a fresh dress before bringing forth a beautiful wedding basket and explaining the significance of its intricate black-and-brown designs. The basket contained prayer feathers, a bull-roarer, arrowheads, and other objects that had come down through the family, and as Katherine Smith talked, she held the basket in her lap, expressing herself with care; though she speaks English better than most elders at Big Mountain, she was transmitting an oral tradition and was obviously taking pains to get it right. Her shy, laughing manner had changed with the change of dress to a certain formality, as if sitting upright on her cot by the cabin window with its long view of Black Mesa, she were speaking for all Big Mountain people. "My story," she began simply. "This I want to say about the mountains. The sacred mountains. My story is the way, a long time ago, my old grandfather and my old grandmother, we say we are from way down in the earth up onto this mountain." She laughed a little, shaking her head. "I don't know what we were when we first started, way down there inside the world." She said that the Sun was the Father and the Earth the Mother, and that the Twins (Child-Born-of-Water and Monster Slayer, the culture heroes of the Dineh) became the tornadoes and the hurricanes; she showed how the whole legend of The People was outlined in the black design upon her basket: "This is a rainbow and this is the earth and this is a door—see, these parts are not joined. . . ."

The most striking object in Katherine Smith's basket was a Mountain Earth Bundle, a beautiful, soft, pale buckskin pouch that contains earth from each of the four sacred mountains of the

Navajo,* including Mount Taylor and the San Francisco Peaks, as well as earth from the two eminences of Big Mountain: according to Craig, who was startled when she brought it out, this sacred object is not often seen. The Mountain Earth Bundle, which represents Creation, has its own *beha sanni*, or law, and gives its holder authority to speak in ceremonial prayer; it is a protection and a blessing that has been in her family "from the beginning," and it also represents her right to stand firm on her ancestral land, which was guaranteed to her as recently as 1960 by a BIA document stamped with a gold seal "By the Authority of the Secretary of the Interior" and now as worthless as most other documents that have been issued to the Indians by "Washington." She held up this white-man document for our inspection. Despite her open manner and warm laugh, Katherine Smith has a remote, unflinching eye that saw through Senator Goldwater in moments, and Craig Carpenter gazed at her in open admiration; his disapproval of "easily led" Navajo who copied the ways of other peoples was dissolving quickly among the Dineh of Big Mountain.

As Ricky Smith had pointed out, the traditional Hopi were supporting his people in protesting the fencing of the Joint Use Area and the evictions. On October 26, 1978, a number of Hopi joined in a protest march from Big Mountain to Flagstaff to confront the Federal Relocation Commission, whose spokesman would later acknowledge to the press that a severe hardship had been visited upon the Navajo. Two days later, the first Navajo fencing crews turned up at Big Mountain, where they were questioned by Katherine Smith's half-sister, Pauline Whitesinger. One of the crew was the brother of her late husband, and another made the lewd suggestion that she take the brother home with her if she had business with him. That day, the small, forty-three-year-old widow was driving her son's pickup truck; she drove at her tormentor with the truck, then jumped out and knocked him down. The foreman warned her that her resistance was useless, the law was the law, that she might be arrested and die of old age in jail, to which she said flatly, "*This* is where I shall die of old age." The

---

*North = De-be-ne-etsa, San Juan Mountain
 East = Dis-na-jki-ui, Mount Elaine
 South = Tsah Dzil, Mount Taylor
 West = Doo-Ko-oslid, San Francisco Peaks

following day, when she challenged the crew again, the foreman went to his truck to report interference from this small, angry, and determined woman, from whom he received a handful of Big Mountain earth full in the face.

"I think there is no way we can survive if we get moved to some other land away from ours," Pauline Whitesinger said later. "We are just going to waste away. People tell us to move, but I've got no place to go. I am not moving anywhere; that is certain. If we uneducated people move out of here, we would probably last just two or three days."

In reference to her sister's confrontation with the fence crew, Katherine Smith said shortly, "We were against that; I saddle my horse, I take my gun over there." A few days later, fences were put in while Pauline Whitesinger was off in Window Rock, seeking in vain for help from the Tribal Council; next day, these fences were torn out by Mrs. Whitesinger, Mrs. Smith, and other neighbors.

In the uneasy summer after our visit, the Big Mountain people were not prosecuted, nor were the fences replaced. Apparently the government wished to avoid armed confrontation and publicity, and for the moment, the Indians lived in suspense: they had no wish to disobey the law, but to abide by it meant spiritual death. "In our traditional tongue there is no word for relocation," Pauline Whitesinger said. "To move away means to disappear and never be seen again."

Meanwhile, they formed the Big Mountain Committee Against the Fence, and pledged resistance to eviction, but realizing how small the chances were that such a committee would find any sort of hearing, they enlisted the support of AIM, which had never been popular among the Navajo. ("We don't like the way these people talk," Katherine Smith had told us. Like all Big Mountain people—and unlike the "flexible" modern Navajo—she is suspicious of outside Indians, "of all the new people coming along with peyote and from other Indian places. Navajo traditionals, we do not change our prayer, but I think pretty soon there's going to be no more Navajo prayer, Navajo singing.") AIM was sure to attract the wary attention of the U.S. government, and the nearest AIM activist was Larry Anderson, who had already led a Big Mountain delegation to the antinuclear demonstrations at Tsah Dzil in order to attract attention to the crisis.

In Washington, there was a good deal of discussion about possible compromises, such as letting elderly Indians remain on their home sites for life, and meanwhile legislators from Utah and New Mexico fought manfully to make sure that none of the homeless Indians would be relocated on Navajo land in their own states. An uneasy peace prevailed until August 1979, when the BIA, under pressure from Peabody Coal, resumed the fencing operation. The Big Mountain people, desperate, angry, and upset because nothing meaningful had been done to help them, made a renewed statement of resolve and warning that scared off the bureaucrats until early September.

On September 16, according to the Los Angeles *Times*, "a sixty-year-old Navajo woman was arrested for firing a rifle at members of a government crew building a barbed-wire fence to partition the disputed land area near Big Mountain." That Navajo woman was Katherine Smith, who did not shoot at members of the crew but only up into the air, in warning. Nevertheless, she was arrested and jailed at Piñon for interfering with the fencing operation, and subsequently transferred to the Keams Canyon jail, where the Hopi police charged her with "felony." "They told me I had broken the laws of the white man and I told them I had my own laws. We the Dineh people have our sacred laws, they were given to us in the Beginning. I don't recognize their laws and I told them that's why I wasn't afraid of them. That's why I would shoot at them again."

At Katherine Smith's trial in October 1979, the charges were dismissed to avoid inviting any more publicity, and the following day about seventy Big Mountain people, threatening to confiscate any fencing equipment on their land, advised the United States of America against further attempts "to intrude on or disrupt the sacred lands at Big Mountain." A sixty-two-year-old woman named Ruth Benally declared that "no matter how small I am, I'll fight all the way to the end," even if she had to use her fists, and a year later, in September 1980, this old lady did just that during a new confrontation at the fence line, upon which she and three of her daughters were maced, handcuffed, and hauled off to jail. That night, half a mile of fencing was ripped out by their neighbors, and the operation was suspended once again. Even without interruptions, the fence was costing the taxpayers $3,500 a mile, or an estimated $10 million altogether.

The only apparent beneficiaries of this costly and painful relocation of thousands of bewildered people were a few prosperous Hopi ranchers such as the Tribal Chairman who with the encouragement of white associates in the mining business were insisting on their legal rights. Even Representative Lloyd Meeds, a man responsible for some of the anti-Indian legislation that inspired the Longest Walk, expressed uneasiness after a visit to the Joint Use Area. "I saw that we were talking about land where people were living as opposed to just raising cattle, which is what the Hopis wanted the land for. There are alternatives to raising cattle, but not too many alternatives for people who are tied to the land." But Senator Morris Udall, who had voted against P.L. 93-531, announced he would fight any repeal attempts, since in his view the Hopi Tribal Council "victory" should be protected. Under the circumstances, it seems unlikely that Congress will undo this piece of legislation that has its origins, not in justice for wronged Indians, but in political manipulations on behalf of the energy corporations.

In 1981, Senator Goldwater supported a constructive plan to transfer to the Hopi a tract of Navajo land elsewhere in the JUA in exchange for the "Hopi" land around Big Mountain; the Hopi Tribal Council agreed to this but the Navajo Tribal Council came out against it, mostly because—or so it appeared—of Peter MacDonald's personal dislike of Goldwater. (Understandably, the Big Mountain people were also wary. "Recently he had a Senate hearing where he had spoke to my great-grandpa, who has been gone the last ten years!" exclaimed Mae Benally. "He claims to know the Navajo people inside out, the same with the Hopis, but he doesn't know a damn thing about us. But that is what he's claiming, and all those people in Washington, D.C., listen to him. . . . I don't know what kind of a person he is.")

On that spring day in 1979, Katherine Smith had led us up to the shrine rocks behind her cabin, on a summit of evergreens and smooth pale rock that has a broad view of Big Mountain. Her Navajo dress—dark-blue velveteen blouse, turquoise skirt, belt, blanket, and moccasins—seemed to gather in the light from the sinking sun. Calm, smiling, yet somehow remote, she pointed out the location of some ancient Anasazi ruins on the ridge to the southward, and told us some of the old legends.

"In my story, they said that there could be a Giant, and the

Father Sun gave those Twins some kind of lightning to kill it; near the highway, over there near Grants, there is some kind of stone, they say that the blood of the Giant is seen there. When there's going to be the end of the world, the Giants will come again. They are going to show themselves at the end of the world."

Katherine Smith was quiet for a while, as if listening to the wind sigh in the piñons. "I am sad on my land," she said at last, turning to contemplate us. "This mountain is sacred, we don't want to leave our mountain." Cocking her head, she fixed us once again with that doomsday eye. "Lightning, rainbow, earth, and night—that's where we came from. Now thousands of white people come, trying to take this land away from us, trying to kill us.... If this government keeps on like that, I think it's going to be the end of the world."

⸱ ⸱ ⸱

In 1982, Tribal Council Chairmen Abbott Sekaquaptewa of the Hopi and Peter MacDonald of the Navajo were turned out of office; their successors, Ivan Sidney and Peterson Zah, are longtime friends who wish to put an end to the dispute between their peoples. Blaming this dispute on the federal government, Navajo Chairman Zah said, "We have to undo all of the hatred that the past leaders have created between the two tribes." In April 1983, they ordered their tribal attorneys to suspend all lawsuits over land; both tribes, Zah said, had spent millions of dollars in legal fees mainly for the benefits of the law firms and the energy corporations. They pledged cooperation in all areas of mutual concern, including contracts with mining and utility companies; a joint committee of Hopi and Navajo would negotiate any further contracts with Peabody Coal in the Joint Use Area. As for the partition ruling and the mass removal of Indian families from the JUA, neither saw an immediate solution. It was hoped that some sort of land exchange might solve the problem, but for the moment the threatened relocation of the Big Mountain Dineh, desired by almost no one but the energy companies, remains the most bitter and dangerous situation in Indian country. The final deadline for relocation is 1986, when those who have not agreed to go will be forcibly removed. However, the Indians intend to fight, and unless Congress comes to its senses, a violent confrontation such as Wounded Knee (1973) appears inevitable.

The new spirit of cooperation between the Hopi and Navajo tribal councils might eventually help to ease the differences between Hopi progressives and traditionals, and meanwhile there are many signs that the Indian nations, although not willing to give up their autonomy, far less join forces behind national spokesmen, are gaining a new sense of themselves as one people, sharing many sustaining customs and traditions despite the diversity of language and culture. The bitter political factions within tribes have learned to recognize that the real enemy is not one another; even on Pine Ridge reservation, where federal policies caused so much violence in the 1970's, even in the Mohawk Nation, the people are resolving differences in peaceable discussion.

An important factor in this new spirit of unity and cooperation is the strange hypocritical cruelty of the Republican administration, waging its mean-spirited war against the most defenseless people in the nation. In May 1983, the conservative National Tribal Chairmen's Association, protesting that this administration had broken promises and ignored the hardships caused by its ruthless budget cuts in social programs and the BIA, denounced President Reagan as "the great forktongued liar and the great deceiver who sits in the White House."

INDEX